Aspects of Ancient Greek Cult

Aarhus Studies in Mediterranean Antiquity (ASMA)

VIII

ASMA is a series published by The Centre for the Study of Antiquity at the University of Aarhus, Denmark.

General editor: George Hinge

The Centre is a network of cooperating departments of Classics, Classical Archaeology, History, and the Faculty of Theology. The objective of the series is to advance interdisciplinary study by publishing proceedings and monographs that reflect the current activities of the Centre.

Aspects of
Ancient Greek Cult

Context, Ritual and Iconography

Edited by
Jesper Tae Jensen, George Hinge, Peter Schultz
and Bronwen Wickkiser

ASPECTS OF ANCIENT GREEK CULT

Cover by Jesper Tae Jensen and Michaelis Lefantzis
Illustration: Votive relief NM 1332 (National Museum, Athens). Large photo: the
Doric Stoa in the Athenian Asklepieion on the South Slope of the Akropolis.
Typeset with Minion
and printed by Narayana Press
Printed in Denmark, 2009

DF
122
.A87
2009

ISBN 978 87 7934 253 8
ISSN 1399 2686

Aarhus University Press
Langelandsgade 177
DK-8200 Aarhus N
www.unipress.dk

White Cross Mills
Hightown, Lancaster, LA1 4XS
United Kingdom
www.gazellebookservices.co.uk

PO Box 511
Oakville, CT 06779
www.oxbowbooks.com

Published with the financial support of
The Aarhus University Research Foundation
Concordia College, Moorhead, MN, USA
The Danish Research Agency, Ministry of Science
Department of Classics at Gustavus Adolphus College
College of Arts and Science at Vanderbilt University
The Centre for the Study of Antiquity at the University of
Aarhus, Denmark

*This book is dedicated to all the wonderful people who have ever worked on
the Athenian Asklepieion on the South Slope of the Akropolis
– above all Alexandros Mantis, Petros Kalligas and Luigi Beschi.*

Contents

Preface

Jesper Tae Jensen, George Hinge, Peter Schultz and Bronwen Wickkiser

Near the end of this labor, only one final matter remains. It is the most pleasant of all tasks involved in producing this book. Namely, to thank the people involved. There have been many wonderful people committed to this project; without them this project – both the 2004 conference and the present book – could never have been completed.

First, for making the conference in Aarhus, *Aspects of Ancient Greek Cult*, such a great success, we would like to thank the hosts of the conference, the Centre for the Study of Antiquity and the Department of Classical Archaeology, University of Aarhus. We would like to express our deepest gratitude in particular to Lise and Niels Hannestad of the Department of Classical Archaeology, University of Aarhus, for all their support and for helping to make this conference possible. We also wish to express our deepest thanks to the Secretary of the Department of Classical Archaeology, Lilian Svenningsen, for her constant assistance with all practical matters, and to the technician at the Museum of Ancient Art, Steffen Ledet Christiansen, for his assistance in every circumstance imaginable. To Stine Birk Toft, who assisted everyone before and throughout the conference, we owe a special debt.

Thanks also go to the core of the conference, the speakers, for making the colloquium such great fun. Throughout the conference, their professionalism and good cheer made all the administrative duties much easier for Lilian, Stine, and Jesper Tae Jensen, the principal organizer of the conference. Finally, we are thankful to the participants and the attendees of the conference; without their fantastic questions, helpful comments, and suggestions our papers would not be what they are.

For financial support of the conference, we are grateful to the Danish Research Agency, Ministry of Science, to the Aarhus University Research Foundation and not least to the Elisabeth Munksgaard Foundation. Our gratitude also goes to the fantastic wine shop Viticole Den Blå Port and Café RIS RAS Filliongongong, both in Aarhus, for providing energy – coffee, wine, beer, and other delicious fuel – to our brains during the conference.

The completion of this book owes much to the talents and assistance of various individuals and organizations. Thanks to Benjamin Millis, Acquisitions at the Blegen Library, American School of Classical Studies at Athens, for assisting us in finding numerous articles and books.

We would also like to thank Craig A. Mauzy, Photographic Department, Agora Excavations, the American School of Classical Studies at Athens, for providing the photo used in Richard Hamilton's article; to Director, Dr. Nikolaos Kaltsas and Eleni Morati, both of the National Archaeological Museum at Athens for providing the photo used in Michaelis Lefantzis's and Jesper Tae Jensen's article; and to Director, Dr. Wolf-Dietrich Niemeier and Oliver Pilz (Fotoabteilung), both of the Deutsches Archäologisches Institut, Athens, for the permission to use the photo (Neg. Nr. : NM 642) for the cover of the book.

We are deeply grateful to the staff at the Aarhus University Press, especially Director Claes Hvidbak, Editor Sanne Lind Hansen, and English editor Mary Waters Lund for all their support in and commitment to producing this book. Thanks also go to Catharina Linneballe, Christina Videbech, and Jens Evald Vandel for bringing photos from Athens, and a special thanks to Amalie Skovmøller for providing much needed help with the photos in general.

For financial support of this book we would like to express our deepest gratitude to Concordia College Moorhead, MN, the Department of Classics at Gustavus Adolphus College, the College of Arts and Science at Vanderbilt University, the Danish Research Agency, Ministry of Science, Aarhus University Research Foundation, and the Centre for the Study of Antiquity, University of Aarhus.

Finally, regarding the technical details: We have used the abbreviations set forth by the Guidelines of *the American Journal of Archaeology* (with the exceptions of *ARG* = *Archiv für Religionsgeschichte*, *ArchEph* = *Archaiologiki Ephemeris*, and *DNP* = *Der Neue Pauly*). There is little consistency among scholars today in the spelling of Greek words and names in English. As a general principle, we, the editors of this volume, have opted for the Greek form (e.g. Apollon, Asklepios, and Strabon instead of Apollo, Asclepius, and Strabo). However, in certain familiar names (like Plato, Piraeus, and Delphi), we have followed the Latin tradition for the convenience of the reader.

This book is dedicated to all the wonderful people who have ever worked on the Athenian Asklepieion on the South Slope of the Akropolis – above all Alexandros Mantis, Petros Kalligas and Luigi Beschi.

Introduction

Jesper Tae Jensen

The articles in this volume are based on an international conference entitled *Aspects of Ancient Greek Cult*, which took place 9-10 January 2004 at the Centre for the Study of Antiquity and the Department of Classical Archaeology, University of Aarhus, Denmark. The conference was organized as part of my Ph.D. program in the Department of Classical Archaeology at the University of Aarhus. Nine scholars working within the fields of architecture, classical archaeology, classical philology, history, musicology, and religion participated. The broad title for this conference reflects my intention to bring together innovative and diverse approaches to the study of ancient Greek cult, particularly those that combine the study of material culture with both textual and epigraphical evidence.

The purpose of the conference was two-fold. First to establish a network among young scholars who deal with ancient Greek cult from different disciplines and countries. Second, to let these young scholars discuss their ideas under the guidance of Professor Richard Hamilton, and then develop these discussions as articles.

The present volume contains revised versions of seven of the papers given at the conference. The paper by Hedvig von Ehrenheim, "Incubation Areas in Pagan and Early Christian Times," will be published in the Proceedings of the Danish Institute at Athens, volume 6. The addition of the article by Vanda Papaefthymiou, archaeologist of the Athenian Asklepieion, was an obvious one since her work encompasses material discussed in several of the conference papers.

Each participant was given free rein regarding the length of their papers, and the editors have not altered their arguments. It is, of course, the editors' hope that these eight articles will offer a fresh look at various aspects of ancient Greek cult.

This book begins, as did the conference, with Lisbeth Bredholt Christensen's penetrating article, "'Cult' in the Study of Religion and Archaeology." Since cult was to be the focal point of the conference, I asked assistant professor Christensen to explore the definition and use of this term within various branches of scholarship. Whereas 'Cult' is not a term widely used in the field of Religion, it is popular and proliferate in the disciplines of Ancient History and Classical and Prehistoric Archaeology. Christensen suggests that the divergence in its use is due largely to the social focus of ancient history and archaeology in contrast to a focus on texts and literature in the study of religion.

The article by Richard Hamilton, "Basket Case: Altars, Animals and Baskets on Classical Attic Votive Reliefs," uses a statistical approach to analyze the relationship between altars, animals and baskets together with worshippers and deities. He demonstrates that groups of worshippers can be found in two-thirds of all the votive reliefs, and altars in almost half, while animals on votive reliefs can be found in only a quarter, and baskets in only an eighth. Hamilton concludes innovatively that the basket is an attractive visual complement to the animal but in no way essential to the offering represented by the votive.

The next four articles present new material and ideas about individual sanctuaries. The first three investigate the Greek healing god Asklepios and his sanctuary on the South Slope of the Athenian Akropolis, followed by a detailed study of the Philippeion at Olympia.

Bronwen Wickkiser's article, "Banishing Plague: Asklepios, Athens, and the Great Plague Reconsidered," questions long-held assumptions about why Athens imported the cult of Asklepios from Epidauros in 420 B.C. Although ancient sources are silent about the cause, scholars have long argued that plague in the years 430-426 B.C. was the most immediate factor prompting the importation. Wickkiser points out, however, that the lag between these events renders a direct cause-and-effect relationship dubious at best, and goes on to argue that the nature of ailments Asklepios is known to have treated – chronic ailments, not fatal ones like plague – also makes the god an unlikely candidate to have cured Athenians of this epidemic. These observations open the door to the possibility, if not the likelihood, that in the context of the Peloponnesian War, factors unrelated to physical health alone prompted the importation.

In "Der Altar des Asklepieions von Athen," Vanda Papaefthymiou gives a brief overview of the Asklepieion and a history of its investigation. Her focus, however, is the results of new excavations conducted during summer 2001 in and around the so-called altar. Papaefthymiou presents the pottery from nine small pits and suggests that some of these pits were used for planting.

Michaelis Lefantzis and I re-study the architectural history of the Asklepieion in "The Athenian Asklepieion on the South Slope of the Akropolis: Early Development, ca. 420-360 B.C." We argue that the original Asklepieion of Telemachos was founded on the east terrace and was designed around a central monument that scholars today identify as an altar. We, unconvinced that this monument is indeed an altar, date the earliest phase of this structure to 418/7-416/5 B.C., and identify at least four distinctive phases of construction. In this article the first two construction phases are investigated in depth after a careful description of the foundations belonging to Phases I-IV.

In "Divine Images and Royal Ideology in the Philippeion at Olympia" Peter Schultz re-examines Leochares' famous portraits of Philip II and his family that were installed in Olympia after the Macedonian triumph at Chaironeia. Three primary questions sustain the paper. First, what is the chronological relationship between the portraits and the architecture of the Philippeion itself? Second, how were the images arranged and what did they look like? And finally, what can the answers to these questions tell us about the function of the Philippeion and role the building played in Philip's pan-Hellenic agenda. Schultz's analysis reveals a number of startling conclusions.

The final two articles move beyond specific sanctuaries to focus on broader contextual issues such as music and ritual. Tore Tvarnø Lind's contribution, "Music and Cult in Ancient Greece: Ethnomusicological Perspectives," investigates the limits of our historical and musical imagination. The article touches upon theoretical, socio-cultural and historical issues, and argues for interdisciplinary and creative approaches to the study of ancient Greek music, including recorded musical reconstructions. Lind sketches how the field of ethnomusicology is valuable to the study of music in ancient Greek culture and cult; he considers the impact of cultural understanding, identity processes and postcolonialism on modern perceptions of ancient music and ritual.

In the final article of the book, "Cultic Persona and the Transmission of the Partheneions," George Hinge argues that the partheneions of Alkman and Pindar were not written for single occasions. Rather, the personal names occurring in these songs were generic role names, or "cultic personae." Both internal and external evidence indicate that the girls were cast for these roles through the kinship structure. Combining literary testimonies and linguistic data, Hinge demonstrates that Alkman's partheneions were part of a living cultic tradition, and that most of the poems were not written down until the Hellenistic age, presumably during the "Spartan Renaissance" under King Agis and King Kleomenes.

"Cult" in the Study of Religion and Archaeology

Lisbeth Bredholt Christensen

Scholars of religion currently study "religion," "ritual," "ritual practice," "myth," and "narrative" in different forms, both theoretical and empirical. "Cult," however, is rarely studied nor is it used as a descriptive term as an object of study. Of the few scholars who do use the word, most are educated theologians. They apply the term to Israelite, early Christian or Hellenistic or Old Norse contexts—in other words, contexts related to the Near Eastern worlds.[1] Among sociologists, the term has acquired its own meaning (see below), not related to a traditional definition but linked to the classification of religious communities. In other academic disciplines such as archaeology (prehistorical and classical) or ancient history, scholars are less reticent when speaking about "cult." In fact, it is more common to refer to "cult" (or "rituals" or "religious practice") than to "religion." In what follows, I will examine how "cult" is used in the disciplines mentioned above. Where, exactly, between "religion" and "ritual," is "cult" to be found?

What is studied as religion?

In the study of religion, "religion" is usually defined as people's relation to transcendent or supernatural powers.[2] This concept of religion mirrors the method by which religion is studied—that is, via texts. Supernatural or transcendent beings are only recognizable in language or text. The only reason we know a statue represents Zeus rather than any other older man is because the texts tell us that Zeus' attribute is a thunderbolt. Using the same logic, however, we cannot know whether the Venus of Willendorf represents a goddess or a "normal" woman because we have no linguistic context. Prehistoric archaeology is thus cut off from working with religion the same way text-based disciplines are.

Like "ritual," "cult" forms a pair with "myth" in what could be called a binary opposition. Traditionally, religion is characterized as consisting of myths and rituals. Which of the two came first and which of the two is the most important has been the subject of innumerable discussions. Fundamental positions are represented by two of the "founding fathers" of the academic study of religion: Edward Burnett Tylor and William Robertson Smith.

In *Primitive Culture* (1871), Tylor claimed myth is the most important element, with religion being basically a "belief in spiritual beings." In his *Lectures on the Religion of the Semites* (1889), Robertson Smith claimed that the performance of rituals is the most important and obligatory part of religion, whereas belief (implied by myth, according to Robertson Smith) is secondary.

According to "the myth and ritual school," myth and ritual are linked in the sense that there is always a ritual connected to a myth and vice versa. Although this view has been criticized as being too rigid, it is still widely assumed that in some way the two complement each other: myth represents "the things said" and ritual represents "the things done." The study of ancient religion being basically a study of texts, it may sometimes be easier to study the myths (written down in texts) than the rituals (action that is now unobservable). For this reason, much scholarship has been occupied with distilling rituals from mythical and other texts. This was the project of both the British and the Scandinavian myth-and-ritual-schools, which attempted to find evidence for rituals of fertility and sacred kingship in Greek, Biblical and Near Eastern texts. This has also been a declared aim in the study of Old Norse religion.[3]

To sum up very briefly some of the more recent trends in the study of religion: first, myth has been "liberated" from an automatic connection with "belief." This "liberation" is to a great extent the product of Classical studies, which have labored to show the differences between Greek religion and Christianity. Also, Classical studies have distilled Christian projections onto the Greek world, the concept of literal belief in the wordings of myths being one of these projections.[4] One of the aims of Classical studies from the beginning was that of "overcoming" Christianity, considered to be the last stage of religion on the way to a scientific view of the world, according to Sir James George Frazer.[5] Second, ritual studies have shown that although rituals may be meaningless in themselves, participation in them is not. Thus, Roy Rappaport has investigated how participation in a ritual is tantamount to signing a form of "contract," taking the ritual seriously.[6] Third, under the influence of speech-act theory ("words are deeds"), the study of religion has become more the study of "religion as practice" or "religion in action" than "religion as belief."[7] While a "religion of the mind" disappeared with the dismissal of a theological approach, it is, however, now reappearing under the auspices of cognitive studies.[8]

Cult in the Study of Religion

Whereas in the past 30 years both "religion" and "ritual" have been the subject of innumerable theoretical discussions about concepts and definitions in religious studies, the study of "cult" has led a life in the shadow. The discipline, together with many other disciplines in the humanities, has turned to theory, method and systematics, and is at the same time largely turning its back on particularistic, descriptive, local studies.

Both "religion" and "ritual" have been developed theoretically, as concepts, being more or less universally applicable. The relatively recent *Guide to the Study of Religion*[9] presents a catalogue of articles relating to a contemporary academic study of religion. Concepts and terms such as "religion," "cognition," "gender," "myth," "ritual," "discourse," "culture" and "ideology" are all discussed at length. There are, however, no articles about "cult," and the word does not appear in the index. The same can be observed in the *Encyclopaedia of Cultural Anthropology*,[10] where there are no entries on cult and no references to articles on related topics.

These two works represent a relatively recent trend where "cult" is not an issue in the study of religion. It was not always so. The standard encyclopaedia of the study of religion, Mircea Eliade's *Encyclopedia of Religion*,[11] likewise lacks a general overview of "cult" and likewise provides no general definition of the term. However, the entry "Worship and Cultic Life" introduces itself by proclaiming that it "… surveys the practical expressions of the religious life … designed to introduce the diverse ways in which adherents of these traditions give concrete expression, both as individuals and as communities, to their ideas and beliefs."[12] Cult is seen as "ritual lived," and the entry proceeds to detailed descriptions of specific religions: Judaism, Christianity, Islam, Buddhism and Hinduism and their primary rituals. Characteristic of these individual articles on particular religions is that each religion is described in terms of history and textual criticism, but with no overall comparison or universalist claims. The description as such is loyal to adherents of the various religions. On Muslim worship and cultic life, we thus hear that "… the cult of idols, the scorning of revelation, and the violation of duties all constitute a chronic disesteeming of God. Pagans do not esteem God duly … By contrast, a true Islamic worship brings to God all that is due from humanity in reverence, awe, submission, and obedience …"[13] No analytic apparatus is at play when describing "cult". "Cult" is a concept that is used with "emic" descriptions.

Remarkably different is the entry in the same encyclopaedia on "Ritual." In this article, the subject is a category, and as such, the issue is scholarship, its history, and suggestions as to how to classify ritual. The article discusses no particular religion but instead various kinds of ritual—transitory, sacrifice, prayer, etc.—as they have been generalized or defined by scholars: "… those conscious and voluntary repetitious and stylized symbolic bodily actions that are centered on cosmic structures and/or sacred presences."[14] Here we have a very "etic" description, perhaps not immediately recognizable to the believers of religions (i.e., outside of scholarly discourse). In this area we can speak of "pioneers" in the study of ritual, such as Henri Hubert and Marcel Mauss, Arnold Van Gennep, and Victor Turner, all of whom contributed valuable models for classifying and understanding ritual. In the study of cult, no such scholars can be found.

Instead, cult studies have largely been replaced by ritual analyses. The difference between the two consists in social vs. model-orientated critiques. "Cult studies" focus on social, historical, political, and economic aspects of worship: the role of diverse people, priests, expenses, prayers, local meanings. Cult studies may, to a certain extent, be diachronic in their perspective and focused on "the special case." Ritual analyses are model-orientated and focus on the synchronic and general "laws" of the rites in question: the elements, stages and classification of particular rituals (e.g., transition, crisis, etc.).

To take Old Norse literary sources as an example, there is hardly any information on religious practice. The result is that all ritual has to be reconstructed out of virtually nothing. What scholars look for and find, then, are not particular rituals specific to the Nordic culture, but rituals in a "model form," mainly as initiation or sacrifice.[15] Thus, whereas careful research seems to be able to extract a framework of ritual from, for example, the sagas, when it comes to the social organization, participants, economy, and paraphernalia linked to the rituals, these seem much more difficult to reconstruct. Consequently, "cult" is not a central issue for most scholars of Nordic religion. The same applies to scholars of many other particular religions.

In contrast to this general trend in religious studies, the fields of Near Eastern religions, Christianity and Classics have maintained an interest in social history and in the term "cult." Consequently, articles on cult can be found in *Religion in Geschichte und Gegenwart (RGG)*,[16] *Neue Pauly*[17] and the Danish *Gads Bibelleksikon*.[18]

What is "cult"?

"Cult" stems from Latin *cultus, colere*: cultivate, "tending" to both soil, education and, as in Cicero, the gods (*cultus deorum, De senectute* 56). Thus in its origin the word is not specifically associated with gods; however, via pagan as well as early and Medieval Christian practice, the meaning of the word has been transformed so that today it cannot be understood in isolation from a religious context. Until the 13th -14th centuries the Christian service was termed "cult." About this time, "Gottesdienst" was introduced in German and "worship" in English.[19] "Gottesdienst" and "worship" are today the best synonyms for "cult." Until 1916, Danish ministers for teaching, science and the church were named "Kultusminister," a term still in use, for example, in Germany.

A rather broad definition of "cult" is found in *RGG*: "die Gesamtheit rel. Praxis im Umgang mit 'spirituellen' oder mit bes. Zuschreibungen versehenen Wesen verstehen (z.B. griech., prot., isl. K)." Cult is here more or less synonymous with religious practice, i.e., practices legitimized by and referring to one or several transempirical powers. Consequently, what this definition frames are "classical" cults such as those of Asklepios or the Virgin Mary.

The *Oxford English Dictionary*[20] reproduces a popular, but outdated, explanation of "cult": "a particular form of system of religious worship; esp. in reference to its external rites and ceremonies." Cult is presented as an "exterior," opposed to a potential "interior," religiosity. The definition here, contrary to the one in *RGG*, seems also to presuppose that "worship" may take place outside the "cult" (e.g., in more "introverted" forms, such as prayer, the writing of hymns or psalms, or life in correspondence with religious rules).

A somewhat narrower definition of cult is found in *Gads Bibelleksikon*: "the religious acts of a culture at a sacred place" (my translation).[21] In this definition, a prayer during a service is cultic while a spontaneous prayer in a situation of crisis is not. Just as rituals can be both religious and non-religious they can, according to this perception of the word, also be cultic and non-cultic. This definition also excludes from "cult" phenomena such as shamanism (the shaman can operate everywhere) and New religions (most New Age spirituality is independent of locale). Via an emphasis on "culture" and "sacred place," this definition potentially delimits "cult" to particular historical contexts, namely religions where space, locality (and territory) are important. Thus, with this definition we may say that cult arose only with the Neolithic where "place" and "border" became issues.[22]

Der Neue Pauly specifies that a "cult" involves (a) an object or a referent of worship, (b) a time, (c) a place, and (d) a group of performers. Contrary to the study of rituals independent of their social context, as a system rather than a lived performance, "cult" in this instance clearly implies that the focus of the scholar is on the social aspects of the phenomenon.

Within sociology, "cult" has acquired a particular use. Here, it is "characterized by a loose association of persons with a private, eclectic religiosity."[23] Cult has a negative relation to society: it "...does not claim to have the truth, and is tolerant of other groups."[24] Entirely contrary to the forementioned more "classical" definitions, cult is here connected to the private rather than the public. Focus also seems to be placed on experience and the individual rather than on the action and the object of worship, which here is absent. Cult has also been shifted to an almost de-institutionalized context. This sociological variant of "cult" seems rather confusing when compared to the more traditional understanding of the term. Although it is still used by some (e.g. Bell 1997), others avoid the term "cult," considering it to be outdated (from a time when the established church was viewed as the norm and all other factions viewed as outsiders). It is, however, the sociological version that underlies such expressions as "cult movie" (e.g., *The Rocky Hor-*

ror Picture Show or *Casablanca*), defined as "films that, in form and content, differ from mainstream films by being odd or … exaggerated."[25] The link between the sociological version of cult and the more "classical" definition seems to arise via "mystery cult." In *Ancient Mystery Cults*, Walter Burkert describes mysteries as being "of a voluntary, *personal*, and secret character that aimed at a change of mind through *experience* of the sacred."[26]

A final comment on definitions relates to Émile Durkheim who said that cult (1) always includes a reference to supernatural beings, and (2) is periodical.[27] Durkheim thus specified that rituals connected with burials or births are not cultic because they are performed occasionally rather than regularly. On the other hand, rituals connected with ancestors are periodical and therefore considered to be cultic. Durkheim's point of departure was the religion of the Australian Aborigines, thought in his time to be the most primitive and therefore a representative of Palaeolithic religion or the origins of religion. By emphasizing the Aboriginal worship of ancestors as intense and cultic, Durkheim saw cult as part of the very most ancient layers of religion. Periodicity and concepts of regularity, according to Durkheim, are also found among the most primitive of peoples. These elements are of course obvious when it comes to agricultural and pastoralist societies but less obvious in hunter-gatherer societies.[28]

The convergence between Durkheim's periodicity and the understanding of "sacred place" in *Gads Bibelleksikon* is important.[29] It puts into question whether we can speak about cult before the Neolithic period. Calendrical systems, and therefore concepts of periodicity, have been demonstrated from the Upper Palaeolithic, dating as far back as 27,000 B.C.[30] Yet, hunter-gatherers are characterized as focusing not on "place" and "territory" but on "markers" and "focuses."[31] "Place" connotes space, gathering, and social events, characteristic for settled people (or hunter-gatherers influenced by a settled way of life), but not for a Palaeolithic lifestyle as we know it.

Summing up, cult is generally viewed within a religious frame, as a collection of religious rituals, as less than "religion," but as more than "ritual." It is question whether cult was introduced already in the Palaeolithic, or whether it must be said to be a Neolithic and post-Neolithic phenomenon.

Prehistoric archaeology

Prehistoric archaeologists work with and from material culture and do not have linguistic sources at their disposal. From the mid 1950s, Christopher Hawkes' pyramidal paradigm reigned for several decades in the discipline: archaeology can speak about the technological level of prehistoric societies with relative ease, with less ease about the economic level, and with still less ease about the social level. Finally, prehistoric archaeology is least able to say anything about the ideological and religious level of an early society.[32] Although it was the specific aim of New Archaeology to work with all levels of prehistoric cultures, in practice interest lay only in the first three levels, and methods and instruments were developed to study these.[33]

In the beginning of the 1980s when Ian Hodder launched postprocessualism, the precondition of this new approach was that material culture is meaningfully structured. Postprocessualism's aim was to study "symbols" and "meaning" in the archaeological record and thereby reinscribe archaeology as an interpretive discipline.[34] Today postprocessualism is time-honored. The interest in symbols and meaning has led to an enormous interest also in the fourth field of Hawkes' pyramid: ideology and religion. Whereas only ten years ago few people worked with this, today the academic market abounds with publications on cult, rituals and religious practice from the Palaeolithic until the beginning of the historical period.

A quick glance at both the titles and content of these publications reveals, as mentioned at the outset, that relatively few scholars write directly about "religion," whereas many refer to "cult," "rituals" and "religious practice."[35] The orientation towards practice is due mainly to the nature of the evidence; prehistoric material culture limits the study of religion to its expression in action. The terminology is not, however, a reflection of what the archaeologists basically think about religion. Thus, to Sir Colin Renfrew, "… the essence of religion is some framework of beliefs."[36] This attitude means (a) that Renfrew, and others with him, belong more to an intellectualist (Tylor) tradition than a ritualist (Robertson Smith) one, and (b) that when Renfrew studies prehistoric ritual as a reflection of religion, it is not because he thinks this is the essential part of religion but that it is the only part available. Renfrew studies ritual because he cannot study belief. From this perspective, prehistoric archaeology does not consider itself capable of contributing fruitfully to the study of religion; rather, the discipline finds itself in a position of shortfall.

The problem with most of prehistory is that we have no gods. This may reflect the actual reality that there were no gods at the time, or it may reflect our method of research: that because we have no texts we have no means of identifying images or figurines as gods. Although theoretically it is possible to speak about sacredness or religion and potentially also cult without the presence of gods (e.g., Buddhism), the usual way of verifying that something is religious is by the presence of deities or other forms of spiritual beings. On this basis, two decades ago Renfrew attempted to define "an archaeology of cult."[37] Although he did not reach lasting conclusions, his study remains a serious attempt at reconciling archaeological material with religious theory. Introducing a new field of study, it also provides a new basis for criticism. By "cult" Renfrew understands that the belief system has found expression in action: "the system of patterned actions in response to religious beliefs."[38] The view expressed again here is that belief is primary and cult or ritual secondary, but also that myth and cult/ritual complement each other.[39]

Renfrew concluded that it is possible to detect evidence of only a very small proportion of all the rituals that actually took place in the past. Significantly, however, his project of defining an archaeology of cult failed. In order to recognize a cultic site, Renfrew considered it necessary that such things as sacred place, sacred building, divine images or expenditure of wealth were present.[40]As such, the project was locked in tautology: in order to define a site as cultic, we need the presence of identified cultic material. Significantly, Renfrew considers "religious ritual" and "cult" synonymous.[41] Their interchangeability implies that "cult" does not refer to a collection of rituals or a specific social focus on rituals; instead, it merely signifies "ritual." In other words, the use of "cult" indicates a view of religion as divided into belief on the one hand and ritual on the other, and the possibility for archaeology to discuss only the latter of the two. If Renfrew's view applies to prehistorians generally, it can be said that the reason prehistorians prefer to use "cult" rather than "religion" is that they thereby avoid asserting something about belief systems, to which they think they have no access.

Classics

Both Classical archaeologists and Classical philologists discuss cult, but tend to use "cult" synonymously with "religion" rather than with "ritual." Thus, characteristicially, the title of the seminar in Aarhus was "Aspects of ancient Greek cult" (in the singular!) and not "Aspects of ancient Greek religion." The preference on the part of Classical archaeologists to use "cult" rather than "religion" should be related to the fields of Classical philology and ancient history more than to archaeology as such.

Where the point of departure of prehistoric archaeology has been the study of stratigraphy, technology and economics, the point of departure of Classical archaeology was originally art history combined with Classical philology.[42] Since material is often scarce for prehistoric archaeologists, they have been forced to include theory in their analysis. The amount of evidence, both material and literary, available to Classical archaeologists, by contrast, is overwhelming and has kept classicists from really entering theoretical discussions until recently.[43] Classicists are now exploring the relation between material and text on both a theoretical and empirical level. Because of the texts available, however, Classical archaeologists naturally rely upon Classical philology and borrow the latter's terminology when relevant.

It is therefore within Classical philology that the term "cult" should be sought, both in terms of terminology and practice. For instance, Robert

Parker (1996), Simon Price (1999), and Mary Beard et al. (1998) extensively discuss "cult" and cults. On the one hand, this is due to a distance from the Christian concept of "religion," i.e. that it should include "belief." Regarding the British in particular (in contrast to the Vernant-school that speaks about both "myth" and "religion"), it is possible to draw a historical link back to the Cambridge ritualists. On the other hand – and this is the more important – it is due to the fact that the word "cult" comes from the Classical world (but the Roman, not the Greek). Despite the awareness that "cult" is a scholarly, "etic" term not immediately recognizable to, e.g., the Athenians, it is still obvious that, perceived as "a complex of religious activities concentrated on one or more deities or heroes and including prayer, ritual, sacrifice, and dedication," cult is there in all of the Greek, Roman and Classical world.[44] We know the gods and it is not a particular problem identifying their places and contexts of worship. To philologists, and therefore also to Classical archaeologists, "cult" appears just "to be there" in the archaeological material and the texts themselves. In this view, Greek and Roman religions *are* cults – i.e., regular worship of gods. In the 1996 edition of the *Oxford Classical Dictionary*, it is therefore not possible to look up cult as a *terminus technicus*, but the reader is referred to the cults of various gods and heros. In contrast to the prehistoric context, it is not possible in a Greek or Roman context to imagine a funeral (cf. Durkheim) that is not, from one perspective or the other, also cultic.

In Classics, speaking about "cult" rather than "religion" is also a way of signalling a resistance to "belief" being of importance in ancient religion. As mentioned above, from the very beginning it has been important to Classicists to mark a distance between Christianity and Greek/Roman religions. As recent a publication as that of Louise Bruit Zaidman and Pauline Schmitt Pantel (1994) finds it necessary to emphasize that the Greek conception of a god was entirely different than the Christian conception.[45] Speaking about "cult" is also, of course, an indication that focus falls upon the action rather than the morals, rules for conduct, anthropology, cosmogony, and everything else that follows from and goes with the term "religion."

Thus "cult" appears not to be as problematic a term for Classical archaeologists as for prehistorians. Classical archaeologists are able to "read" references to the transcendent in their (material) material, even if such references are only implicit. Classical archaeologists may do so because we know from the texts that, for example, Greece was full of gods.

However, this apparent lucidity may turn out to be a forgery. We may ask if Classical archaeologists are not trying to avoid a problem by speaking about cult rather than religion, namely the problem of defining their issue. When speaking about cult, they tend to refer to philologists rather than to the source material. As such, Classical archaeologists miss an opportunity to investigate whether or not the archaeological material and the texts actu-

ally "agree" on what comprises worship. Since Classicists investigate archaeological material together with texts, they face the unique possibility of
actually defining the word "cult" rather than reproducing old assumptions.

Conclusion

Even if "cult" is not "cultic" in the study of religion for the time being, it is
so elsewhere. Despite the popularity of the term, however, it can be difficult
to understand exactly what people mean when they speak about cult. Most
often the word is not defined, and when it is, it turns out that people are
speaking about different things in different ways. "Cult" is, in other words,
not a very precise or useful word to use.

While Classical archaeologists use "cult" in "its own context" and therefore do not think they need to define the term, prehistoric archaeologists
approach "cult" as a theoretical concept. But while in both Classical and
Near Eastern contexts we can speak about god-worshipping societies, the
area is rather more muddy when it comes to prehistory. "Cult" includes
rituals and presupposes a religion that again presumes gods or other spiritual beings bestowed with authority. Concerning the prehistoric material it
is therefore problematic to use "cult" because the word implies gods that
we have no chance to verify.

As far as scholars of religion are concerned, it would appear (for the time
being) that they, like Classicists, link "cult" to a specific, limited context. On
the other hand, "cult" is also tied to a research tradition with which people
no longer identify. Instead, focus is for the time being on stringent analyses
of ritual structures. This interest has qualified theory and methodology but
(temporarily?) moved focus away from the (equally important!) social, economic and political aspects of religion such as time, place, objects and participants.

Scholars of religion have for the past many years focused on and studied
ritual rather than cult to the extent that today the term has almost disappeared from the discipline. Classical archaeologists have never really studied rituals because a ritual consisting of performance, words, smells, etc.,
cannot be reconstructed from material remains. Likewise, the study of ritual, at least as it has been practiced until now, is bound up with textual studies, implying and presupposing knowledge about the identity of the supernatural agents involved and the characteristics of the phases of the
ritual – particularities that mainly come from texts and are verbally communicated and accessible. Again, information of this sort does not show up
in the archaeological material. For Classical archaeologists, who are more
historians than anthropologists, to choose between "ritual" and "cult" has
not therefore been difficult. As a point of departure, "cult" is assumed to

have been there all along. Making "cult" the focus of study does not require applying models that, after all, do not fit the material.

Acknowledgements:

I would like to thank the participants in the seminar for comments on the oral paper. I would like to thank Jesper Tae Jensen, Giuseppe Torresin and David Warburton for comments on the written version.

Notes

 1 E.g. Jensen 2001; Bilde 1998, ch. 2; Mack 1998; Brink 2001.
 2 Bilde 1991; Geertz 1999; Schjødt 2001; Tylor 1871; Durkheim 1995.
 3 Cf. Schjødt 2003.
 4 Calame 2003 is one recent exponent of this effort.
 5 Cf. Gras 1997.
 6 Rappaport 2000.
 7 E.g. McCutcheon 2003.
 8 E.g. Boyer 2001.
 9 Braun & McCutcheon 2000.
10 Levinson & Ember 1996.
11 Eliade 1987a.
12 Eliade 1987b.
13 Cragg 1987, 454.
14 Zuesse 1987, 405.
15 Schjødt 2003.
16 Betz et al. 2001.
17 Cancik & Schneider 1999.
18 Hallbäck & Jensen 1998.
19 *RGG* s.v. "Kult", *Neue Pauly* s.v. "Kult."
20 Simpson et al. (2008).
21 Hallbäck & Jensen 1998.
22 Wilson (1988) has argued how the introduction of "wall" and "house" in the early Neolithic transformed the world not only physically and visibly but also socially by follow-on effects in the form of new concepts such as "border", "space", "territory", "neighbour" and even "war."
23 McGuire 1987, 117.
24 McGuire 1987, 121.
25 *Den store danske encyklopædi* s.v. "kultfilm."
26 Burkert 1987, 11; my italics.
27 Durkheim 1995, 59-60.
28 Today we know, however, that all existing hunter-gatherer societies, including the Australian Aborigines, have been in contact with and influenced by settled communities for at least several hundred years, and most often several thousand. David 2002. The Australians are, in many ways, not therefore as "primitive" as Durkheim thought they were, and it is not surprising that we find customs related to a settled lifestyle connected to a hunter-gatherer community.

29   Hallbäck & Jensen 1998.

30   Marshack 1999.

31   Wilson 1988; Ingold 1999.

32   Hawkes 1954.

33   On the aim of New Archaeology to work with all levels of prehistoric societies, see Binford 1972, 20-32.

34   Hodder 1992.

35   On "religion," Cauvin 2000; Watkins 2001. On "cult", "rituals" and "religious practice," Renfrew 1985; Rollefson 1998; Kuijt 2000; Gebel 2002; Verhoeven 2002.

36   Renfrew 1985, 12.

37   Renfrew 1985.

38   Renfrew & Bahn 1991, 359.

39   The concept of ideology or beliefs as being independent of, and coming before, material expression has, however, recently been revised by Renfrew himself (Renfrew 2001). Here, he argues that material culture is the precondition for concepts as such. Applied to the discussion of belief, religion and rituals, the same argument must be that materials or rituals come first and beliefs afterwards.

40   Renfrew 1985, 19-20.

41   "We are concerned here…with religious ritual or cult…," Renfrew 1985, 15.

42   Andrén (1998, 17) cites Alexander Conze for claiming, "Where the cross-section of Classical philology and the longitudinal section of art history intersect, there, and precisely there, lies the field of Classical archaeology."

43   Andrén (1998, 17) describes early Classical archaeology as "so strongly tied to ancient texts and philological criticism that … [t]he starting point for the major excavations was normally texts."

44   Aleshire 1994, 12.

45   Zaidman & Schmitt Pantel 1994, 9.

Bibliography

Aleshire, S.B. 1994. "Towards a Definition of 'State Cult' for Ancient Athens." In *Ancient Greek Cult Practice from the Epigraphical Evidence, Proceedings of the Second International Seminar on Ancient Greek Cult, Athens, 1991*, edited by R. Hägg, 9-16. SkrAth 8°, 13. Stockholm: Svenska Institutet i Athen, distribution Paul Åströms Förlag.

Andrén, A. 1998. *Between Artifacts and Texts: Historical Archaeology in Global Perspective*. Translated by A. Crozier. New York: Plenum Press.

Beard, M., J. North & S.R.F. Price. 1998. *Religions of Rome*. 2 Vols. Cambridge: Cambridge University Press.

Bell, C. 1997. *Ritual: Perspectives and Dimensions*. New York & Oxford: Oxford University Press.

Betz, H.D. et al. (eds.). 2001. *Religion in Geschichte und Gegenwart: Handwörterbuch für Theologie und Religionswissenschaft*. Vol. 4. Tübingen: Mohr-Siebeck.

Bilde, P. 1991. "Begrebet religion: Et indlæg i debatten om religionsviden-skabens objekt drøftet i lyset af beslægtede begreber." *Chaos* 15: 3-24.

Bilde, P. 1998. *Den hellenistisk-romerske verden: Religiøse tekster*. Verdensreli-gionernes hovedværker. Copenhagen: Spektrum.

Binford, L. 1972. *An Archaeological Perspective*. Studies in Archaeology. New York, San Francisco & London: Seminar Press.

Boyer, P. 2001. *Religion Explained: The Evolutionary Origins of Religious Thought*. New York : Basic Books.

Braun, W. & R.T. McCutcheon. (eds.). 2000. *Guide to the Study of Religion*. London & New York: Cassell.

Brink, S. 2001. "Mythologizing Landscape: Place and Space of Cult and Myth". In *Kontinuitäten und Brüche in der Religionsgeschichte*, edited by M. Stausberg, 76-112. Berlin: de Gruyter.

Burkert, W. 1987. *Ancient Mystery Cults*. Cambridge, MA & London: Harvard University Press.

Calame, C. 2003. *Myth and History in Ancient Greece: The Symbolic Creation of a Colony*. Translated by D.W. Berman. Princeton & Oxford: Princeton University Press.

Cancik, H. & H. Schneider. (eds.). 1999. *Der Neue Pauly: Enzyklopädie der Antike*. Vol. 6. Stuttgart & Weimar: J.B. Metzler.

Cragg, K. 1987. "Muslim Worship and Cultic Life." In Eliade 1987a, vol. 15, 454-63.

Cauvin, J. 2000. *The Birth of the Gods and the Origins of Agriculture*. New Stud-ies in Archaeology. Translated by T. Watkins. Cambridge: Cambridge University Press.

David, B. 2002. *Landscapes, Rock-Art and the Dreaming: An Archaeology of Preun-derstanding*. London: Leicester University Press.

Durkheim, E. 1995. *The Elementary Forms of Religious Life*. Translated by. K.E. Fields. New York: Free Press.

Eliade, M. (ed.). 1987a *Encyclopedia of Religion*. 16. vols. New York: Collier Macmillan.

Eliade, M. 1987b. "Worship and Cultic Life." In Eliade 1987a, vol. 15, 445.

Gebel, H.-G.K. et al. (eds.). 2002. [2004]. *Magic Practices and Ritual in the Near Eastern Neolithic*. Studies in Early Near Eastern Production, Subsistence, and Environment 8. Berlin: Ex Oriente.

Geertz, A. 1999. "Definition as Analytical Strategy in the Study of Religion." *Historical Reflections/Réflections Historiques* 25.3: 445-75.

Gras, V. 1997. "Cambridge Ritualists." In *The Johns Hopkins Guide to Literary Theory and Criticism*, edited by M. Groden & M. Kreiswirth. http://www.press.jhu.edu/books/hopkins_guide_to_literary_theory/b-contents.html

Hallbäck, G. & H.J.L. Jensen. (eds.). 1998. *Gads Bibelleksikon*. Copenhagen: Gad.

Hawkes, C. 1954. "Archaeological Theory and Method: Some Suggestions from the Old World." *American Anthropologist* 56: 155-68.

Hodder, I. 1992. *Theory and Practice in Archaeology*. Material Cultures. Interdisciplinary Studies in the Material Construction of Social Worlds. London & New York: Routledge.

Hornblower, S. & A. Spawforth. (eds.). 1996. *Oxford Classical Dictionary*. 3rd ed. Oxford: Oxford University Press.

Ingold, T. 1999. "On the Social Relations of the Hunter-Gatherer Band." In *The Cambridge Encyclopedia of Hunters and Gatherers*, edited by R.B. Lee & R. Daly, 399-410. Cambridge: Cambridge University Press.

Jensen, H.J.L. 2001. "Myte, kult og visdom i Det Gamle Testamente." In *Religionsvidenskabelige sonderinger*, edited by V. Andersen, 106-18. Aarhus: Aarhus University Press.

Kuijt, I. 2000. "Keeping the Peace: Ritual, Skull Caching, and Community Integration in the Levantine Neolithic." In *Life in Neolithic Farming Communities: Social Organization, Identity, and Differentiation*, edited by I. Kuijt, 137-64. Fundamental Issues in Archaeology. New York, Boston, Dordrecht, London & Moscow: Kluwer Academic/Plenum Publishers.

Levinson, D. & M. Ember. (eds.). 1996. *Encyclopedia of Cultural Anthropology*. New York: Henry Holt & Company.

Lund, J. et al. (eds.). 1994-2001. *Den store danske Encyklopædi*. Copenhagen: Danmarks Nationalleksikon.

McCutcheon, R. 2003. *The Discipline of Religion: Structure, Meaning, Rhetoric*. London & New York: Routledge.

McGuire, M. 1987. *Religion: The Social Context*. Belmont: Wadsworth Publishing Company.

Mack, B. 1998. *A Myth of Innocence*. Augsburg: Fortress Publishers.

Marshack, A. 1999. "Space and Time in Preagricultural Europe and the Near East: The Evidence for Early Structural Complexity." In *Urbanization and Land Ownership in the Ancient Near East. A Colloquium held at New York University, November 1996, and the Oriental Institute, St. Petersburg, Russia, May 1997*, edited by M. Hudson & B.A. Levine, 19-63. Cambridge, MA: Peabody Museum of Archaeology and Ethnology, Harvard University.

Parker, R. 1996. *Athenian Religion: A History*. Oxford: Clarendon Press.

Price, S.R.F. 1999. *Religions of the Ancient Greeks*. Key Themes in Ancient History. Cambridge: Cambridge University Press.

Rappaport, R. 2000. Reprint. *Ritual and Religion in the Making of Humanity*. Cambridge Studies in Social and Cultural Anthropology 110. Cambridge: Cambridge University Press. Original edition, Cambridge: Cambridge University Press, 1999.

Renfrew, C. 1985. *The Archaeology of Cult: The Sanctuary at Phylakopi*. British School of Archaeology at Athens Suppl. 18. London: British School of Archaeology at Athens, distrubution Thames & Hudson.

Renfrew, C. 2001. "Symbol before Concept: Material Engagement and the Early Development of Society." In *Archaeological Theory Today*, edited by I. Hodder, 122-40. Cambridge: Polity Press.

Renfrew, C. & P. Bahn. (eds.). 1991. *Archaeology: Theories, Methods, and Practice*. London: Thames & Hudson.

Robertson-Smith, W. 1889. *Lectures on the Religion of the Semites*. Edinburgh: A. & C. Black.

Rollefson, G. 1998. "Ain Ghazal (Jordan): Ritual and Ceremony III." *Paléorient* 24.1: 43-58.

Schjødt, J.P. 2001. "Det 'Hellige' i religionsvidenskaben: En diskussion af det hellige som konstituerende for vor opfattelse af begrebet religion." In *Religionsvidenskabelige sonderinger*, edited by V. Andersen, 189-98. Aarhus: Aarhus University Press.

Schjødt, J.P. 2003. "Myths as Sources for Rituals – Theoretical and Practical Implications." In *Old Norse Myths*, edited by M.C. Ross, 261-78. Odense: University Press of Southern Denmark.

Simpson, J.A. et al. (eds.). *Oxford English Dictionary. OED Online*. http://dictionary.oed.com. (20 December 2008).

Tylor, E.B. 1871. *Primitive Culture: Researches into Development of Mythology, Philosophy, Religion, Language, Art and Custom*. London: Murray.

Verhoeven, M. 2002. "Ritual and its Investigation in Prehistory." In Gebel et al. 2002, 5-42.

Watkins, T. 2001. "The Beginning of Religion at the Beginning of the Neolithic." Paper read at the 2001 conference of the Bristish Association for Near Eastern Archaeology, 4-6 January 2001, Liverpool. http://www.arcl.ed.ac.uk/arch/watkins/watkins_conference.html.

Wilson, P.J. 1988. *The Domestication of the Human Species*. New Haven & London: Yale University Press.

Zaidman, L.B. & P. Schmitt Pantel. 1994. *Die Religion der Griechen: Kult und Mythos*. Munich: Beck.

Zuesse, E.M. 1987. "Ritual." In Eliade 1987a, vol. 12, 405-22.

Basket Case:
Altars, Animals and Baskets on Classical Attic Votive Reliefs

Richard Hamilton

Attic votive reliefs have a limited iconography: divinity, altar, worshipper(s), attendant(s), sacrificial animal.[1] In fact, the reliefs are so stereotyped that it is sometimes difficult to distinguish Zeus from Asklepios or a "banqueting hero."[2] Nonetheless, there do seem to be a few meaningful juxtapositions susceptible to a statistical approach and worth describing at some length, in hope that such correlations can prove useful to students of Greek religion.

The advantages of a statistical approach are that it requires both precise description of one's thesis and consideration of the converse of that thesis. If I can show that Århus has a high percentage of intelligent graduate students, I must also show the converse, that the rest of Denmark (the world?) does not have a high percentage, or at least that the percentage of intelligent Århus graduate students is *much* higher than the others, if my findings are to be significant statistically.[3] The disadvantages of a statistical approach are first that it concentrates on the most common elements and ignores the more interesting unique examples and secondly that it is useful only when a fairly large sample can be assembled. Also, it's not very lively reading so I will be brief.

The first task is to collect a sample. Since there is no Beazley Archive of Attic votive reliefs to give us a handy sample, it seemed to me prudent first to consult the largest, newest and most complete collections.[4]

1. Altars and animals

If we analyze van Straten's excellent catalogue of sacrifice scenes on Classical votive reliefs, we find that most scenes show a sacrificial animal being led to an altar, as we can see in an unpublished fragmentary relief from the Agora (S 800) showing a servant with a ritual basket (*kanoun*) and pig at an altar and two (larger) gods standing to the left (fig. 1).[5] Thus we find that 86 Attic reliefs in van Straten's list have an animal and only 23 do not, and 63 of those 86 have an altar. Conversely, only 10 of the 23 reliefs without a sacrificial animal have an altar. If we subject these data to a simple

Fig. 1

statistical test (called a "chi-square test") of the probability of this relationship being by chance, we find that the probability is only one in a hundred
(p=.01), which is significant.

Table 1.

	animal	no animal
altar	63	10
no altar	23	13

chi square 7.27, p=.01

This relationship should not surprise us since van Straten built his catalogue
on the basis of sacrificial animals and what he calls "indications pointing to

sacrificial ritual" such as altar, god, fillets on the animal or *kanoun*.[6] Thus, reliefs lacking altar and animal are likely to be ignored.

What should surprise us is that this relationship is the opposite of that between altar and the large straight-sided cylindrical basket, generally called a *kiste*, that we often see carried by a woman at the end of a procession of worshippers.[7]

Table 2.

	kiste	no *kiste*
altar	16	57
no altar	21	15

chi square 14.26, p=.001

Thus, while animal occurs with altar 63 times in van Straten's list and only 23 without, *kiste* occurs with altar only 16 times but 21 times without.[8] Equally important is the fact that the converse is true: when there is no animal there usually is no altar but when there is no *kiste* there usually is. These strong correlations suggest that the *kiste* was imagined as having a different destination than the altar. We might wish to interpret the occurrences of *kiste* and animal in the same scene as representations of a double offering with separate destinations' but we will see below that there is a strong correlation between *kiste* and animal.

Beyond interpretative uncertainties, the main problem here is that the sample is not random. Van Straten is interested only in sacrifice scenes, not in votive reliefs in general, and so his sample is skewed toward reliefs with altars and animals; as he notes, "among the whole class of votive reliefs, the ones with depictions of sacrifice are only a minority."[9] The question remains, then, whether these strong correlations hold more generally for votive reliefs.

One way to test this is to consider M. Edelmann's very full catalogue of worshippers on votive reliefs.[10] Though she illustrates only 36 reliefs, Edelmann catalogues over 450 and describes them quite fully. Using those descriptions and limiting ourselves to Attic reliefs, we find that we have more examples of animal without altar than we had with van Straten (25 vs. 17) and many more examples of altar without animal (34 vs. 13). Now altar appears hardly more often with animal than without, and now there is usually no *kiste* when there is no altar, but the relationships we found with van Straten's catalogue still hold statistically: altar is associated with the presence of animal and the absence of *kiste*.[11]

Table 3.

	animal	no animal		*kiste*	no *kiste*
altar	39	34	altar	16	57
no altar	25	53	no altar	32	46
chi square 7.05, p=.01			chi square 6.35, p=.025		

Although these relationships are still statistically significant, the probability has dropped considerably.[12] More worrisome, when I checked Edelmann's descriptions against van Straten's illustrations, I found that she often over-looked either altar or animal, and therefore any results derived from her lists are questionable.[13]

So, in the end these shortcuts proved unsuccessful, and it was necessary to construct a new catalogue, which can be found in the appendix. Given the accessibility of the *Lexicon iconographicum mythologiae classicae* (LIMC) and the relative lack of illustrated museum catalogues, it seemed best to collect by divinity: three non-Olympians (Nymphs, Asklepios, the banqueting hero) and three Olympians (Apollon, Artemis, Athena) seemed a large enough sample, to which I added Zeus, who though the archetypal Olympian is in the votive reliefs almost always the "other" Zeus, Zeus Meilichios or Zeus Philios, often pictured as a snake.[14]

Table 4.[15]

god	total	altar	worshipper	animal	kiste
Apollon	4	2	4 (2)	2 (2)	0
Artemis	18	4	12 (4)	2 (1)	2 (1)
Apollon+Artemis	6	2	3 (2)	1 (0)	1 (0)
Zeus	36	19	32 (15)	11 (8)	4 (1)
Athena	9	3	8 (3)	2 (1)	1 (1)
Nymphs	31	15	9 (3)	0	0
Asklepios	57	30	47 (26)	24 (21)	10 (6)
banqueting hero	63	19	52 (16)	20 (16)	10 (4)
total	224	94	167 (71)	62 (49)	28 (13)

Here, once again, the relationship between altar and animal is statistically significant, but the relationship between altar and *kiste* is now not significant.

Table 5.

	animal	no animal		kiste	no kiste
altar	50	40	altar	13	71
no altar	13	116	no altar	15	111
chi square 53.51, p=.001			chi square.56, p= not significant		

It is immediately apparent when looking at our list of gods that the Nymphs are anomalous. Although they are often pictured with altars, they are never seen with *kiste* and hardly ever with animal.[16] Thus, altar, which suggests animal sacrifice in the other reliefs, must have a different meaning in Nymph reliefs. In the present context, this anomaly suggests that we should exclude the Nymph reliefs in our calculations. But even without the Nymphs, the statistics remain virtually the same:

Table 6.

	animal	no animal		kiste	no kiste
altar	49	26	altar	13	56
no altar	13	100	no altar	15	96
chi square 59.10, p=.001			chi square.92, p= not significant		

2. Basket

If *kiste* is not related to altar, the question then becomes whether it is related to anything else, and the answer is that it is related to child, animal, and group of three or more worshippers.

Table 7.

	child	none	group	none	animal	none
kiste	22	4	24	2	18	9
no *kiste*	61	113	71	101	35	146
chi-square		22.88 p=.001		23.56 p=.001		27.72 p=.001

Relation to animal is surprising, especially given lack of relation to altar, which is closely related to animal. Van Straten surmised that the *kistai* "refer to the bringing of bloodless offerings such as cakes," but this will not explain the absence of any connection between *kiste* and altar.[17]

The association between *kiste* and child or group is less surprising and

receives support from Edelmann's catalogue of worshippers, where we find
kiste (maidservant) almost exclusively with a family of worshippers. We find
no *kiste* on reliefs that show a single worshipper (Katalog B Einzelne Adorant-
en) or paired young and old worshippers (Katalog E Erwachsene und Kind),
and only one on reliefs with married pairs (Katalog C Ehepaare) or groups
of men or women (Katalog G Frauen- oder Männergruppen). By contrast,
twelve reliefs depicting a family of worshippers have a *kiste* (Katalog D
Familie) and twenty depicting a family group (Katalog F Familiengruppen).[18]
The contrast is statistically significant:[19]

Table 8.

	maid	no maid
family	32	71
no family	2	161

chi-square 50.42, p=.001

The association between *kiste* and child or group receives further support
from what seem to be *kistai* depicted on Classical Athenian vases, that is,
depictions from the same period and from the same geographical area. There
we repeatedly find a straight-sided footless container, often carried by a
woman on her head or in her hands, sometimes in precisely the same pose
we see on the reliefs.[20] The decoration of the containers on the vases makes
it clear that they are (woven) baskets not (wooden) boxes, something we
might have suspected anyway from their relative size on the reliefs and from
their location on a servant's head.[21] Amyx, in his study of baskets on vases,
differentiated the straight-sided one from two other main types not only in
look and construction but also function for it "appears in scenes having to
do with women's indoor activities … especially in nuptial subjects," whereas the other two are associated with banquets.[22] This association ties in well
with our earlier finding that the *kiste* on votive reliefs is associated with
children and family. The *kiste* then is more likely to hold the bride's (or
mother's or child's) clothing than van Straten's sacrificial cakes.[23]

What about *kiste* and altar on these vases? I have found ten vases showing *kiste* at altar, and at first that might seem to offer a significant counter-
weight against the lack of association between *kiste* and altar on reliefs, but
these ten vases are a small percentage of the total number of vases depicting
kistai.[24] Furthermore, on only one of them is there anything resembling a
scene or tableau, that is, something possibly comparable to the scene we find
on the reliefs, and here the figures are labelled Eunomia and Thaleia, suggesting a mythological scene.[25] The other vases show a single individual in
a space defined only by the altar (and in one case a door).[26] Since half of the

individuals are winged and therefore unrealistic, one may surmise that the depiction on the vase is more an abstract idea than a concrete representation.[27] *Kistai* on vases, then, are shown with altars infrequently, and, when they are, one cannot speak of a representational scene.

The vases, it appears, support both the dissociation of *kiste* and altar and the association of *kiste* with children and family group. This emphasis on the feminine connotation of the *kiste* may help explain the relationship between *kiste* and animal. Since animal is strongly associated with altar but *kiste* is neither associated with nor dissociated from altar, we must reject both the possibility that *kiste* belongs to the sacrifice (that is, the combination of altar and animal) and the possibility that it represents an alternative to sacrifice. If the *kistai* on vases are associated with women and marriage, then we may wish to see the *kiste* on reliefs likewise as part of the representation of women. It is always carried by a woman, it is usually located close to the mother, nurse and children, and at opposite side of relief from the men, male servant, altar and animal.

We need finally to put the *kiste* in the larger context of the votive reliefs in general. Whereas we find a group of worshippers in two-thirds of the reliefs and altars in almost half, we find animal in only a quarter and *kiste* in only an eighth. The *kiste*, then, is a grace note, an attractive visual complement to the animal but in no way essential to the offering that is represented by the votive. We always find the divinity and usually find the worshipper, often with family, sometimes with offering, rarely with *kiste*. This is what the numbers tell us.

Statistics, then, have limits. They can show that there is likely to be a relationship between two variables but they cannot measure the strength of that relationship or explain the relationship. Their final value may be in the negative, requiring us to ask about the other, the absence, and showing that often what we think is significant is not.

Acknowledgements:

This essay is a rather dry distillation of what I hope was a more lively presentation at an energetic conference before an enthusiastic audience. I am grateful especially to Jesper Tae Jensen for introducing me to the numerous delights of Hamlet's fatherland and to his helpful and friendly colleagues for making the conference wonderful fun. I am grateful also to Jan Jordan and Carol Lawton for their cheerful and efficient assistance with the Agora relief and to Jon Owens for checking some numbers I thought I had botched (and had).

Notes

1 One could study all votive reliefs as I did at first, but, since Attic votive reliefs comprise over half the total I collected (224/426) and are almost all before the Hellenistic period, it seemed possible to still have a sufficiently large sample and at the same time to have one that is much more meaningful since it is chronologically and geographically limited.

2 And conversely the same iconography can be attributed to different divinities, as the fortuitous discovery of the numerous votive reliefs in the Pankrates sanctuary on the Ilissos shows us. There one of the two basic iconographic typologies is labeled indifferently Plouton (A2), Pankrates (A4), Palaimon (A10) or "the god" (A11). See Vikela 1994.

3 Even then statistical significance does not show causality but simply the probability of a relationship not being by chance.

4 I am delighted to hear that Anja Kloeckner of the University of Saarbrücken is in the process of constructing one.

5 van Straten 1995.

6 van Straten 1995, 12. These indications are presumably the same as the "characteristics [that] may identify the scene as a sacrificial one" listed two pages earlier: altar, god, fillets on the sacrificial animal, woman with basket on her head.

7 It may seem odd to use the term *kiste* since the well-known "mystic *kiste*" suggests a small box rather than a large basket, but *kiste* seems to be the generic term for basket. See the full discussion by Amyx (1958, 270) who concludes "the term was, to a certain degree, generic."

8 If we consider only relatively complete reliefs, the numbers are considerably smaller, but the statistical significance remains:

	animal	no animal		*kiste*	no *kiste*
altar	31	3	altar	14	20
no altar	10	10	no altar	17	3
chi square 11.68, p=.001			chi square 9.89 p=.01		

I should say that I am depending largely on van Straten's descriptions; comparison with available illustrations suggests his descriptions are very accurate. Truth in advertising requires that I give the data on which my numbers are based and so here is a list of the reliefs in van Straten and what I think they show. K= *kiste*, A= altar, B= animal (fragmentary/doubtful reliefs have a minus sign) so that van Straten's R5 shows *kiste*, altar and animal; his fragmentary R1 shows altar and animal, and so on.

KAB: R5, 7, 8, 20, 26, 28, 33, 44, 68, 73, 74, 115, 124-, 126, 128
AB: R1-, 3, 4-, 6-, 9, 13-, 15-, 21-, 23, 25-, 27, 29-, 32-, 41-, 42-, 43-, 48, 60-, 61-, 63-, 67, 84-, 86, 87, 89, 91-, 97, 99, 101-, 116-, 121-, 122-, 123-, 125-, 127-, 129, 130, 131, 132, 134, 135, 136-, 212-, 213-, 216-, 229-, 231-, 237-
KB: R18, 19, 31, 37-, 39, 45, 75, 90,
KA: R59-

A: R10- (van Straten calls it a table), 16, 40-, 46-, 47, 62-, 100, 117-, 120-
K: R11-, 22, 64, 66-, 98, 195, 197, 199, 202, 203, 206, 207, 233-
B: R17-, 24-, 30, 36-, 58, 65-, 93-, 18-, 119-, 133, 214-, 215-, 235-, 236-, 241-

9 van Straten 1995, 58.

10 Edelmann 1999. Güntner (1994) offers more illustrations of reliefs than Edelmann (62 vs 36) but does not describe the other reliefs that are catalogued and so provides too small a sample to be of use.

11 Edelmann speaks of maidservant not *kiste*, but a check of this against van Straten suggests she means "maid with kiste."

12 The statistics expert on whom I depend, Professor Clark McCauley of the Department of Psychology at Bryn Mawr, tells me I should not be impressed by a difference in statistical significance between .05 and .001.

13 In fact, correction of her numbers produces a much stronger probability of a relationship between animal and altar. She missed the altar in C12, 15, D6, 312, 2, E3, F10, 12, 13, 22, 32, 36, G7, 13, 37, 39, and U76; she missed the pig in F10 and the sheep in D41, F2, and U135. The revised numbers then are altar alone 28x; altar plus animal 46, animal alone 11. The chi-square here is 36.81, p.=.001.

14 Kybele was not considered, even though Güntner lists 48 reliefs, since only six in her list are dated to the fourth century (B1, B44, B45, B46, B47, B48, the last three with other gods), the rest being "spätklassisch-frühhellenistisch." Van Straten lists none, Edelmann only three (C20, D29, F46).

15 The figures in parentheses are occurrences with altar.

16 "Among the numerous Nymph reliefs, depictions of animal sacrifice are surprisingly rare," van Straten 1995, 91.

17 van Straten 1995, 97. "The things that were needed for the sacrifice in addition to the animal, such as sacrificial cakes or loaves, could be prepared at home and brought to the sanctuary in this *kiste*," (van Straten 61). This works much better for the covered tray shown in the relief of Herakles in the Epigraphical Museum at Athens (inv. 3942) illustrated in van Straten (fig. 93) than the boxlike *kiste* that is usually depicted. Van Straten offers no visual evidence for such a function, and his literary evidence is not strong: he offers *Thesmophoriazusai* 284f. as an "illustration" where a *kiste* holds a sacrificial cake but then goes on to undercut this by noting that there was "a different type of basket" (hemispherical with strings) used to bring food to a banquet (citing *Acharnians* 1085f.). Since the term *kiste* is found in both passages, there is no assurance that the *kiste* used in *Thesmophoriazusai* is any different from the one used in *Acharnians*, especially since both carry food. Also, the large size of the *kistai* on the reliefs (which are never labeled as *kistai*, we should remember) argues against them holding sacrificial cakes. On the different kinds of basket called *kiste*, see above n. 7.

18 0 of 85 single (B), 1 of 20 married pair (C6), 0 of 18 young and old (E), and 1 of 40 group of men/women (G36) but, by contrast, 12 of 55 family (D14, 15, 16, 19, 20, 30, 32, 35, 42, 45, 53, 55), 20 of 48 family group (F4, 9, 12, 13, 16, 17, 18, 19, 22, 23, 27, 28, 29, 31, 34, 37, 38, 39, 40, 42).

19 If we restrict ourselves to Attic reliefs the contrast between family and non-family is about the same:

	maid	no maid
family	21	51
no family	2	87

chi-square 25.56, p=.001

20 The connection was made already by Richter (1926, 99) who illustrated (fig. 244) the pose on a red-figure lebes gamikos by the Washing Painter in Athens (NM 14791); for another parallel by the Washing Painter see the red-figure lebes gamikos in New York (MMA 16.73) illustrated in Oakley and Sinos 1993, fig. 37. It is surprising that van Straten (1995, 60) says these women with *kistai* are not "encountered" on vases but presumably he means "in the same context."

21 The lack of decoration on the *kistai* shown on reliefs may be thought to undermine the parallel, but such decoration may well have been painted on (and subsequently wore off).

22 Amyx 1958.

23 This would explain why the *kiste* is so rare, 10%. There are other possible functions. One is that the *kiste* is meant to hold meat that will result from the impending sacrifice, which will be shared with family and friends, and so is a symbol of the dedicator's generosity. Pamela Webb ingeniously suggested to me that the *kiste* holds clothes and so is in effect a suitcase, showing that the worshippers have come from far away to honor the god.

24 To give you a rough idea, on 7 August 2004 the Beazley Archive listed 1065 "box" and 1132 "basket," both terms that describe our *kiste*, though these lists include other types of box and basket.

25 BA (= Beazley Archive) 220622 (= *LIMC* Eunomia 6, Thaleia V.1) a red-figure lekythos, once Bauville collection Paris, in the manner of the Meidias Painter (ARV2 1326.67), shows a goddess (?) with scepter seated on a stool beside an altar and a statue on a column, with women named [Th]aleia and Eunomia nearby, one holding a *kiste*.

26 BA 210092 Louvre G 477, a red-figure cup by the Painter of London E 80 shows a woman alone at an altar beside a door. Other vases depicting women alone at an altar include: BA 9082, a red-figure oinochoe in the D.J. collection in Ostwestfalen; BA 43561, a red-figure lekythos in the Mormino collection in Palermo (inv. 3309); and BA 340008, a red-figure hydria near the Washing Painter in the Antikensammlungen in Munich (inv. 2436). Five vases show Nike alone at altar: BA 239 Bryn Mawr P103, a red-figure hydria by Shuvalov Painter; BA 12419 Braunschweig 261, a red-figure lekythos; BA 24444 Oxford 1934.327, a red-figure alabaston; BA 41488 Moscow Pushkin 587, a red-figure lekythos; Providence 11.013 (*CVA* Providence pl. 25.3), a white-ground lekythos.

One might add the late BA 230853, a fourth-century red-figure lekanis lid in the Museo Nazionale di Spina in Ferrara (inv. 4252) showing Eros with a *kiste* or box flying to an altar next to a large female head, with another Eros on the other side at an altar chasing a woman (*ARV2* 1500.6).

27 For this complicated subject see now Ferrari 2002.

Appendix: List of Classical Attic Reliefs

(?= non-Attic?; *= with *kiste*; #= with animal; += child worshipper)[1]

Nymphs[2]
altar

Edwards 1 (= Güntner A8) Athens NM 1329, 410/400 B.C.: three Nymphs
  Pan worshipper rock altar

Edwards 14 (= *LIMC* Artemis 1280; Güntner A54) Athens Agora I 7154,
  340/330 B.C.: Demeter Apollon Artemis Zeus Pan Acheloos head Hermes
  delivering baby Dionysos to three Nymphs rock altar

Edwards 22 (= *LIMC* Pan 236; Güntner A18) Athens NM 4466, 330/320 B.C.:
  three Nymphs Hermes worshipper servant Pan kantharos oinochoe rock
  altar

Edwards 23 (= *LIMC* Acheloos 176) Athens NM 2008, 340/330 B.C.: Acheloos
  head Hermes three Nymphs Pan rock altar

Edwards 26 (= *LIMC* Acheloos 186) Athens NM 1859, 330/320 B.C.: Hermes
  three Nymphs Acheloos head rock altar

#Edwards 28 (= *LIMC* Acheloos 174) Worsley, 330/310 B.C.: five worshippers
  servant animal rock altar Hermes three Nymphs Acheloos head

Edwards 30 (= *LIMC* Acheloos 202; Güntner A53) Berlin Staatliche Museen
  K 87, 320/310 B.C.: upper register= head of Acheloos Hermes three
  Nymphs Pan; lower register= Demeter Kore carved altar Hero Equitans
  (?)

Edwards 34 (= *LIMC* Acheloos 187; Güntner A34) Athens NM 1447, 320/300
  B.C.: Hermes three Nymphs rock altar

?Edwards 38 (= *LIMC* Acheloos 178; Güntner A23) Athens NM 1445, 320/300
  B.C.: head of Acheloos Pan three Nymphs single-stone altar

Edwards 40 (= *LIMC* Acheloos 177) Athens NM 2009, 320/300 B.C.: Hermes
  three Nymphs rock altar face of Acheloos Pan

Edwards 43 (= Fuchs 1962, pl. 64.2) Athens NM (no inventory number)
  320/300 B.C.: Hermes three Nymphs rock altar

?Edwards 44 (= *LIMC* Acheloos 183) private coll. Kent, 320/300 B.C.: Hermes
  three Nymphs Pan Acheloos head altar

Edwards 53 (= *LIMC* Acheloos 192) Athens NM 3835, 310/290 B.C.: Hermes
  Pan two Nymphs rock altar Acheloos head

Edwards 54 (= *LIMC* Acheloos 188; Güntner A44) Athens NM 1448, 310/290
  B.C.: Pan Hermes three Nymphs Acheloos head single-stone altar

?Edwards 58 (= *LIMC* Apollon 804) Treviso, 310/290 B.C.: three Nymphs rock
  altar, seated male w. phiale

non-altar

+Edwards 3 (= *LIMC* Acheloos 197, Apollon 968, Artemis 1182) Athens NM
2756, 405/390 B.C.: Apollon six gods two worshippers (one child) three
Nymphs Acheloos head[3]

Edwards 4 (= *LIMC* Acheloos 210, Artemis 1028) Athens NM 1783, 400/390
B.C.: side A= Kephisos Artemis hero three Nymphs; side B= hero Ech-
elos abducts Iasile[4]

?Edwards 5 (= *LIMC* Acheloos 166) Berlin Staatliche Museen K 83, 400/390
B.C.: Hermes three Nymphs Acheloos head worshipper

Edwards 11 (= *LIMC* Fluvii) Avignon Calvet E 19, 380/370 B.C.: three Nymphs
Pan seated male (Dionysos?)

Edwards 15 (= *LIMC* Hermes 355) Athens NM 2011, 340/330 B.C.: Pan three
Nymphs Hermes (holding baby Dionysos?)

Edwards 19 (= *LIMC* Asklepios 211, Bendis 4) Copenhagen NCG 462, 329
B.C.: below= Bendis Deloptes two worshippers; above= Hermes three
Nymphs Pan head

Edwards 20 (= *LIMC* Pan 236) Athens NM 4465, 330/320 B.C.: three worshippers Pan Hermes three Nymphs

Edwards 29 (= *LIMC* Acheloos 179) Athens NM 2012, 320/310 B.C.: Pan hunt-
er Acheloos head three Nymphs

Edwards 31 (= *LIMC* Acheloos 182) Berlin Statliche Museen K 84, 320/310
B.C.: three Nymphs Acheloos head (fragmentary)

Edwards 33 (= *LIMC* Kynnes 2) Athens NM 2010, 320/310 B.C.: three Nymphs
Hermes (maybe more)

Edwards 47 (= *LIMC* Acheloos 173) Riehen, 320/300 B.C.: Hermes Pan three
Nymphs Acheloos head

+?Edwards 50 (= Svoronos pl. 137) Athens NM 2796, 320/300 B.C.: three
worshippers (one child) Hermes two Nymphs (fragmentary)

Edwards 51 (= *LIMC* Acheloos 184) Athens NM 2007, 310/290 B.C.: Hermes
three Nymphs Pan Acheloos head

Edwards 52 (= *LIMC* Acheloos 191) Athens Kerameikos K170, 310/290 B.C.:
Pan two Nymphs Acheloos head

Edwards 57 (= *LIMC* Hera 263) Athens NM 1459, 310/290 B.C.: Zeus Agathe
Tyche(?) Artemis heads of Hermes and three Nymphs

Güntner A2 (= *LIMC* Pandrosos 25, Hermes 321) Athens Akropolis Museum
702, 500 B.C.: Hermes three Nymphs boy[5]

Asklepios
altar

+#van Straten R1 (= Walter #188) Athens Akropolis Museum 2410, 4th C.:
snake altar four worshippers (one child) servant *kanoun* pig (gods lost)

+#van Straten R3 (= Walter #106) Athens Akropolis Museum 2559+3264, 4th
C.: Asklepios altar three worshippers (one child) servant *kanoun* sheep

#van Straten R4 (= Walter #101) Athens Akropolis Museum 4718, 4th C.: Asklepios altar servant sheep (worshippers lost)

*#van Straten R5 (= Walter #315) Athens Akropolis Museum 4738, 4th C.: A= altar three worshippers servant pig; B= altar three worshippers servant *kanoun* pig maid kiste (fragmentary)

#van Straten R6 (= *LIMC* Asklepios 63) Athens NM 1330, 4th C.: Asklepios Hygieia disk on pillar altar two worshippers servant *kanoun* pig

*#van Straten R7 (= *LIMC* Asklepios 386) Athens NM 1331, 4th C.: Asklepios Hygieia altar three worshippers servant cow maid kiste

+*#van Straten R8 (= *LIMC* Asklepios 66) Athens NM 1333, 4th C.: Asklepios Hygieia tree altar five worshippers (two children) servant sheep bowl maid kiste

+#van Straten R9 (= *LIMC* Asklepios 338) Athens NM 1334, 4th C.: Asklepios Hygieia altar three worshippers (two children) servant pig

van Straten R10 (= *LIMC* Asklepios 96) Athens NM 1335, 4th C.: Asklepios Hygieia tree altar two worshippers servant *kanoun*

+#van Straten R13 (= Svoronos pl. 40) Athens NM 1362, 4th C.: Asklepios two sons(+) altar four worshippers (two children) servant sheep

+van Straten R14 (= *LIMC* Epione 4) Athens NM 1368, 4th C.: two goddesses phiale four worshippers (one child) altar? ("chest" Svoronos) thymiaterion

#van Straten R15 (= Svoronos pl. 47) Athens NM 1370, 4th C.: two sons(+) altar worshipper(+) servant *kanoun* pig

van Straten R16 (= Svoronos pl. 35) Athens NM 1372, 4th C.: two sons(+) altar two worshippers

+*#van Straten R20 (= Svoronos pl. 147) Athens NM 2401, 4th C.: altar six worshippers (two children) servant *kanoun* sheep maid kiste (fragmentary)

#van Straten R21 (= *LIMC* Epione 2, Asklepios 59) Athens NM 2418, 4th C.: Asklepios Hygieia two sons three daughters altar two worshippers(+) servant animal

+#van Straten R23 (= *LIMC* Asklepios 64) Louvre MA 755, 4th C.: Asklepios Hygieia disk on pillar altar six worshippers (two children) servant *kanoun* cow

#van Straten R25 (= Mitropoulou 1968 #239) Agora S 800, 4th C.: Asklepios Hygieia altar two worshippers(+) servant *kanoun* pig

+*#van Straten R26 (= Svoronos pl. 93) Athens NM 2681, 4th C.: Asklepios altar five worshippers (one child) servant *kanoun* sheep maid kiste

+#van Straten R27 (= *LIMC* Asklepios 202) Athens NM 1407, 4th C.: Asklepios snake altar four worshippers (one child) servant *kanoun* sheep

+*#van Straten R28 (= Svoronos pl. 37) Athens NM 1429, 4th C.: altar eight worshippers (one child) servant cow maid kiste (fragmentary)

+#van Straten R29 (= Karouzou 1974) Athens NM 3304, 4th C.: altar three
  worshippers (one child) servant cow (fragmentary)
+#?van Straten R32 (= *EA* 561) Palermo, 4th C.: Hygieia(+) altar two worshippers servant *kanoun* pig
Güntner C14 (= *LIMC* Asklepios 86) Athens NM 1338, 400/390: Asklepios
  Hygieia altar worshipper
+Edelmann D17 (= Svoronos pl. 50) Athens NM 1356, 4th C.: Hygieia(+) four
  worshippers (two children) altar
+Edelmann D25 (= Svoronos pl. 156) Athens NM 2520, early 4th C.: three
  worshippers (one child) altar (gods missing)
#Edelmann U76 (= *LIMC* Asklepios 78) Athens NM 2390, 4th C.: Asklepios?
  servant ox sheep goat altar
LIMC Hygieia 28 Athens NM 1383, 4th C.: Hygieia altar pillar w. relief horse
?#*LIMC* Hygieia 131 (= *LIMC* Amphiaraos 65) Athens NM 1396 (stele from
  Oropos), 320 B.C.: Asklepios Hygieia altar worshipper victim
+*LIMC* Asklepios 93 Athens NM 2417, first quarter 4th C.: Asklepios Hy-
  gieia altar three worshippers (one child?)[6] two columns
LIMC Asklepios 104 Athens NM 2925, 350 B.C.: Asklepios two daughters
  altar phiale?

no altar

+*van Straten R11 (= *LIMC* Asklepios 344) Athens NM 1345, 4th C.: Asklepios
  Hygieia seven worshippers (two children) maid kiste (middle lost, perhaps including altar and animal)
van Straten R12 (= Güntner C25) Athens NM 1346, early 4th C.: Asklepios
  two daughters table (fragmentary)
+*#van Straten R18 (= *LIMC* Asklepios 201) Athens NM 1377, 4th C.: Asklepios
  Hygieia Epione ten worshippers (two children) servant *kanoun* pig kiste,
  herm Hekate
+*#van Straten R19 (= *LIMC* Asklepios 248) Athens NM 1402, 4th C.: Asklepios
  Hygieia two sons three daughters six worshippers (two children) maid
  kiste pig
+*van Straten R22 (= *LIMC* Asklepios 89) Kassel SK 44, 370 B.C.: Asklepios
  patient on couch four worshippers (two children) maid kiste
#van Straten R30 (= Ziehen 1892, 234 fig. 5) Piraeus, 4th C.?: Asklepios god-
  dess woman? patient on couch four worshippers servant pig
+Güntner C2 (= *LIMC* Asklepios 105, Hygieia 138) Piraeus 405, late 5th C.:
  Asklepios Hygieia patient on couch four worshippers (one child)
?Güntner C5 (= *LIMC* Hygieia 48) Athens NM 2926, early 4th C.: Asklepios
  Hygieia two worshippers
+Güntner C16 (= *LIMC* Asklepios 92) Athens NM 1354, late 4th C.: Asklepios
  Hygieia four worshippers (one child)

Güntner C21 (= *LIMC* Asklepios 71; Svoronos 36 pl. 38.1) Athens NM 1339, middle 4th C. Asklepios Hygieia? worshipper

Güntner C24 (= *LIMC* Asklepios 395) Athens NM 1341, late 5th C.: Asklepios two daughters worshipper chariot ("saved from large rocks")

+Güntner C31 (= *LIMC* Asklepios 75) Athens NM, first half 4th C.: Asklepios son six worshippers (four children)

+Güntner C33 (= *LIMC* Asklepios 70) Athens NM 1344, second half 4th C.: Asklepios Hygieia son five worshippers (two children)

+Güntner C40 (= Svoronos pl. 50.1) Athens NM 1361, second half 4th C.: Asklepios Hygieia son five worshippers (three children)

Güntner C43 (= *LIMC* Hygieia 37, Alkon 1) Athens NM 1365, mid-4th C.: Asklepios Hygieia two others

Güntner C49 (= *LIMC* Asklepios 60, Hygieia 140)[7] Athens NM 1388, 410/400 B.C.: Asklepios Poseidon goddess

Güntner C51 (= *LIMC* Asklepios 313) Athens NM 1332, 340/330 B.C.: Asklepios Demeter Kore six worshippers

Edelmann B13 (= *LIMC* Asklepios 200) Athens NM 1347, first half 4th C.: Asklepios worshipper

Edelmann B14 (= Svoronos pl. 46) Athens NM 1373, first half 4th C.: Asklepios worshipper

Edelmann B15 (= *LIMC* Asklepios 203) Athens NM 1376, second half 4th C.: Asklepios worshipper

+Edelmann D24 (= *LIMC* Asklepios 54) Athens NM 1841, first half 4th C.: Asklepios son? patient on couch two worshippers (one child?)[8]

+Edelmann D40 (= *LIMC* Asklepios 102, Hygieia 137) Brockleby Park 10, 415 B.C.: Asklepios Hygieia three worshippers (one child)

LIMC Hygieia 29 (= *LIMC* Asklepios 76) Athens NM 2557, 4th C.: Asklepios Hygieia pillar

LIMC Hygieia 148 (= *LIMC* Asklepios 205) Athens NM 2406, 4th C.: Asklepios Hygieia

?*LIMC* Asklepios 82 Vatican 799, 400 B.C.: Asklepios w. phiale goddess w. oinochoe worshipper

LIMC Asklepios 87 (= Svoronos pl. 150) Athens NM 2416,[9] first quarter 4th C.: Asklepios Hygieia four daughters

LIMC Asklepios 337 (= Svoronos pl. 193) Athens NM 2958, 4th C.: Asklepios Hygieia worshipper pillar (w. relief?)

[*LIMC* Asklepios 5 Athens NM 1351 = Artemis 1279]

[*LIMC* Asklepios 211 Copenhagen NCG 462 = Nymphs Edwards 19]

Zeus[10]

altar

#van Straten R41 (= Svoronos pl. 219) Athens Epigraphical Museum 8738, 324 B.C.: Zeus bird altar pig phiale (worshippers lost)

#van Straten R42 (= Svoronos pl. 143) Athens NM 2383, 4th C.: Zeus bird altar? sheep? *kanoun*? (worshippers lost)

#van Straten R43 (= Svoronos pl. 140.5 "Asklepios") Athens NM 2390, 4th C.: Zeus(?) altar servant cow two goats (worshippers lost)

+*#van Straten R44 (= Mitropoulou 1975, 120 fig. 3) Piraeus 3, 4th C: Zeus w. cornucopia altar five worshippers (three children) servant *kanoun* pig maid kiste

?van Straten R46 (= Mitropoulou Snakes fig. 46) Eleusis 5126, 4th C.: Zeus bird altar servant *kanoun* (worshippers lost)

+van Straten R47 (= *Praktika* 1979 pl. 3b) Rhamnous 102, 4th C: Zeus bird altar five worshippers (three children)

+#?van Straten R48 (= Svoronos pl. 45.1) Athens NM 1433, 4th C.: Zeus altar six worshippers (one child) servant *kanoun*? sheep

+#van Straten R97 (= *LIMC* Pankrates 7, Vikela A4) Fetiye Camii P56B, 4th C.: Zeus/Hades cornucopia phiale altar four worshippers (one child) servant pig *kanoun*

#*LIMC* Pankrates 5 (= Vikela A1) Fetiye Camii P26B, middle 4th C.: Zeus/Hades altar? servant ram, *kanoun* three worshippers

LIMC Pankrates 8 (= Vikela A5) Fetiye Camii P4A, 330/325 B.C.: Zeus/Hades phiale altar two worshippers

+*LIMC* Pankrates 12 (= Vikela A9) Fetiye Camii P53B, 330/320 B.C.: Zeus/Hades cornucopia phiale altar servant *kanoun* pig four worshippers (two children)

+*LIMC* Pankrates 15 (= Vikela A14) Fetiye Camii P89A, 340 B.C.: Zeus/Hades phiale altar four worshippers (one child)

+*LIMC* Pankrates 16 (= Vikela A15) Fetiye Camii P14A, 330 B.C.: Zeus/Hades altar four worshippers (one child)

+*LIMC* Pankrates 17 (= Vikela A16) Fetiye Camii P46B, 320/310 B.C.: Zeus/Hades phiale square rock altar four worshippers (two children)

LIMC Pankrates 18 (= Vikela A18) Fetiye Camii P20A, third quarter 4th C.: Zeus/Hades altar worshipper

#*LIMC* Pankrates 19 (= Vikela A20) Fetiye Camii P31B, 300 B.C.: Zeus/Hades phiale? rock altar animal kneeling worshipper

LIMC Pankrates 24 (= Vikela A10) Fetiye Camii P3A, late 4th C.: Zeus/Hades cornucopia phiale altar kneeling worshipper, two+ worshippers[11]

+Edelmann D23 (= *LIMC* Zeus 200) Athens NM 1431, second half 4th C.: Zeus phiale altar three worshippers (one child)

+Edelmann E4 (= *LIMC* Zeus 201) Athens NM 1779, 4th C. Zeus phiale rock altar two worshippers (one child)

no altar

+*#?van Straten R45 (= Svoronos pl. 65) Athens NM 1408, 4th C.: Zeus four worshippers (one kneeling, two children) servant sheep *kanoun* maid kiste

*van Straten R98 (= Pankrates 14) Fetiye Camii P8A, 300 B.C.: Zeus/Hades cornucopia phiale kneeling worshipper table worshipper maid kiste

+Edelmann E8 (= *LIMC* Zeus 204) Athens NM 1405, 4th/early 3rd B.C.: Zeus two worshippers (one child)

LIMC Pankrates 6 (= Vikela A3) Fetiye Camii P10A, 340/330 B.C.: Zeus/Hades cornucopia phiale goddess w. phiale three worshippers (one kneeling)

+*LIMC* Pankrates 11 (= Vikela A8) Fetiye Camii P25A, 320 B.C.: Zeus/Hades phiale, goddess? five worshippers (two children)

+*#*LIMC* Pankrates 13 (= Vikela A11) Fetiye Camii P48B, 310 B.C.: Zeus/Hades cornucopia phiale servant pig *kanoun* maid kiste seven worshippers (four children)

LIMC Pankrates 21 (= Vikela A13) Fetiye Camii P1A, late 4th C.: Zeus/Hades cornucopia phiale worshipper

+*LIMC* Pankrates 23 (= Vikela A2) Fetiye Camii P18A, 340 B.C.: Zeus/Hades cornucopia phiale ("Pluton") three+ worshippers (child)

#*LIMC* Pankrates 25 (= Vikela A17) Fetiye Camii P7A, 300 B.C.: Zeus/Hades worshipper w. fish

Edelmann B20 (= Svoronos pl. 142) Athens NM 2356, late 4th C.: Zeus phiale(?) worshipper

Edelmann B26 (= Mitropoulou Snakes fig. 59) Piraeus, second half 4th C.: snake worshipper

Edelmann B34 (= Mitropoulou Snakes fig. 58) Paris Louvre 1430, second half 4th C: snake worshipper

+Edelmann D28 (= Mitropoulou Snakes fig. 48a) Athens NM 3329, second half 4th C.: snake three worshippers (one child)

+Edelmann D33 (= Mitropoulou Snakes fig. 40) Piraeus 51, second half 4th C.: Zeus three worshippers (one child)

Edelmann D37 (= Blümel 1966, fig. 122) Berlin 723, first half 4th C.: snake three worshippers

+?Edelmann D44 (= Mitropoulou Snakes fig. 47a) Göttingen 18a/b, 4th C.: Zeus five worshippers (three children)

Edelmann G40 Athens NM, 4th C.: snake two worshippers

Athena[12]
altar

*van Straten R59 (= Mangold pl. 7.1) Athens Acropolis Museum 2413+ 2515+3003, 4th C.: Athena altar worshipper(s) servant (animal?) maid kiste

#van Straten R60 (= Mangold pl. 7.2) Athens Akropolis Museum 3007, 4th
   C.: Athena altar eight worshippers servant *kanoun* pig
Svoronos pl. 37.5 Athens NM 1369, 4th C.: Athena Asklepios worshipper
   altar

no altar
+#van Straten R58 (= *LIMC* Athena 587) Athens Akropolis Museum 581,
   500/480 B.C.: Athena four worshippers (two children) servant pig phiale
LIMC Athena 52 Athens Akropolis Museum 577, 480/70 B.C.: Athena artisan
   tripod(?)
Edelmann B2 Athens Akropolis Museum 2435, late 5th C: Athena worshipper
Edelmann U32 (= Svoronos pl. 212) Athens Epigraphical Museum 2812, 4th
   C.: Athena worshipper
+Rühfel 1984, fig. 87 Athens Akropolis Museum 3030, 4th C.: Athena two
   worshippers (one child[13])
LIMC Athena 148 Athens NM 82, early 5th C.: two Athenas in frame

Artemis
altar

+*#van Straten R73 (= *LIMC* Artemis 974) Brauron 1151, 330 B.C.: Artemis w.
   bow phiale deer altar twelve worshippers (four children) servant *kanoun*
   cow maid kiste
+?van Straten R76 (= *LIMC* Artemis 461) Athens NM 1950 (Aigina), second
   half 5th C.: Artemis w. torches six worshippers (two children) four-step
   altar phiale fawn goose
Edelmann C13 (= Philadelpheus 1927, 158 no. 1, pl. 8) Athens NM, late 4th
   C.: Artemis altar two pithoi two worshippers
LIMC Artemis 508 Athens NM 1403, late 4th C.: Artemis w. torches altar
   worshipper (fr.)

no altar

+*#van Straten R75 (= *LIMC* Artemis 673) Brauron 1153, middle 4th C.: Ar-
   temis deer eight worshippers (three children) servant goat maid kiste
+Edelmann F30 (= *LIMC* Artemis 459) Brauron 1171, late 5th C.: Artemis w.
   torch deer nine worshippers (two children) (fragmentary)
?Edelmann G25 (= *LIMC* Bendis 3) London BM 2155, second half 4th C.:
   Bendis ten worshippers (torchracers)
?Edelmann G38 (= *LIMC* Artemis 505) Athens NM 2376, first half 4th C.:
   goddess w. torches, goddess??, two worshippers
LIMC Artemis 234 Brauron 1175, late 5th C.: Artemis dog (fragmentary)[14]

LIMC Artemis 287 (= Walter #111) Athens Akropolis Museum 3316+3370 (date?): Artemis dog (fragmentary)[15]

LIMC Artemis 397 Kassel 774, late 5th C.: Artemis deer

LIMC Artemis 412 Athens Agora S 100, 400/375 B.C.: Artemis w. torch (fragmentary)

LIMC Artemis 413 Athens NM 208: Artemis w. torch tree deer pillar(?)

LIMC Artemis 462 (= Walter #110) Athens Akropolis Museum 2674, 400 B.C.: Artemis w. torches deer worshipper (fragmentary)[16]

LIMC Artemis 463 Brauron 1182, 4th C.: Artemis w. torches worshipper

(#)*LIMC* Artemis 621 Brauron 1157, late 5th C.: Artemis, four sheep

LIMC Artemis 674 Athens NM 2361, third quarter 4th C.: Artemis seated on hill deer worshipper

LIMC Artemis 724 Brauron 1183, 400 B.C.: Artemis(?) worshipper

LIMC Artemis 1036a Brauron 1172, 400 B.C.: Artemis(?) five worshippers

[*LIMC* Artemis 1028 Athens NM 1783 = Edwards 4]

[*LIMC* Artemis 1182 Athens NM 2756 = Edwards 3]

[*LIMC* Artemis 286 (= Walter #297) Athens Akropolis Museum 2596 (date?): Artemis (too fragmentary)]

[*LIMC* Artemis 418 (= Svoronos pl. 152) Athens NM 2445 4th C.: Artemis w. torches worshipper(?)[17]

Artemis and Apollon
altar

Güntner E2 (= Voutiras 1982, pl. 31.3) Athens NM 3075, 330 B.C.: Artemis w. torch Apollon altar worshipper omphalos phiale

LIMC Artemis 911 (= Vermeule 1981, #62) Boston MFA 1977.171, 323 B.C.: Artemis(?) Apollon(?) altar four worshippers

no altar

+*#van Straten R74 (= *LIMC* Apollon 957, Artemis 1127) Brauron 1152, 340/330 B.C.: Artemis w. torch Apollon Leto servant animal maid kiste seven worshippers (four children)

Güntner E3 (= *LIMC* Apollon 657) Athens NM 1389, late 5th C.: Apollon seated on tripod Artemis Leto

?Güntner E9 (= *LIMC* Artemis 1225) Brauron 1180, 420/400 B.C.: Zeus Artemis Apollon Leto deer

*LIMC Artemis 1279 (= *LIMC* Asklepios 5) Athens NM 1351, 350 B.C.: Artemis Apollon palm dog snake *liknon*

[Güntner E6 (= *LIMC* Artemis 1130) Athens NM 3917, 330 B.C.: Artemis w. torches Apollon Leto (too fragmentary)

[Güntner E7 (= *LIMC* Apollon 731) Athens NM 3061, 330 B.C. Artemis Apollon Leto (too fragmentary)

Apollon
altar

+?#van Straten R83 (= *LIMC* Apollon 956) Copenhagen NCG 2309, 4th C.:
  Apollon w. kithara altar five worshippers (two children) servant *kanoun*
  sheep
?#van Straten R84 (= Voutiras, 1982, pl. 30.1-2) Detroit 25.14, 4th C.: Apollon
  altar two+ worshippers servant *kanoun* sheep

no altar

?Edelmann U1 (= *LIMC* Apollon 418a) Aigina, second half 4th C.: Apollon
  kithara phiale worshipper omphalos
LIMC Apollon 145c (= Walter #50) Athens Akropolis Museum 2970, 4th C.:
  Apollon worshipper

Banquet Reliefs[18]
altar

+*#van Straten R115 (Dentzer R 103) Athens Akropolis Museum 3013, 4th C.
  A= six worshippers (four children); B= six worshippers (four children)
  altar servant *kanoun* sheep maid kiste (fragmentary)
+#van Straten R116 (Dentzer R 99) Athens Akropolis Museum 2451, 4th C.:
  hero five worshippers (two children) altar servant sheep maid (kiste?)
#van Straten R117 (Svoronos pl. 186) Athens NM 2929, 4th C.: heroine altar
  worshipper servant *kanoun*
van Straten R120 (Dentzer R 156) Athens NM 2363, 4th C.: hero heroine
  oinochoos altar (worshippers lost)
#van Straten R121 (Dentzer R 163) Athens NM 2816, 4th C.: hero heroine
  altar servant *kanoun* pig (worshippers lost)
#van Straten R122 (Dentzer R 165) Athens NM 2850, 4th C.: oinochoos altar
  three worshippers servant sheep *kanoun* (hero lost)
(#)van Straten R123 (Dentzer R 177) Athens NM 2912, 4th C.: hero heroine
  altar three worshippers pig? horsehead
+*#van Straten R124 (Dentzer R 154) Athens NM 2927, 4th C.: hero heroine
  altar? five worshippers (two children) servant *kanoun* pig maid kiste
#van Straten R125 (Dentzer R 189) Athens NM 2942, 4th C.: altar worshipper(s)
  servant *kanoun* pig (hero lost)
+*#van Straten R126 (Dentzer R 195) Athens NM 3873, 4th C.: hero heroine
  oinochoos horsehead altar five worshippers (three children) servant
  kanoun pig maid kiste
#van Straten R127 (Dentzer R 201b) Athens excavation, 4th C.: hero heroine
  oinochoos altar servant *kanoun* pig (worshippers lost)
+*#van Straten R128 (Dentzer R 201a) Athens excavation, 4th C.: hero heroine horsehead altar five worshippers (three children) servant *kanoun* pig
  maid kiste

#van Straten R129 (Dentzer R 466) Madrid, 4th C.: hero heroine altar worshipper servant *kanoun* pig (fragmentary)

+#van Straten R130 (Dentzer R 394) Athens NM 1516, 4th C.: hero heroine oinochoos dog altar four worshippers (one child?) servant *kanoun* pig

+#van Straten R131 (Dentzer R 402) Athens NM 1538, 4th C.: hero heroine oinochoos horsehead altar five worshippers (two children) servant pig

+#van Straten R132 (Dentzer R 229) from Piraeus, 4th C.: hero heroine oinochoos horsehead altar five worshippers (two children) servant *kanoun* pig

+#van Straten R134 (Dentzer R 233) from Dagla, 4th C.: hero heroine horsehead altar six worshippers (three children) servant *kanoun* pig

+#van Straten R135 (Dentzer R 244) market, 4th C.: hero heroine oinochoos altar four worshippers (two children) servant *kanoun* pig

Dentzer R 100 (= Walter 115) Athens Akropolis Museum, 4th C.: altar? four worshippers?[19] (hero) heroine

non-altar

#van Straten R118 (Dentzer R 107) Athens Akropolis Museum 4697, 4th C.: hero heroine krater servant sheep *kanoun* (worshippers lost)

+#van Straten R119 (Dentzer R 121) Athens Agora S 538, 4th C.: four worshippers (two children) servant pig (fragmentary; perhaps with altar)

?#van Straten R133 (Dentzer R 344) Bardo C 1200, 4th C.: hero heroine oinochoos two worshippers servant *kanoun*? pig

+#van Straten R136 (Dentzer R 455) Rome Barracco 138, 4th C.: hero heroine oinochoos horsehead three worshippers (one child) servant *kanoun* sheep

+*van Straten R195 (Dentzer R 153) Athens NM 1537, 4th C.: oinochoos four worshippers (two children) maid kiste (hero lost)

+*van Straten R197 (Dentzer R 237) Athens NM, 4th C.: hero heroine oinochoos horsehead four worshippers (two children) maid kiste

*van Straten R199 (Dentzer R 205) Berlin 817, 4th C.: hero heroine two worshippers dogs maid kiste (damaged)

+*van Straten R203 (Dentzer R 440) Kassel, 4th C.: hero heroine oinochoos four worshippers (two children) maid kiste

?*van Straten R206 (Dentzer R 469) Nice, 4th C.: hero heroine two worshippers maid kiste

+*van Straten R207 (Dentzer R 225) Paris Louvre MA 747, 4th C.: hero heroine oinochoos horsehead six worshippers (three children) maid kiste

+Dentzer R 119 Athens Agora S 396: hero heroine four worshippers (one child)

Dentzer R 124 Athens Agora S 713: hero oinochoos

Dentzer R 126 Athens Agora S 834: worshipper hero heroine

Dentzer R 139 Athens Agora S 1630: worshipper hero heroine

+Dentzer R 143 Athens Agora I 4707: two worshippers (one child) hero hero-
    ine
Dentzer R 144 Athens NM 4802: hero heroine oinochoos
Dentzer R 145 Athens NM 1371: three worshippers (hero) heroine oinochoos
    horsehead
+Dentzer R 146 Athens NM 1512: three worshippers (one child) hero heroine
    oinochoos
+Dentzer R 148 Athens NM 1518: four worshippers (two children) hero
    heroine
Dentzer R 150 Athens NM 1523: worshipper hero heroine oinochoos
+Dentzer R 151 Athens NM 1524: four worshippers (two children) hero
    heroine oinochoos
+Dentzer R 152 Athens NM 1530: four worshippers (one child) hero heroine
    oinochoos?
+Dentzer R 169b Athens NM 2904: four worshippers (two children) oinochoos
    (hero heroine)
+Dentzer R 174 Athens NM 2909: three? worshippers (one child) hero heroi-
    ne oinochoos
Dentzer R 186 Athens NM 2921: hero heroine oinochoos?
+Dentzer R 192 Athens NM 3527: five worshippers (two children) hero her-
    oine oinochoos
+Dentzer R 193 Athens NM 3715: hero heroine four worshippers (two chil-
    dren) oinochoos
Dentzer R 194 Athens NM 3872: hero heroine oinochoos
+Dentzer R 196 Athens NM 3937: three worshippers (one child) hero heroine
    oinochoos
Dentzer R 197 Athens: worshipper hero heroine oinochoos
Dentzer R 198a Athens Tower of Winds 117: oinochoos? two heroes hero-
    ine
+Dentzer R 200 Athens four+ worshippers (two+ children) hero heroine
    oinochoos
+Dentzer R 203 Berlin 819:[20] four worshippers (two children) hero heroine
    oinochoos
Dentzer R 204? Berlin 818 hero heroine oinochoos?
Dentzer R 222 Athens NM 1501: worshipper?[21] hero heroine oinochoos
Dentzer R 223 Piraeus 208: hero heroine oinochoos?
Dentzer R 224 Piraeus 2: three worshippers hero heroine oinochoos[22]
Dentzer R 226 Piraeus 4: three worshippers hero heroine horse plaque
Dentzer R 228 Copenhagen NCG 1558: three worshippers hero heroine
    oinochoos
?Dentzer R 446 Basel market: two+ worshippers hero heroine oinochoos
?Dentzer R 470 Paris Louvre: two worshippers?[23] hero heroine oinochoos

+Dentzer R 479 Copenhagen NCG 1656: four worshippers (two children) hero heroine oinochoos horsehead

+Dentzer R 483 Cambridge Fitzwilliam GR 16.1865: four worshippers (two children?) hero heroine oinochoos horsehead

LIMC Pankrates 22 Fetyie Camii P76A, 4th C.: hero heroine oinochoos? worshipper

[Dentzer R 199 Athens Kerameikos: figure in boat two heroes two heroines]

Notes (Appendix)

1. Güntner = Güntner 1994, van Straten = van Straten 1995, Edelmann = Edelmann 1999, Svoronos = Svoronos 1908-37, Walter = Walter 1923, Mitropoulou Snakes = Mitropoulou 1977, Mangold = Mangold 1993, Vikela = Vikela 1994. The number of worshippers given below includes children.
2. This list is based on Edwards 1985. It does not include document reliefs such as #47 (NCG 402) in Lawton 1984 or the anomalous Agora 2905 330/320 B.C. (= Van Straten R101, Edwards 59) showing a dancer, a carved altar, two worshippers and a pig; "the well-made altar finds no parallel on Nymph reliefs of 4th C." (Edwards 640).
3. "It is clear that some deities not mentioned in the "Opferordnung" [*IG* II2 4547] must also be present on the relief" (Edwards 319).
4. The accompanying inscription (*IG* II2 4546) speaks of Kephisodotos establishing a bomos but there is no bomos on the relief.
5. The boy is more likely a human than a god (Güntner 14, following Himmelmann-Wildschütz 1956).
6. Or perhaps one worshipper and a servant; the stone is very poorly preserved.
7. Poseidon is identified as a worshipper in *LIMC*.
8. "deux personnages drapés de petit format" (*LIMC*).
9. This is incorrectly listed as NM 1416 in *LIMC*.
10. I do not include the following fragmentary reliefs: *LIMC* Pankrates 10 (Fetyie Camii P34B), *LIMC* Zeus 149 (Athens NM G95), *LIMC* Zeus 209 (= Artemis 1280 = Edwards 14), *LIMC* 210 (= Dentzer R 228), van Straten R46 Eleusis 5126. The banquet relief found in the Pankrates sanctuary Fetyie Camii P76A (= *LIMC* Zeus 22) is listed with the other banquet reliefs.
11. There are probably no children.
12. I do not include document reliefs (Mangold 6.1, 6.3, 8.2, 9.2, *LIMC* 606-9, Lawton passim), *LIMC* Demeter 449 (= Svoronos pl. 256) Athens NM 2668 showing a series of gods; Svoronos 71 pl. 244 (not seen); Edelmann U27 Athens Akropolis Museum 3003 (+2413?) 4th C. (too fragmentary).
13. He is a naked "fat baby".
14. No altar or animal is likely.
15. No altar or animal is likely.
16. The worshipper is facing away from Artemis, suggesting that there is another set of gods (and perhaps an altar) missing.
17. The worshipper is the same size as the god.

18 I do not indicate kline and table, which are always found with the hero, or krater, which is always found with oinochoos.
19 Three worshippers with somewhat larger figure approach the kline.
20 Dentzer fig. 461, mislabelled R 202.
21 The worshipper is the same size as hero and heroine.
22 What looks like a basket is probably a krater on a stand (see Dentzer R 446).
23 They are the same size as the hero and heroine.

Bibliography

Amyx, D. 1958. "The Attic Stelai Part III: Vases and Other Containers." *Hesperia* 27: 164-310.

Blümel, C. 1966. *Die Klassisch griechischen Skulpturen der Staatlichen Museen zu Berlin*. Berlin: Akademie Verlag.

Edelmann, M. 1999. *Menschen auf griechischen Weihreliefs*. Quellen und Forschungen zur Antiken Welt 33. Munich: Tuduv.

Edwards, C. M. 1985. "Greek Votive Reliefs to Pan and the Nymphs." Ph.D. diss., New York University, Institute of Fine Arts.

Ferrari, G. 2002. *Figures of Speech. Men and Maidens in Ancient Greece*. Chicago & London: University of Chicago Press.

Fuchs, W. 1992 "Attische Nymphenreliefs." *AM* 77: 242-9.

Güntner, G. 1994. *Göttervereine und Götterversammlungen auf attischen Weihreliefs. Untersuchungen zur Typologie und Bedeutung*. Beiträge zur Archäologie 21. Würzburg: Konrad Triltsch.

Himmelmann-Wildschütz, N. 1956. *Studien zum Ilissos-Relief*. Munich: Prestel.

Karouzou, S. 1974. Reprint. *National Archaeological Museum. Collection of Sculpture: A Catalogue*. Translated by H. Wace. Athens: General Direction of Antiquities and Restoration. Original edition, Athens: General Direction of Antiquities and Restoration, 1968.

Lawton, C. 1995. *Attic Document Reliefs of the Classical and Hellenistic Periods. Art and Politics in Ancient Athens*. Oxford: Oxford University Press, Clarendon Press.

Mangold, M. 1993. *Athenatypen auf attischen Weihreliefs des 5. und 4. Jhs.v. Chr.* Hefte des Archäologischen Seminars der Universität Bern BH 2. Bern: Institut für Klassische Archäologie der Universität Bern.

Mitropoulou, E. 1968. "Attic Votive Reliefs of the Fourth Century B.C." Ph.D. diss., London University.

Mitropoulou, E. 1975. "Attic Workshops." *AAA* 8: 118-23.

Mitropoulou, E. 1977. *Deities and Heroes in the Form of Snakes*. Athens: Pyli.

Oakley, J.H. & R.H. Sinos. 1993. *The Wedding in Ancient Athens*. Wisconsin Studies in Classics. Madison: University of Wisconsin Press.

Philadelpheus, A. 1927. "Le sanctuaire d'Artémis Kalistè et l'ancienne rue de l'Académie." *BCH* 51: 153-63.

Richter, G.M.A. 1926. *Ancient Furniture. A History of Greek, Etruscan and Roman Furniture.* Oxford: Oxford University Press.

Rühfel, H. 1984. *Das Kind in der griechische Kunst: Von der minoisch-mykenischen Zeit bis zum Hellenismus.* Kulturgeschichte der antiken Welt 18. Mainz am Rhein: Philipp von Zabern.

Svoronos, J.N. 1908-37. *Das Athener Nationalmuseum.* Translated by W. Barth. Athens: Eleftheroudakis.

van Straten, F.T. 1995. *Hiera Kala: Images of Animal Sacrifice in Archaic and Classical Greece.* Religions in the Graeco-Roman World 127. Leiden, New York & Cologne: E.J. Brill.

Vermeule, C.C. 1981.*Greek and Roman sculpture in America: Masterpieces in Public Collections in the United States and Canada.* Berkeley: University of California Press.

Vikela, E. 1994. *Die Weihreliefs aus dem Athener Pankrates-Heiligtum am Ilissos. Religionsgeschichtliche Bedeutung und Typologie. AM-BH* 16.

Voutiras, E. 1982. "A Dedication of the Hebdomaistai to the Pythian Apollo." *AJA* 86: 229-33.

Walter, O. 1923. *Beschreibung der Reliefs im kleinen Akropolismuseum in Athen.* Vienna: Österreichische Verlagsgesellschaft.

Ziehen, J. 1892. "Studien zu den Asklepiosreliefs." *AM* 17: 229-51.

Banishing Plague: Asklepios, Athens, and the Great Plague Reconsidered

Bronwen Wickkiser

The cult of the renowned healing god Asklepios arrived in Athens from his sanctuary at Epidauros in the Peloponnese in 420/19 B.C.[1] Asklepios' arrival in Athens has often been attributed to the great plague that decimated Attika in the early years of the Peloponnesian War: it is said that plague created the need for a healing god, and since Athens' resident healing gods were unsuccessful in banishing the pestilence, Athens imported Epidaurian Asklepios.[2] This paper reexamines the evidence for the great plague and Athens' reaction to it, as well as evidence for the nature of Asklepios-cult, and argues that plague alone cannot well account for the cult's importation to Athens.

Sources and motives for Asklepios' arrival in Athens

No ancient source explains the reasons for the importation of Asklepios-cult to Athens. In fact, only one ancient source addresses the cult's importation at all: the Telemachos Monument, named after the man it celebrates for his part in establishing Asklepios' sanctuary on the south slope of the Athenian Akropolis.[3] This now-fragmentary monument—consisting of an inscribed *stele* surmounted by reliefs depicting scenes from the cult—provides important information about the early history of Asklepios-cult in Athens, including the year of the god's arrival.[4] It does not, however, state why the cult was imported nor does it make any reference to plague as Thukydides describes it.

Scholars have inferred from events in the 420s B.C. that plague prompted Athens to import the cult. In the summer of 430 B.C. a major plague broke out in Attica, with recurrent outbreaks until the winter of 426/5 B.C. Thukydides vividly recounts the suffering and loss caused by the plague and the failure of the gods to help (Thuc. 2.47-54). Athens was surely desperate for a cure and so, it is argued, Athens imported the successful new healing god Asklepios from Epidauros, just across the Saronic Gulf, where his sanctuary had already attracted panhellenic fame.[5]

This makes sense: Asklepios was a healer and Athens had a major epidemic on its hands. Or did it? The chronology of events leaves a remarkable gap between cause and effect. Asklepios arrived in Athens ten years after the plague initially struck, and six years after its last major outbreak.[6]

Plague and the Peloponnesian War

To explain the gap between the last outbreak of the plague and the importation of Asklepios-cult, Jon Mikalson has argued that the Peloponnesian War hindered Athens from importing the cult until 420 B.C. He reasons that because Epidauros lay in enemy territory, Athens had to wait until the Peace of Nikias in 421 B.C. to successfully obtain the cult.[7] The war did have a major impact on Athens' importation of Asklepios, as I have argued elsewhere, but it is not certain that war in itself would have prevented the god's importation.[8]

In the Classical period, efforts were made at maintaining cult and festival traditions, even among warring states. Sacred truces, for example, were declared between enemy states to allow for participation in panhellenic festivals.[9] Matthew Dillon notes that these truces were observed with few exceptions.[10] While a clause in the Peace of Nikias guaranteeing safe passage to those wishing to consult oracles or visit common sanctuaries indicates that the Peloponnesian War posed hindrances (Thuc. 5.18.2), there is no reason to suppose that the dangers prompting this clause were operative throughout the first ten years of the war. Moreover, efforts such as sacred truces to support panhellenic festival activity during wartime suggest that Athens might have negotiated the importation despite the war, especially given the dire circumstances of the plague as Thukydides describes it.[11]

More striking, however, is the fact that Athens could have imported Asklepios-cult from a city other than Epidauros. Although Epidauros was the most popular of the god's sanctuaries at the time, it was not the only one nor did it control a monopoly on the export of Asklepios. According to Strabon, the earliest sanctuary of Asklepios was at Trikka in Thessaly (Strabon 9.5.17 [C 437]).[12] This sanctuary later exported Asklepios-cult to other cities.[13] Thessaly, moreover, was an ally of Athens throughout much of the fifth century B.C. and therefore would not have presented Athens with the same problems entailed in obtaining a cult from a Peloponnesian city during the Peloponnesian War. Aristophanes' *Wasps* produced in 422 B.C. mentions another sanctuary of Asklepios, this one on Aigina (*Vesp.* 121-3).[14] Aigina's proximity to Athens, as well as reference to the sanctuary in a comedy produced for an Athenian audience, indicate that Athenians were familiar with this sanctuary. Moreover, Aigina had been a member of the Delian League since 458/7 B.C. when compelled to join (Thuc. 1.108.4), and in 431 B.C., Athens colonized the island and evicted at least some of its inhabitants (Thuc. 2.27.1). All of this indicates that Athens exerted considerable control over the island and probably also its cults.[15] If Athens had needed Asklepios in particular because of plague, then Athens could have imported the god earlier in the 420s B.C. from another center of his cult.

Instead, sources indicate that Athenians turned to other gods for assistance in averting the plague, like Apollon Ἀλεξίκακος and Herakles Ἀλεξίκακος, literally "Warder off of evil." According to Pausanias, Apollon received the epithet Ἀλεξίκακος for ending the Athenian plague (Paus. 1.3.4), and a scholiast to Aristophanes' *Frogs* gives the same reason for Herakles' epithet Ἀλεξίκακος (schol. ad Ar. *Ran.* 501).[16] According to Diodoros, Athens purified Apollon's island Delos in the winter of 426/5 B.C. in order to end the plague (Diod. Sic. 12.58.6-7). Other cities struck by the same plague are likewise said to have turned to gods other than Asklepios. Pan Luterios is credited with ending the plague in Troizen (Paus. 2.32.6) and Apollon with ending the plague in Kleonai (Paus. 10.11.15).

Of course, all of these sources are late and problematic. The evidence Pausanias and the scholiast to the *Frogs* adduce for linking Apollon and Herakles to the plague are statues of each as *Alexikakos* crafted by Kalamis and Ageladas, respectively; but these artists, if the same as the famous fifth-century B.C. sculptors, were active too early in the century to have produced statues as late as the 420s.[17] Regarding Delos, Thukydides, too, speaks of its purification (Thuc. 3.104). But while the purification coincides chronologically with mention of the last outbreak of the plague in his account, Thukydides does not associate these events.[18]

However problematic and ultimately inaccurate these accounts may be, it is nonetheless striking that no ancient source credits Asklepios, the healing god *par excellence* of the Greco-Roman world, with ending the plague of the 420s. This suggests that Asklepios was not associated with the cessation of this plague in Athens or anywhere else. It also suggests that Asklepios was not perceived as a plague-healing god generally in antiquity; otherwise, some ancient source would probably have given such a prominent healing god the credit for Athens. In this case, silence is eloquent.

Healing in Asklepios-cult

What we know of Asklepios' healing is consistent with this silence. I am aware of only two instances where Asklepios is given any credit for treating plague, and both require caveats. The first instance is Rome, which in ca. 291 B.C. imported Asklepios (or Aesculapius, as the Romans called him) from Epidauros in response, ancient sources say, to a plague. But these sources date more than two-and-a-half centuries after the importation and may reflect a geographic and/or temporal shift in perception about what the god was capable of healing.[19] For instance, Livy, who is the earliest of these sources, has a penchant for medical metaphor that may have carried over into his discussion of Aesculapius. It is possible that he conflated an actual plague with political and military threats to Rome that more immediately motivated the importation from Epidauros, especially given that Rome was beginning its military contact with Greece.[20] The other instance is Ailios Aristeides, a second-century A.D. orator and fervent devotee of Asklepios. In the *Sacred Tales*, where he recounts his interactions with Asklepios, he thanks Asklepios and Athena together for saving him from a plague in A.D. 165 (*Or.* 48.37-45, 50.9), but Athena plays a much greater role in this event than does Asklepios, and her participation here (her presence otherwise in the *Sacred Tales* is rare) suggests that Asklepios alone was unable to cure Aristeides of this ailment.

The lack of evidence for Asklepios as a plague-healer can be explained in large part by the sorts of illness Asklepios is known to have treated. The vast majority of ailments recorded on healing inscriptions and dedications, and those described by literary sources as having been cured by the god, are chronic conditions. Among the earliest recorded cases, which date no later than the fourth century B.C., are blindness, deafness, baldness, infertility, prolonged pregnancies, festering sores, paralysis, tumors, gout, muteness, dropsy, stones in the penis, ulcers, abscesses, persistent headache accompanied by insomnia, stomach disorder, worms in the belly, leeches in the chest, lice, and even a case of epilepsy.[21] These are not typically fatal ailments, but recurrent or lingering ones.[22]

Since plague was often fatal, especially the great plague as described by Thukydides, it is not the sort of illness Asklepios would have treated. A much more likely deity to help against plague was Asklepios' father Apollon who could banish from (or send upon) communities *en masse* the *miasma* believed to be responsible for such pestilence.[23] And as we have seen, ancient sources credit Apollon, not Asklepios, with ending the plague of the 420s B.C.

Conclusions

It is unlikely that plague, even the great plague that afflicted so many Athenians including prominent leaders like Perikles, was the most immediate factor motivating the importation of Asklepios-cult. I do not mean to imply that plague had nothing to do with the arrival of Asklepios in Athens. Quite the contrary. The physical suffering and death left in its wake, exacerbated by ailments due to the war, must have increased anxiety about health and healthcare, and any healing god would have been welcome.[24] But in 420 B.C., Asklepios arrived too late and without the proper credentials to relieve Athens of the plague itself.

It is much more likely that a constellation of factors motivated Asklepios' importation to Athens, nor should we assume, simply because Asklepios is a healing god, that all or even the most important of these factors concerned physical health. Political and military concerns must have played a prominent role as well given not only Athenian precedent for importing or modifying cults in response to territorial interests, but given also the context of the Peloponnesian War and the Peloponnesian origin of the cult.[25]

Acknowledgements:

This article develops one section of the paper "Plague, Politics, and the Peloponnesian War: The Arrival of Asklepios in Athens in 420/19 B.C." delivered at Aarhus in January 2004. Both the article and conference paper stem from material discussed in my monograph, *Asklepios, Medicine, and the Politics of Healing in Fifth-Century Greece* (Johns Hopkins, 2008). My great thanks to Jesper Tae Jensen and the Department of Classical Archaeology at the University of Aarhus, and to all the participants, for a dynamic, productive, and enjoyable conference. Many thanks also to Carol Lawton, who kindly read an earlier draft of this paper and shared with me her forthcoming article on votive reliefs (see bibliography), and to Jesper Tae Jensen and Alan Shapiro for their enlightening comments on this topic. All errors are my own.

Notes

1 The source for the date is *SEG* 25.226, an inscription that records the arrival of Asklepios in Athens and the early development of his sanctuary on the south slope of the Akropolis. On the inscription and the larger monument of which it is a part (known as the Telemachos Monument), see n. 3 and 4 below.

2 E.g., Kern (1963, vol. 2, 312) attributes the god's arrival to his having helped against the great plague; Dodds (1951, 193 with n. 83) speculates that the god's fame at Athens dates from the same plague; Mikalson (1984, 220) argues that the memory of the plague was one of the reasons Athens imported the god; Garland (1992, 130-2) states, "The cult was established primarily in connection with the plague which broke out in Athens in 430"; Parker (1996, 180) agrees with Mikalson that the plague and importation were connected, but adds that Asklepios would have arrived in Athens eventually regardless of plague.

3 *SEG* 25.226 = *IG* II² 4961 + 4960, associated by Beschi 1967-8; and Beschi 1982 (a new fragment). For a reconstruction of the monument and discussion of its complex iconography, see Beschi 1967-8; Beschi 1982; Beschi 2002, 19-29; see Riethmüller 2005, vol. 1, 241-50, for further bibliography and discussion. The only other reference to the importation is the twelfth-century *Etymologicum Magnum*, which states that the poet Sophokles was called "*Dexion*," or "Receiver," for having received Asklepios into his own *oikia* and setting up an altar to the god (*Et.M.* sv Ἀεξίων'). Sources beginning in the third century A.D. indicate that Sophokles composed a paean to Asklepios (Lukian *Dem.Enc.* 27, Philostr. *VA* 3.17, Philostr.Jun. *Im.* 13; a portion of a paean by Sophokles, probably to Asklepios, is preserved in a third-century A.D. inscription—*IG* II² 4510, part of a larger monument known as the Sarapion Monument, for which see Oliver 1936 [who argues that the paean does not celebrate Asklepios], *SEG* 28.225, and Aleshire 1991, 49-74). It is possible that the Sophokles-Dexion tradi-

tion arose in the Hellenistic period or later as a result of this paean, even though none of the sources for the paean associate it in any way with Asklepios' arrival. On fictionalizing within Hellenistic biographies, including that of Sophokles, see Lefkowitz 1981. For ancient testimonia and recent bibliography on Sophokles' relationship to Asklepios, see Clinton 1994, 25 with ns. 26-7; also Connolly 1998, who concludes that Dexion was not the heroized Sophokles.

4 Some have argued that Telemachos' involvement in establishing the god's sanctuary demonstrates that the cult was a "private" foundation, and that the city had little involvement in the effort. See, e.g., Aleshire 1989, 7; Garland 1992, 128-30; Stafford 2000, 155 with n. 33. Two cautions must be raised. First, the inscription on the Telemachos Monument mentions Telemachos' involvement only in transferring the cult from the Eleusinion to the god's permanent sanctuary on the south slope of the Akropolis; it does not indicate that Telemachos was responsible for bringing the cult from Epidauros to Athens. Second, even if Telemachos had played a larger role in the importation, the Athenian assembly would nevertheless have had to approve both the importation itself and the placement of the cult on the slopes of the newly refurbished Akropolis. On the role of the *demos* in approving new cults, see Rudhardt 1960, 92-3; Garland 1984, 78; 1992, 19; Clinton 1994, 24-5 and 28; Parker 1996, 180 and 214-7; Price 1999, 76-8. Recent work on this sanctuary by Vanda Papaefthimiou, and by Jesper Tae Jensen and Mihaelis Lefantzis, sheds valuable new light on the cult; see their contributions in this volume.

5 The panhellenic nature of the cult in the fifth century B.C. is attested by the *iamata*, or healing narratives inscribed on *stelai* erected in the sanctuary (*IG* IV² 121-4). Although the earliest of the Epidaurian *iamata* were inscribed in the fourth century B.C., LiDonnici (1995, 76-82) has convincingly argued that they narrate events that took place in the fifth century B.C. These *iamata* often mention the city from which a visitor traveled, and in the earliest *iamata* include Pellene, Athens, Thessaly, and Epidauros itself. Moreover, Pind. *Nem.* 3.84 and 5.52, and *Isth.* 8.68, all mention athletic contests at Epidauros in which victors from Aigina competed.

6 The plague, although over, had a lingering impact that surely added to Asklepios' appeal. In his description of preparations for the expedition to Sicily in 415 B.C., Thukydides remarks that Athens had only recently recovered from the plague (Thuc. 6.12.1, 6.26.2). My thanks to Carol Lawton for bringing these references to my attention. The identity of the plague has long been debated, and suggestions include measles, typhus, smallpox, and Ebola; for bibliography, see Mikalson 1984, n. 1. More recently, a study of ancient dental pulp from a mass grave in the Kerameikos cemetery of Athens, published in the *International Journal of Infectious Diseases* in 2006, argues that typhoid fever was a probable cause of the plague. On the rhetoric of Thukydides and the likelihood of his having embellished the severity of the plague, see Woodman 1988, 1-69, esp. 28-40.

7 Mikalson 1984, 220; also Parker 1996, 180.

8 In Wickkiser 2008, ch. 4-6, I argue that Athens imported Epidauros' signature cult as a way of opening diplomatic relations with this city whose geography (on major sea and land routes between Attica and the Peloponnese) made it critical to Athenian success against Peloponnesian aggression. Athens' interest

in Epidauros during the First Peloponnesian War, during the first ten years of the Peloponnesian War, and in 419 B.C. when hostilities resumed subsequent to the Peace of Nikias, all indicate its strategic importance to Athens (Thuc. 1.105.1, 2.56.4-5, 4.45.2, 5.53, 5.56.1-2; Diod. Sic. 11.78).

9   Dillon 1997, 1-26. These truces guaranteed safe passage through warring territories for those attending particular festivals.

10   Dillon 1997, 4.

11   Nor was negotiation the only method of obtaining a cult. Mikalson (1984, 220) proposes that Athens tried to appropriate the cult by force in the first year of the war when Athenian troops unsuccessfully attacked Epidauros.

12   No conclusive evidence corroborates Strabon's statement. Strabon 14.1.39 [C 647]; Hyg. *Fab.* 14.21; and Euseb. *Praep.Ev.* 3.14.6 all mention Trikka as the birthplace of Asklepios. In the *Iliad*, Machaon and Podaleirios are said to be from Trikka, which may be the source of Strabon's claim (Hom. *Il.* 2.729-33, 4.198-202; cf. Eustath. *Il.* 2.729 and 4.202). A fifth-century B.C. coin depicting Asklepios has been found in neighboring Larissa, as have coins of the fourth century B.C. in Trikka (the coin from Trikka: *LIMC* II.2, s.v. 'Asklepios,' nos. 40, 52; the coin from Larissa: *A Catalogue of the Greek Coins*, British Museum, 7.28.44). Excavators have identified a site at Trikka as an Asklepieion on tentative material evidence. On Asklepieia in Thessaly, including Trikka, see Melfi 2003, 418-37; Riethmüller 2005, vol. 1, 91-106; vol. 2, 289-315.

13   E.g., to Gerenia in Messenia: Strabon 8.4.4 [C 360]; to Kos: Herondas 2.97, 4.1-2. See also Edelstein 1945, vol. 2, 238-42.

14   No remains of this sanctuary have yet been located.

15   On Athens' colonization of Aigina, see Figueira 1991. In 405 B.C., Lysander returned the island to the Aiginetans (Xen. *Hell.* 2.2.9).

16   According to the *Presbeutikos*, a speech ascribed to Hippokrates' son Thessalos, Hippokrates traveled to Delphi to ask Apollon to save the Greeks from plague (*Presb.* 7 = Littré 9.418-20). Smith (1990, 3) argues that this plague, which came from the north and threatened the entire Greek mainland, is not based on an historical event. Jouanna (1999, 32) argues that if the plague is historical, the chronology of the speech indicates that it must have occurred during the years 419-416 B.C. On the pseudepigraphia of Hippokrates, see Smith 1990; Pinault 1992, esp. 35-60 as it relates to the plague.

17   For sources and bibliography on Ageladas and Kalamis, see Pollitt 1990, 32-3, 46-8. It is possible that their statues of Apollon and Herakles, sculpted earlier in the century, acquired the title *Alexikakos* at the time of the plague; see Harrison 1996, 65. On dangers of using late sources as evidence for the association of fifth-century B.C. monuments with the plague, see also Keesling 2005, esp. 67-70 with n. 90.

18   Apollon's role in averting the plague in Athens is striking inasmuch as Apollon-cult was never strong there, possibly because of his association with Delos from which Athens moved the treasury of the Delian League. Gomme (1956, 414), Garland (1992, 131), and Parker (1996, 150) argue that plague did motivate the purification of Delos. Mikalson (1984, 221-2 and 224) argues against a causal link since, according to Thukydides, the purification was carried out in response to an oracle, and Thuc. 2.47.4 had claimed that oracles were useless against the plague. Mikalson (1984, 224) further argues that Athens' destruction and de-

secration of Delion in winter 424/3 B.C. suggest "either the Athenians had a very short memory or else they did *not* credit Apollon with assistance in ending the pestilence." For the presence of Asklepios-cult at Delos, see Melfi 2007, 456-69.

19 For ancient accounts of Aesculapius' importation to Rome, see Edelstein 1945, vol. 1, T 845-55.

20 See Wickkiser 2003, ch. 7-9.

21 These cases are reported in fourth-century B.C. *iamata* from Epidauros. *Iamata* have also been found at Asklepios' sanctuary at Lebena on Krete (*ICr* I, xvii, 8-24, dating to the second century B.C.), at Rome (*IGUR* 148, dating to the second century A.D.), and at Pergamon (*AvP* VIII 3). Strabon 8.6.15 (C 374) reports that there were *iamata* also at Asklepios' sanctuary at Trikka in Thessaly, and on Kos (as does Pliny *NH* 29.1 and 29.4, quoting Varro), but none of these have been recovered. On the Epidaurian *iamata*, see also n. 5 above.

22 On the chronic nature of the ailments Asklepios treated, see also Nutton 2004, 109; and for a remarkable parallel, see Park 1992, 72-5, on chronic cases typical of the healing of early Christian saints. I have argued elsewhere that Asklepios, by treating chronic cases, picked up where Hippokratic medicine left off inasmuch as chronic ailments are among the sorts of illnesses that, according to fifth-century B.C. medical treatises, physicians deemed beyond the limits of their *techne*, or craft (Wickkiser 2006). The popularity of Asklepios-cult beginning in the late fifth century B.C. was fueled in large part by Asklepios' ability to fill this particular void; see Wickkiser 2008, ch. 1-3.

23 On *miasma* and plague, see Parker 1983, 271-6.

24 The *iamata* from Epidauros include among the ailments cured by Asklepios weapon wounds, like spearheads and arrowheads (*IG* IV² I 121.95-7, *IG* IV² I 122.55-60; the latter is said to have been incurred "in some battle," ἐμ μάχαι τινί), and the earliest literary evidence for Asklepios places his sons Machaon and Podaleirios on the battlefield of Troy where they perform the invaluable service of treating the most difficult war wounds (Hom. *Il.* 4.193-218, 11.833-6). It is therefore likely that some soldiers, especially those suffering hard-to-treat wounds like those mentioned in the Epidaurian *iamata*, would have sought Asklepios' help. Lawton (forthcoming) argues that the war and plague had a direct impact on the dedication of votive reliefs to Asklepios in Athens, which begin to appear around 420 B.C. in the Agora.

25 Prominent examples are the cult of Theseus, whose mythology by the late sixth century B.C. included a cycle of labors reflecting contemporary Athenian interest in the Megarid (Walker 1995; Calame 1996, 421-32); the cult of Bendis imported into Piraieus in ca. 430 B.C. probably to consolidate an alliance with Thrace (Nilsson 1951, 45-8; Garland 1992, 112-3); and the Dioskouroi whose prevalence and changing iconography in Attic vase painting during the fifth century suggest Athenian interest in co-opting these Spartan heroes (Shapiro 1999). The limits of this paper do not allow me to make the full argument here, but see Wickkiser 2008, ch. 4-6, and n. 8 above.

Bibliography

Aleshire, S.B. 1989. *The Athenian Asklepieion: the People, their Dedications, and the Inventories.* Amsterdam: J.C. Gieben.

Aleshire, S.B. 1991. *Asklepios at Athens: Epigraphic and Prosopographic Essays on the Athenian Healing Cults.* Amsterdam: J.C. Gieben.

Beschi, L. 1967-68a [1969]. "Il monumento di Telemachos: fondatore dell'Asclepieion ateniese." *ASAtene* 45-46 (n.s. 29-30): 381-436.

Beschi, L. 1982. "Il rilievo di Telemachos ricompletato." *AAA* 15: 31-43.

Beschi, L. 2002 [2003]. "Culti Stranieri e fondazioni private nell'Attica Classica: alcuni case." *ASAtene* 80 (n.s. 3.2): 13-42.

Calame, C. 1996. *Thésée et l'imaginaire athénien: légende et culte en Grèce antique.* Lausanne: Editions Payot.

Clinton, K. 1994. "The Epidauria and the Arrival of Asclepius in Athens." In *Ancient Greek Cult Practice from the Epigraphical Evidence, Proceedings of the Second International Seminar on Ancient Greek Cult, Athens, 1991,* edited by R. Hägg, 17-34. SkrAth 8°, 13. Stockholm: Svenska Institutet i Athen, distribution Paul Åströms Förlag.

Connolly, A. 1998. "Was Sophocles Heroised as Dexion?" *JHS* 118: 1-21.

Dillon, M. 1997. *Pilgrims and Pilgrimage in Ancient Greece.* London & New York: Routledge.

Dodds, E.R. 1951. *The Greeks and the Irrational.* Berkeley, Los Angeles & London: University of California Press.

Edelstein, E.J. & L. Edelstein. 1998. Reprint. *Asclepius. Collection and Interpretation of the Testimonies.* 2 vols. Baltimore & London: Johns Hopkins University Press. Original edition, Baltimore: Johns Hopkins University Press, 1945.

Figueira, T.J. 1991. *Athens and Aigina in the Age of Imperial Colonization.* Baltimore & London: Johns Hopkins University Press.

Garland, R.S.J. 1984. "Religious Authority in Archaic and Classical Athens." *BSA* 79: 75-123.

Garland, R.S.J. 1992. *Introducing New Gods: The Politics of Athenian Religion.* London: Duckworth.

Gomme, A.W. 1956. *A Historical Commentary on Thucydides.* Vol. 2, *The Ten Year's War, Books II-III.* Oxford: Clarendon Press.

Harrison, E.B. 1996. "Pheidias." In *Personal Styles in Greek Sculpture,* edited by O. Palagia & J.J. Pollitt, 16-65. Yale Classical Studies 30. Cambridge: Cambridge University Press.

Jouanna, J. 1999. *Hippocrates.* Translated by M.B. DeBevoise. Baltimore & London: Johns Hopkins University Press.

Keesling, C.M. 2005. "Misunderstood Gestures: Iconatrophy and the Reception of Greek Sculpture in the Roman Imperial Period." *ClAnt* 24: 41-79.

Kern, O. 1963. *Die religion der Griechen.* 3 vols. 2nd ed. Berlin: Weidmann.

Lawton, C. Forthcoming. "Attic Votive Reliefs and the Peloponnesian War."
    In *Art in Athens during the Peloponnesian War*, edited by O. Palagia. Cam-
    bridge: Cambridge University Press.

Lefkowitz, M.R. 1981. *The Lives of the Greek Poets*. London: Duckworth.

LiDonnici, L.R. 1995. *The Epidaurian Miracle Inscriptions: Text, Translation and
    Commentary*. Society of Biblical Literature. Texts and Translations 36.
    Graeco-Roman Religion Series 11. Atlanta: Scholars Press.

Littré, E. 1973-1989. Reprint. *Oeuvres complètes d'Hippocrate: traduction nouvelle
    avec le texte grec en regard, collationné sur les manuscrits et toutes les éditions*.
    10 vols. Paris: J.B. Baillière. Original edition, Amsterdam: A.M. Hakkert,
    1839-61.

Melfi, M. 2003. "I santuari di Asclepio in Grecia." Ph.D. diss.: University of
    Messina.

Melfi, M. 2007. *I santuari di Asclepio in Grecia. I. StArch* 157. Rome: L'Erma di
    Bretschneider.

Mikalson, J.D. 1984. "Religion and Plague in Athens, 431-423 B.C." In *Stud-
    ies Presented to Sterling Dow on his Eightieth Birthday*, edited by K.J. Rigs-
    by, 217-25. *GRBM* 10.

Nilsson, M.P. 1951. *Cults, Myths, Oracles, and Politics in Ancient Greece*. SkrAth
    8°, 1. Lund: C.W.K. Gleerup.

Nutton, V. 2004. *Ancient Medicine*. Series of Antiquity. London & New York:
    Routledge.

Oliver, J.H. 1936. "The Sarapion Monument and the Paean of Sophocles."
    Hesperia 5: 91-122.

Park, K. 1992. "Medicine and Society in Medieval Europe, 500-1500." In
    Medicine in Society: Historical Essays, edited by A. Wear, 59-90. Cambridge:
    Cambridge University Press.

Parker, R. 1983. *Miasma: Pollution and Purification in Early Greek Religion*.
    Oxford: Clarendon Press.

Parker, R. 1996. *Athenian Religion: A History*. Oxford: Clarendon Press.

Pinault, J.R. 1992. *Hippocratic Lives and Legends*. Studies in Ancient Medicine
    4. Leiden, New York & Cologne: E.J. Brill.

Pollitt, J.J. 1990. *The Art of Ancient Greece: Sources and Documents*. Cambridge:
    Cambridge University Press.

Price, S.R.F. 1999. *Religions of the Ancient Greeks*. Key Themes in Ancient His-
    tory. Cambridge: Cambridge University Press.

Riethmüller, J. 2005. *Asklepios: Heiligtümer und Kulte*. Studien zu antiken
    Heiligtümern. 2 vols. Heidelberg: Archäologie und Geschichte.

Rudhardt, J. 1960. "La définition du délit d'impiété d'après la législation
    attique." *MusHelv* 17: 87-105.

Shapiro, H.A. 1999. "Cult Warfare: The Dioskouroi between Sparta and
    Athens." In *Ancient Greek Hero Cult: Proceedings of the Fifth International
    Seminar on Ancient Greek Cult, organized by the Department of Classical*

Archaeology and Ancient History, Göteborg University, 21-23 April 1995, edited by R. Hägg, 99-107. SkrAth 8°, 16. Stockholm: Svenska Institutet i Athen, distribution Paul Åströms Förlag.

Smith, W.D. (ed.). 1990. *Hippocrates: Pseudepigraphic Writings: Letters—Embassy—Speech from the Altar—Decree*. Studies in Ancient Medicine 2. Leiden: E.J. Brill.

Stafford, E. 2000. *Worshipping Virtues: Personification and the Divine in Ancient Greece*. London: Classical Press of Wales & Duckworth.

Walker, H.J. 1995. *Theseus and Athens*. New York & Oxford: Oxford University Press.

Wickkiser, B.L. 2003. "The Appeal of Asklepios and the Politics of Healing in the Greco-Roman World." Ph.D. diss., University of Texas at Austin.

Wickkiser, B.L. 2006. "Chronicles of Chronic Cases and Tools of the Trade at Asklepieia." *ARG* 8: 25-40.

Wickkiser, B.L. 2008. *Asklepios, Medicine, and the Politics of Healing in Fifth-Century Greece: Between Craft and Cult*. Baltimore: Johns Hopkins University Press.

Woodman, A.J. 1988. *Rhetoric in Classical Historiography: Four Studies*. London & Sydney: Croom Helm.

Der Altar des Asklepieions von Athen

Vanda Papaefthymiou

Im Jahr 420/19 v. Chr. gründete der Privatmann Telemachos aus dem Demos Acharnai das Athener Asklepieion. Das neue Heiligtum wurde im freien Raum am Südabhang der Akropolis, nordwestlich des Dionysostheaters, eingerichtet (Abb. 1). Zu diesem Asklepiosheiligtum existiert eine Tempel-chronik in Form eines Pfeilers, der ein Doppelrelief trägt. Auf dem Pfeiler ist eine Inschrift mit der Gründungslegende des Asklepieions angebracht. Nach dem in der Inschrift erwähnten Gründer wird die Doppelstele auch das Telemachosmonument genannt (Abb. 2).[1]

Die Ikonographie des Telemachosmonuments – dargestellt ist die Ankunft des Gottes und seiner Tochter Hygieia in Athen – ist einmalig und absolut untypisch, wie A. Verbanck-Pierard richtig bemerkt hat: das Monument wurde bestellt, um einen bestimmten historischen Vorgang festzuhalten.[2] Die Inschrift auf dem Telemachosmonument berichtet, dass Asklepios aus Epidauros, dem Zentrum seines Kultes in klassischer Zeit, über das Meer kam und zunächst im Hafen Zea an Land ging. Von dort aus gelangte er nach Athen, wo er im Monat Boedromion, am dritten Tag der großen eleu-sinischen Mysterien, eintraf. Die Kerykes, die Priester des Eleusinions am Südabhang der Akropolis, traten einen Teil des Heiligtums der Demeter und Kore an den neuen Heilgott ab. Daraus ist wohl abzuleiten, dass die Einfüh-rung des Gottes in Athen auf langfristige Planung durch das athenische Priestertum zurückgeht.[3] Pausanias (2.26.8) berichtet, dass ab diesem Zeit-punkt der dritte Tag der eleusinischen Mysterien, der 18. Boedromion, im athenischen Festkalender Epidauria genannt worden sei, und dass Asklepios von da ab als "athenischer Gott" betrachtet wurde.

Im letzten Viertel des 5. Jhs. v. Chr. besaß das Heiligtum einen Tempel und einen Altar des Gottes sowie ein hölzernes Propylon an seinem Eingang. Eine Stoa ionischer Ordnung, die als Xenon diente,[4] wurde, nach M. Korrés,[5] um die Zeit der Gründung des Heiligtums errichtet (Abb. 1).

Aus der Inschrift *IG* II[2] 4355[6] ist außerdem zu entnehmen, dass Telemachos dem Asklepios und seinen Kindern, sowie anderen Gottheiten, deren Namen in der Inschrift nicht mehr zu lesen sind, einen Altar weihte.[7] Es ist bekannt, dass in antiken Heiligtümern der Altar geweiht wurde, wenn das erste Opfer für den Gott bzw. die Götter stattfand. Ab diesem Zeitpunkt bleibt der Altar in der Regel an seinem Ort, auch wenn Umbauten am Heiligtum vorgenom-

Abb. 1. Plan des Asklepieions
(nach Travlos 1971, 129,
Fig. 171).

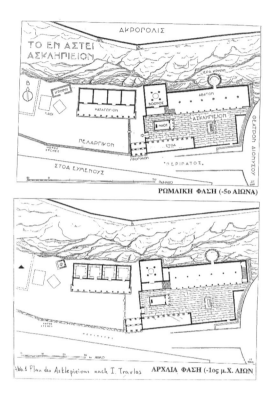

men werden.[8] Der Altar stand vor der Front des Tempels, ist aber nicht zu diesem hin orientiert, sondern dorthin, von wo man sich die Gottheit wirkend dachte. Man wendete sich also nicht zum Tempel hin, um zu opfern, sondern gewöhnlich nach Osten.[9] Daher sind die Fundamente des hier zu besprechenden Monuments, das an dem zu erwartenden Ort, etwa 17 m östlich des Tempels liegt, unabhängig davon, in welche Zeit sie zu datieren sind (s.u.), sicher die Fundamente eines Altars. Die Spuren des Altars im Asklepieion sind also nicht gänzlich verloren gegangen, wie behauptet wurde.[10] Bemerkenswert ist es auch, dass sich die Fundamente des Altars (5,80 m) und des Tempels (5,90 m) in der Breite fast entsprechen, was auch bei anderen Heiligtümern vorkommt, so z. B. beim Asklepieion von Korinth[11] oder beim Zeustempel von Nemea.[12]

Im Asklepieion wurde nach der Inschrift *IG* II[2] 974 zu Ehren des Gottes auf dem Altar dreimal pro Jahr geopfert: Erstens beim Fest der Epidauria am 18. Boedromion, dem dritten Tag der eleusinischen Mysterienfeier. Der Archon Basileus war an diesem Tag für die Durchführung einer pompe zu Ehren des Asklepios verantwortlich.[13] Zweitens fand das Fest der Asklepieia am 8. Elaphebolion statt, zur Zeit der städtischen Dionysien; es war ebenfalls mit einem Opfer für den Gott verbunden. Schließlich bringt der Priester des Asklepios am Fest der Heroa ein Rinderopfer dar:

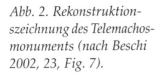

*Abb. 2. Rekonstruktion-
szeichnung des Telemachosmonuments (nach Beschi
2002, 23, Fig. 7).*

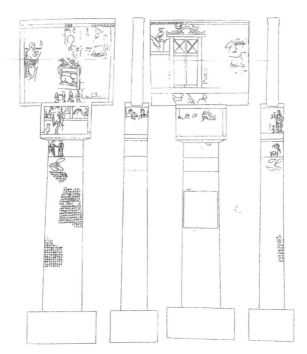

Ἐβουθ[ύτησεν Ἀσκληπιείοις] καὶ Ἐπιδαυρίοις καὶ Ἡρώοις
παρὰ τ[ῷ Ἀσκληπιείῳ τῷ ἐν ἄστει κ]αὶ τὰς τούτων παννυχίδας
συν[ετέλεσεν...

Außerdem waren alle drei Feste mit Nachtfeiern verbunden. Es ist auch
bekannt, dass nach einer alten Sitte, welche später durch einen Volksbe-
schluss bestätigt wurde, die Ärzte der Stadt zweimal im Jahr im Asklepieion
ein Opfer darbrachten.[14]

Obwohl die Gründung des Asklepiosheiligtums in Athen ursprünglich
auf private Initiative zurückging, wurde der Kult des Gottes sehr populär
und schnell bedeutender als die Kulte der älteren und etablierten athenischen
Heilgottheiten, wie Athena Hygieia, Zeus Hypsistos und Amynos, der Heil-
heros Athens, dessen Priester der große Tragödiendichter Sophokles gewe-
sen ist.

Sophokles hat nach den antiken Schriftquellen als erster in Athen den
Gott empfangen.[15] Er hat auch einen Paian zu Ehren des Gottes gedichtet,
der bis zum Ende der Antike gesungen wurde.[16]

Auch aus Inschriften geht hervor, dass der Kult des Asklepios mit der
Zeit sehr populär geworden ist. Zu diesem Aufschwung wird entscheidend
beigetragen haben, dass der Kult um die Mitte des 4. Jhs. v. Chr. verstaatlicht

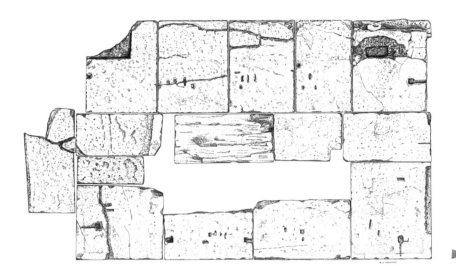

Abb. 3. Grundriss des Altars vor der Ausgrabung.

wurde.[17] Die Ehrung eines Priesters des Asklepios, Theophanes aus dem Demos Acharnai, durch die Polis (*IG* II[2] 304+604) zeigt, dass die Stadt in der Mitte des 4. Jhs. v. Chr. den Kult des Asklepios im Heiligtum übernommen hatte. Das Dekret wurde dann auf Staatskosten im städtischen Asklepieion aufgestellt. Als Beispiel dient auch das bekannte Weihrelief der Ärzte an Asklepios und die eleusinischen Göttinnen aus der Mitte des 4. Jhs. v. Chr.[18] Auf dem Relief werden links Asklepios, Demeter und Kore wiedergegeben und rechts insgesamt 6 Männer (5 davon Ärzte), die inschriftlich benannt und bekränzt sind. Nach Ansicht von S. Aleshire dankt die Stadt mit dieser Ehrung durch Kränze den Ärzten, die zur Durchsetzung der städtischen Kontrollen im Asklepieion beigetragen haben.[19]

Die wachsenden Bedürfnisse des Heiligtums führten zum Neubau von Monumenten: am Ende des 4. Jhs. v. Chr. wird nach Aussage der Bauin- schrift[20] eine zweistöckige Halle dorischer Ordnung gebaut, die als Abaton (d.h. als Raum für den Inkubationsschlaf) diente (Abb. 1). In die Halle[21] einbezogen wurden der heilige Bothros und eine Quelle, die sich in einer Höhle im Akropolisfelsen befand. U. Köhler und nach ihm F. Robert[22] stellten fest, dass der runde, von Mauerwerk umgebene, und mit einem Baldachin überdeckte Bothros dem Kult der Heroen geweiht war und bei den Heroa eine Rolle spielte.[23] Wegen der chthonischen Natur des Kultes folgerten sie, dass der Bothros für diesen Zweck am besten geeignet sei, und erklärten ihn als die alte Opferstätte, an welcher zu den Heroa geop- fert wurde.[24]

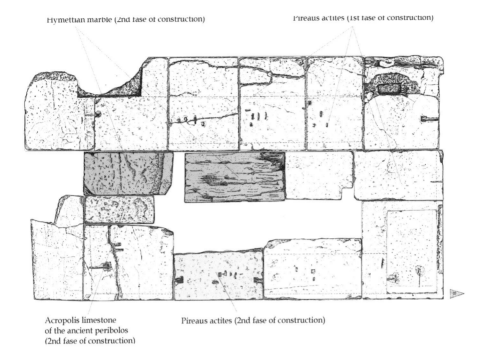

Abb. 4. Grundriss des Altars nach der Ausgrabung.

Der Altar des Asklepieions befindet sich, wie gesagt, etwa 17 m östlich vom Tempel. Er liegt aber nicht in derselben Achse wie dieser, sondern er ist gegenüber dem Tempel etwas nach Süden verschoben (Abb. 1).

Die Baugeschichte des Altars in der Antike ist heute nicht mehr genau rekonstruierbar; wir wissen aber, dass der Altar sowie der Tempel des Asklepios in frühchristlicher Zeit (nach der Mitte des 5. Jhs. n. Chr.) in das Mittelschiff einer großen christlichen Basilika aufgenommen wurde.

Das Monument wurde 1876 von der Griechischen Archäologischen Gesellschaft unter der Leitung von S. Koumanoudis zusammen mit dem Heiligtum ausgegraben.[25] Im topographischen Plan des Architekten M. Lambert von 1877[26] sieht man, dass von dem Altar nur die Fundamente erhalten sind. Aleshire notierte,[27] dass die Erde um den Altar bis zum Niveau des natürlichen Felsens abgegraben wurde (Abb. 3).

Der Altar hat eine Länge von 5,90 m; die Schmalseiten sind 3,40 m breit (Abb. 4).[28] Er besteht hauptsächlich aus Kalksteinen,[29] die untereinander nicht durch horizontale Eisenklammern verbunden sind. Nur die vier Ecksteine tragen rechteckige Einlassungen mit Gusskanälen für die Aufstellung der Steinplatten, aus denen der Aufbau des Altars besteht. Zwei rechteckige Einarbeitungen auf dem nördlichen und dem südlichen Eckstein der westlichen Seite des Altars waren wohl für die Befestigung von Stelen oder So-

Abb. 5. Innerer Teil des Altars der nur mit Erde gefüllt ist (Photo vom N und S).

ckeln bestimmt. Festzuhalten ist, dass nicht alle Steine des Fundaments aus Piräuskalk bestehen: Drei der vier im Inneren des Altars eingesetzten Steine bestehen aus anderem Material, nämlich aus hymettischen Marmor sowie aus Burgkalk, d.h. Kalkstein des Akropolisfelsens (Abb. 4).

Auf der östlichen Langseite ist der dritte Stein von Norden, der wie die anderen aus Piräuskalk besteht, mit dem Zahneisen sehr gut geglättet, und trägt in der Mitte seiner Schmalseiten Einlassungen für Eisenklammern. Einen Hinweis auf die Zweitverwendung dieses Bauteils im Fundament des Altars gibt die Tatsache, dass die Klammerlöcher auf den Nachbarsteinen keine Entsprechung haben.[30] Überhaupt sind die einzelnen Fundamentblöcke des Monuments untereinander nicht mit Klammern verbunden.

Es ist möglich, dass die Piräuskalksteine des Fundaments auf eine frühere Phase hindeuten, d.h. dass sie von einem früheren Asklepiosaltar am selben Ort stammen und hier wiederverwendet sind.[31]

Das Innere des Altars ist nicht ganz mit Steinen ausgefüllt, ein Teil davon entlang der östlichen Seite des Monuments (Länge: 2,90 m, Breite: 0,65 m) ist nur mit Erde gefüllt (Abb. 5). Schon der erste Plan des Altars von Lambert zeigt diesen Befund bereits nach der ersten Ausgrabung des Heiligtums im

Jahr 1876. Es ist schwer zu beurteilen, ob dieser Teil des Altars ehemals ebenfalls mit Steinen gefüllt war, und wann gegebenenfalls diese Steine entfernt worden sind (in der Antike oder zu einem späteren Zeitpunkt).

Die neuen Grabungen

Insgesamt sechs Grabungsflächen wurden angelegt, zwei im inneren Teil des Monuments und vier außerhalb, jeweils an den Ecken des Altars.

Die Ausgrabung im inneren Teil des Monuments fand in zwei Bereichen statt: erstens in dem Teil des Altars, der nur mit Erde gefüllt war (Abb. 6) und zweitens unter den drei eingesetzten Steinen aus heterogenem Material, die schon erwähnt wurden (Abb. 7). Die Hebung dieser Steine war zu Restaurierungszwecken notwendig geworden. Nach der Restaurierung wurden sie wieder an ihren Platz gebaut.

Die Ausgrabung in der Nordhälfte des Altars im inneren wie im äußeren Teil, zeigte, dass der natürliche Fels nur 0,05 m unterhalb der Oberfläche der Grabung lag, mit anderen Worten: Die nördliche Hälfte des Altars sitzt fast direkt auf dem anstehenden Fels (Abb. 8). Nach Süden hin fällt der Hang ab; unter der Südseite des Monuments liegt deshalb eine etwa 0,30 m hohe Aufschüttung; ebenso sind die Fundamentblöcke etwa ab der Mitte des Monuments mit kleineren Steinen unterfüttert worden (Abb. 9).

Ein bedeutendes Ergebnis der Ausgrabungen innerhalb und außerhalb des Altars ist die Entdeckung von insgesamt neun Gruben, die in den anstehenden Fels gehauen sind (Abb. 10).[32] Diese Gruben haben verschiedene Grundrisse (viereckig oder oval) und unterschiedliche Tiefe. Beispiele sind die Gruben Nr. IV, die sich an der südlichen Außenseite des Altares befindet (1,10 x 0,75 m; Tiefe 0,52 m) (Abb. 11) und die Grube Nr. V an der Ostseite des Altars (0,63 x 0,54 m; Tiefe 0,39 m) (Abb. 12). Wie man im Abb. 10 sieht, sind diese Gruben nicht in regelmäßigen Reihen angelegt.

Folgende Merkmale sind den Gruben gemeinsam: Erstens, sie sind in den natürlichen Fels gehauen, die Seiten der Gruben sind schräg und verengen sich nach unten (der Durchmesser des Bodens ist kleiner als der der Mündung). Zweitens, der Boden dieser Gruben ist nicht flach eingeebnet, sondern felsig und unregelmäßig. Drittens sind alle Gruben mit aufgeschütteter Erde gefüllt. Die Keramik aus der Füllung der Gruben ist von prähistorischer Zeit bis an das Ende des 5. Jhs. v. Chr. zu datieren. Sie besteht aus Scherben von unbemaltem Kochgeschirr, die etwa 80% des gesamten Scherbenmaterials ausmachen, sowie aus bemalten Scherben von Feinkeramik (Abb. 13). Leider sind nur sehr wenige Fragmente für eine präzise Datierung auswertbar. Die signifikanten Scherben, bei denen die Form des Gefäßes rekonstruiert werden kann, zeigen, dass der größte Teil der Keramik, bis auf wenige Fragmente prähistorischer, geometrischer und archaischer Zeit, in die klassische Zeit gehört, und zwar in die zweite Hälfte des 5. Jhs. v. Chr. (Abb. 14). Zu

Abb. 6. Innerer Teil des Altars nach der Ausgrabung.

Abb. 7. Innerer Teil des Altars nach der Ausgrabung unter den drei eingesetzten Steinen (Photo von S).

dieser Datierung stimmen auch die Fragmente der Dachziegel, die aus der Ausgrabung stammen: die Mehrzahl gehört zum korinthischen Typus, aber auch der lakonische Typus ist vertreten. Es sind gut gefirnisste Ziegel klassischer Zeit, und zwar bis zum Ende des 5. Jhs. v. Chr. vertreten (Abb. 15).[33] Es ist deutlich, dass das Verfüllen der Gruben und die Nivellierung des Areals nach dem Ende des 5. Jhs. V. Chr. stattfand und offensichtlich in Zusammenhang steht mit der ersten Einrichtung eines Altars an dieser Stelle, der aber nicht dem Monument entspricht, das wir vor uns haben.

Es ist festzuhalten, dass die Gruben wegen der Art und Weise ihrer Anlage, sowie wegen ihres Inhalts, nicht als prähistorische Schachtgräber oder als Bothroi (Abfallgruben im Heiligtum) interpretiert werden können. Einen Hinweis auf die Interpretation dieser Gruben gibt uns die Inschrift des Telemachosmonuments. Wir wissen aus dieser Inschrift, dass in der Zeit des Archons Kleokritos (413/2 v. Chr.) das Heiligtum bepflanzt und geschmückt war.[34] Die Bepflanzung mit Bäumen, die ein Heiligtum in einen heiligen Hain verwandeln kann, ist ein bekannter und weit verbreiteter Brauch im antiken Griechenland.[35] Es ist also möglich, dass diese Gruben unter dem

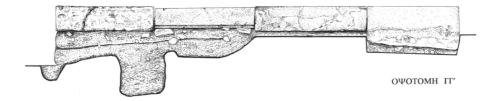

ΟΨΟΤΟΜΗ ΓΓ΄

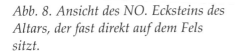

Abb. 8. Ansicht des NO. Ecksteins des Altars, der fast direkt auf dem Fels sitzt.

Altarfundament als Pflanzgruben für Bäume gedient haben; vielleicht sogar, bevor das Asklepieion gegründet wurde, nämlich zu der Zeit, als das Areal noch zum athenischen Eleusinion gehörte. Ähnliche Gruben mit genau demselben Inhalt notiert bei seiner Ausgrabung von 1963 auch N. Platon, und zwar in der Apsis der frühchristlichen Basilika des Asklepieions, die etwa 3 m nordöstlich des Altars liegt.[36]

Es ist bekannt, dass viele Asklepiosheiligtümer der klassischen Zeit heilige Haine innerhalb des Temenos hatten; die berühmtesten davon waren in Epidauros, Korinth, Titane, Kos und Lampsakos zu sehen.[37] Demnach braucht das Vorhandensein eines Haines im athenischen Asklepieion nicht zu überraschen.[38] Es ist sogar möglich, dass dieser Hain vor der Gründung des Heiligtums existierte, bereits zu der Zeit, als das Areal des späteren Asklepieion der Kontrolle des Eleusinions und damit der Priesterfamilie der Keryken unterstand.

Abb. 9. Ansicht der Südhälfte des Altars. Zu sehen sind die Ausgleichsschicht und die kleinen Steine unter den Altarblöcken.

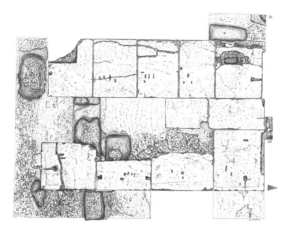

Abb. 10. Plan der Gruben.

Es handelt sich um eine bekannte Praxis der priesterlichen Familien in der Antike, die Orte der Heiligtümer als Heilige Haine zu deklarieren und Bäume zu pflanzen. Damit wurden diese Orte vor Übergriffen durch die Stadt oder durch einzelne Bürger geschützt. Für die Bewahrung der heiligen Haine wurden Heilige Gesetze aufgestellt. Durch diese Gesetze war das Niedertreten oder Holzfällen innerhalb des Hains der Stadt und den Bürgern verboten und konnte mit Geldstrafen belegt werden, wie aus einer Inschrift des 5. Jhs. v. Chr., die im Asklepieion von Kos gefunden wurde, hervorgeht.[39]

Die Bepflanzung des Bezirks scheint auf einigen aus dem Asklepieion stammenden Reliefs angedeutet zu sein, z. B. auf den Weihreliefs im Athener Nationalmuseum, bei denen in der Mitte des Reliefs jeweils ein Baum dargestellt ist, an den sich Hygieia lehnt.[40] Dieser Baum ist nicht innerhalb des Tempels zu denken, sondern stellt die Bepflanzung in dem Bezirk dar. Ein weiteres Indiz für die Bepflanzung des Heiligtums ist auf dem Telemachos-

ΟΨΟΤΟΜΗ ΛΛ'

Abb. 11. Ansicht der Grube IV.

monument zu sehen, und zwar auf der Rückseite des Doppelreliefs. Dort wird außerhalb des Temenos ein Baum mit einem Storch gezeigt, der die Bäume des heiligen Hains als pars pro toto repräsentiert (Abb. 16).[41]

Interessante Ergebnisse für die Datierung des Monuments hat die Ausgrabung im inneren Teil des Altars ergeben, und zwar sowohl die Grabung der Schichten unter den Steinen im Inneren des Fundamentes als auch an der südlichen Schmalseite außerhalb des Altars.

Die aus diesen Schnitten stammende Keramik besteht hauptsächlich aus Scherben die von der prähistorischen bis zu der klassischen Zeit zu datieren sind (Abb. 17),[42] enthält aber auch ein wichtiges Indiz für die Datierung des Fundaments.

Abb. 12. Ansicht der Grube V.

Es handelt sich um das Fragment einer Kassettendecke aus pentelischem Marmor, welches von der östlichen Prostasis des Erechtheions stammt, wie Korrés erkannt hat (Abb. 18).[43] Dieses Fragment kann nur nach der Eroberung der Akropolis unter dem römischen Feldherrn Sulla 86 v. Chr. und der damit verbundene Zerstörung des Erechtheions durch Feuer an die Stelle des Altars des Asklepieions gelangt sein.[44]

Für die Datierung des Monuments in die römische Zeit (und definitiv nach 86 v. Chr.) sprechen auch weitere Indizien. Nicht nur das heterogene Steinmaterial des Fundamentes erweckt den Eindruck, dass, wie Aleshire bemerkt hat, "the Altar has been so completely rebuilt in later times that any statements about it are quiet hazardous".[45] Als zusätzliches Argument kann gelten, dass die Form der Klammerlöcher auf den vier Seiten des Fundamentes, die in Abb. 3 zu sehen sind, ebenfalls charakteristisch für die römische Zeit ist. Diese Klammerlöcher sind viereckig und bemerkenswert tief (6,3 bis 6,5 cm), wobei die Gusskanäle mit 0,18 m sehr lang sind. Klammerlöcher und Gusskanäle sind den Klammerlöchern der Euthynterie des Asklepiostempels sehr ähnlich, dessen Datierung in die römische Zeit F. Versakis als erste richtig erkannt hat.[46]

Die antiken Schriftquellen und die Inschriften zum Altar des Asklepieions sind spärlich. Es ist sicher, dass Telemachos, der Gründer des Athener Asklepieions, als erster Priester des Gottes einen Altar gründete, wie die Inschrift auf dem Telemachosmonument belegt:

Abb. 13. Keramik aus der Füllung der Grube IV.

Abb. 14. Keramik aus der Füllung der Grube V.

[Τ]ηλέμαχος ἱδ[ρύσατο τὸ ἱε]ρὸν καὶ τὸν βω̃[μον τῶι Ἀσκλ]
ηπιῶι πρῶτ[ος καὶ Ὑγιείαι] τοῖς Ἀσσ[κληπιο(ῦ) Θυγατράσιν]
κα[ὶ...

Von großer Bedeutung ist auch eine fragmentarisch erhaltene Inschrift, die
ein heiliges Gesetz enthält. Diese Inschrift stammt aus der Agora von Athen,

Abb. 15. Dachziegelfragmente.

und ist von K. Clinton publiziert worden,[47] der sie in die Zeit zwischen 410 und 404 v. Chr. datiert. In der Inschrift werden Kosten eines Opfers aufgeführt, welches die Polis Athen dem Asklepios und seinen Kindern dargeboten hat und das in dem neu gegründeten Asklepieion stattfand. Wo dieser Altar war, und wo dieses Opfer stattfand, ist nicht sicher. Aber wenn man bedenkt, dass der Altar für das erste Opfer dem Gott bzw. den Göttern geweiht worden sein muss, dann darf man annehmen, dass vielleicht schon der erste Altar des Asklepieions hier seinen Platz hatte. Eine der Voraussetzungen für diese Annahme ist die Feststellung von J. Travlos, dass seit der Zeit der Gründung des Asklepieions sich das eigentliche Heiligtum im Osten der Anlage befand, während der westliche Teil, der von der Pelargikon-Mauer begrenzt wurde, nur zum umgebenden Raum des Heiligtums gehörte.[48] Tatsache ist, dass das Fundament, das wir vor uns haben, in römischer Zeit verlegt wurde. Als terminus post quem gilt die Eroberung und die Zerstörung vieler Monumente am Südabhang der Akropolis durch Sulla im

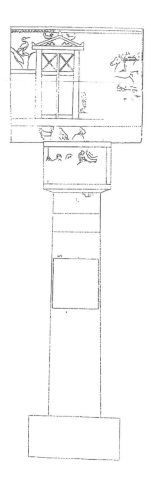

*Abb. 16. Detail aus der Umzeichnung des Telema-
chosmonuments: Storch und Baum (nach Beschi
2002, 22, Fig. 6).*

Jahr 86 v. Chr.[49] Vielleicht kommt die augusteische Zeit in Frage, da damals
viele monumentale Teile des Asklepieions erst gebaut worden sind (z. B. die
römische Südstoa) oder renoviert wurden (z. B. das Propylon).[50]

Wenn man aber – anders als hier und von Travlos vertreten – annehmen
will, dass das Asklepieion zunächst im Westteil der Terrasse gegründet
wurde,[51] dann wäre es möglich, dass der erste Altar auf der westlichen Terrasse gebaut wurde. Davon ist aber keine Spur erhalten. Zudem wäre möglich, dass der Altar zu einem unbekannten Zeitpunkt von der westlichen zu
der östlichen Terrasse transportiert worden wäre. Ein Ortswechsel ist bei-
spielsweise für den Zwölfgötteraltar auf der Agora von Athen belegt, aber
in diesem Fall wurde auch der Kult selbst an eine andere Stelle versetzt.[52]
Für das Asklepieion entfällt ein derartiger Grund; es spricht also alles dafür,
dass sich das römische Altarfundament an der Stelle des früheren Asklepios-
altars befindet.

Abb. 17. Keramik aus den Schichten der Füllung in der Südhälfte des Altars.

Danksagung

Der Präsident des Komitees für die Monumente am Südabhang der Akropolis, Herr P. Kalligas, Ehrendirektor der 1. Ephorie für prähistorische und klassische Altertümer, hat mir im Sommer 2001 die Ausgrabung an diesem Monument anvertraut. Ich möchte mich bei ihm, sowie auch beim Herrn Dr. A. Mantis, Präsidenten des Komitees für das Dionysostheater und das Asklepieion am Südabhang der Akropolis und Direktor der 1. Ephorie für prähistorische und klassische Altertümer bedanken, für die Erlaubnis, hier die ersten Gedanken über die Ausgrabung präsentieren zu dürfen. Ferner möchte ich Herrn Prof. M. Korrés für seine Hilfe und unsere fruchtbaren Diskussionen danken. Besonderen Dank schulde ich auch Frau Prof. E. Vikela für Auskünfte, Hinweise und unsere zahlreichen Gespräche. Frau Dr. J. Stroszeck hat meinen Text mit großer Aufmerksamkeit gelesen und sprachlich verbessert. Unsere Gespräche haben mir sehr geholfen, und ich möchte mich bei ihr herzlich bedanken.

Abb. 18. Zeichnung des Fragments von der Kassettendecke des Erechtheions.

NK4201. Κλίμακα 1 : 2

Anmerkungen

1. Grundlegende Artikel zur Zusammenstellung der in verschiedenen Museen aufbewahrten Teile des Monuments und seiner Interpretation: Beschi 1967-68; 1982; 2002. Vgl. auch Mitropoulou 1975 und Iliakis 1992-98.
2. Verbanck-Pierard 2000, 303. S. auch Vikela 1997, 190 Abb. 3.
3. Clinton 1994, 29-34.
4. Die ionische Stoa (Καταγώγιον) befindet sich auf der Westseite des Asklepieions und besteht aus vier quadratischen Räumen mit je 6 m Seitenlänge. Die Räume dienten als Bankettsäle für je 11 Klinen und wurden von den Besuchern, möglicherweise auch von den Priestern des Heiligtums, benutzt.
5. Korrés 1996, 97.
6. *IG* II² 4355 [Τηλέμαχ]ός σε ἱέρωσε Ἀσσκληπιῶι ἠδὲ ὁμοβώμοις | πρῶτος ἱδρυσάμενος θυσίαις θείαις ὑποθήκαις. Koumanoudis 1877a, 137-8 Nr. 14, s. auch Köhler 1877, 241.
7. Vielleicht ist auf dem Telemachosmonument das erste Opfer für die Einweihung des Heiligtums dargestellt, und zwar in dem Fries unter der Hauptdarstellung der zweiten Seite des Doppelreliefs, wie Verbanck-Piérard annimmt. Auf diesem Fries wird eine τρίττοια abgebildet d.h. das Opfer von drei Tieren: Rind, Widder und Schwein. Verbanck-Pierard 2000, 302.
8. Burkert 1977, 146-7.
9. Şahin 1972, 1-2. S. auch Yavis 1949; Étienne 1992.
10. Kutsch 1913, 25 Anm. 11.
11. De Waele 1933; s. auch Roebuck 1951, 28-30.
12. Blegen 1927.
13. Arist. [*Ath. Pol.*] 56.4: πομπῶν δ᾽ ἐπιμελεῖτ[αι (ὁ βασιλεύς) τῆς τ]ε τῷ Ἀσκληπιῷ γιγνομένης (θυσίας), ὅταν οἰκουρῶσι μύσται. Vgl. Clinton 1994, 27 Anm. 36.
14. *IG* II² 772, 9-13. s. auch Aleshire 1989, 94-5; Cohn-Haft 1956.

15 Über den Beinamen "Dexion", den Sophokles nach seinem Tod übernommen
    hätte, s. Walter 1953 und oben S. 57 in dem Artikel von Wickkiser. Dagegen:
    Connolly 1998.

16 Der Paian ist auf dem bekannten Sarapionmonument (*SEG* 28.225) wiederge-
    geben. Um 125 n. Chr. weihte Κόϊντος Στάτιος Σαραπίων Χολλείδης einen
    Dreifuß zu Ehren seines Großvaters Σαραπίων. Auf der Basis dieses Monu-
    ments wurden sowohl ein philosophisches als auch ein medizinisches Gedicht
    angebracht. Um 200 n. Chr. ist auf dem Sarapionmonument zusätzlich eine
    weitere Weihung angebracht worden: Auf den Seiten der Basis wurde Sopho-
    kles' Paian eingetragen, der damals, zur Zeit des Archons Mounatios Themison,
    von einem siegreichen Chor gesungen wurde. Zum Sarapionmonument, s.
    Oliver 1936; Edelstein & Edelstein 1945, 200 Anm. 5; Aleshire 1989, 9-11; 1991,
    49-74.

17 Aleshire 1989, 14-5.

18 Athen, NM 1332, Svoronos 1908-37, 247-52, Taf. 36.2. Vikela 1997, 192 Anm. 79.

19 Aleshire 1989, 94-5.

20 *IG* II² 1685, s. Aleshire 1991, 13-32.

21 Travlos 1939/41.

22 Köhler 1877, 245-54; Robert 1939, 143, 233-40, 325.

23 *IG* II² 974-975. Die Inschrift ist in die erste Hälfte des 2. Jhs. v. Chr. zu datieren
    und enthält die erste Erwähnung des Festes der Heroa in diesem Zusammen-
    hang.

24 Vgl. für diese Annahme Riehmüller 1999. Dagegen und für die Deutung des
    heiligen Bothros als Zisterne für die Wasserversorgung des Asklepieions, s.
    Aleshire 1989, 26-7 Anm. 7; Verbanck-Piérard 2000, 329-32. s. auch Eckroth
    2002, 60 Anm. 165, 226 Anm. 55.

25 Koumanoudis 1876, 14-35; 1877b, 6-12.

26 Lambert 1877.

27 Aleshire 1989, 6.

28 Zu den Abweichungen zwischen den Plänen des Altars, die auf Abb. 3 und 4
    zu sehen sind, bedarf es folgender Erklärung: dem originalen Zustand des
    Altars in römischer Zeit entspricht Abb. 4. Im Verlauf der Arbeiten im Askle-
    pieion, die 1989 ausgeführt wurden, gelang es den Restauratoren Happas und
    Anastasias, dem Altar einen Block zuzuweisen, der den Abschluss des Monu-
    mentes als Eckblock an der SW-Seite bildete (vgl. die tiefe, rechteckige Einar-
    beitung, die sich auf dem benachbarten Block fortsetzt); ferner ist es den ge-
    nauen Beobachtungen beiden zu verdanken, dass die ursprüngliche Position
    des schon früher bekannten südöstlichen Eckblocks genauer bestimmt werden
    konnte. Entsprechend einem Vorschlag, den der Architekt Lefantzis beim Ko-
    mitee für die Monumente des Südabhangs der Akropolis im Dezember 2001
    eingereicht hat, sind beide Ecksteine wieder an ihren richtigen Platz gesetzt
    worden.

29 Dieser Kalkstein wurde in der Antike im Piräus gebrochen, und ist als Piräus-
    kalk (πειραϊκός ακτίτης) bekannt.

30 Fraglich bleibt, ob dieser Stein zu einem bislang unbekannten Monument am
    Südabhang der Akropolis gehört, oder ob er unter Umständen, wie Prof. Kor-
    rés mündlich geäußert hat, vom Oberbau einer früheren Phase des Altars stam-
    men könnte. Es ist möglich, dass die Piräuskalksteine des Fundaments zu einer

früheren Phase des Monuments gehören, bevor sie, zusammen mit den anderen Steinen aus heterogenem Material, für den Altar verwendet wurden.

31 Für die Datierung des Altars, s. den in diesem Band erschienenen Artikel von Lefantzis und Jensen.

32 Die Gruben sind mit lateinischen Zahlen nummeriert worden.

33 Über Dachziegel, s. Winter 1994.

34 *IG* II² 4961 + 4960a + 4960b, stoich. 38-42. [Κλεόκρι]τος ἐπὶ τοῦ[το ἐφυτεύθ]η καὶ κατέστ[ησε κοσμή]σας τὸ τέμεν[ος ἅπαν τέ]λει τῶι ἑαυ[το(ῦ).

35 Für ähnliche Pflanzungen beim Hephaisteion auf der Athener Agora vgl. Burr Thompson & Griswold 1963, 7-11 (Abb. 11-15); Thompson & Wycherley 1972, 149, Taf. 76; Camp 1986, 86-7, Abb. 64. Für Pflanzungen in Nemea, s. Birge 1992.

36 Platon 1963, 20.

37 Birge 1982, 72-3, 175, 194, 342.

38 Graf 1992, 181-3.

39 Herzog 1928, 32-3 Nr. II.

40 Athen, NM 1333: Svoronos 1908-37, 252-4, Taf. 36.3. Athen, NM 1335: Svoronos 1908-37, 254-6, Taf. 36.4.

41 Walter 1930, 98 Anm. 55; Wegner 1985, 133-6.

42 Vergleichsbeispiele für die Gebrauchskeramik, s. Sparkes & Talcott 1970, 32-40. Für die rotfigurige Keramik und speziell für das rotfigurige Scherbe mit der Darstellung einer nach rechts schreitenden Frau, s. Moore 1997, 149, Nr. 107, Taf. 18; Vgl. auch Burn 1988, 106-7.

43 Das Fragment hat die Inv. Nr. NK 4201 und wird im Asklepieion aufbewahrt. L.: 0,19 m; B.: 0,13 m; D.: 0,095 m. Auf der Vorderseite des Fragments ist nur ein Teil des reliefierten ionischen Kymations der Kassettendecke erhalten, die Rückseite ist grob mit dem Spitzmeißel bearbeitet. Zum Vergleich sollten die Beispiele der Kassettendecken der östlichen Prostasis des Erechtheions dienen in Paton, Caskey, Fowler & G.P. Stevens 1927, 27-30, Abb. 16, Taf. 16, 18.

44 Reparaturen und Ausbesserungsarbeiten wurden im Erechtheion vor dem Ende des 1. Jhs. v. Chr. ausgeführt, s. Bruskari 1984.

45 Aleshire 1989, 20 Anm. 5.

46 Versakis 1908.

47 Clinton 1994.

48 Travlos 1971, 127; Aleshire 1989, 27.

49 Über Sulla, s. Berve 1966, 130-50.

50 Aleshire 1989, 16 Anm. 4.

51 Girard 1881, 5-6; Townsend 1982, 77 Anm. 5.

52 Stillwell 1933, 140-8; Thompson & Scranton 1943, 299-300 Anm. 38; Thompson 1952, 50-1 Anm. 18.

Bibliographie

Aleshire, S.B. 1989. *The Athenian Asklepieion: The People, their Dedications, and the Inventories*. Amsterdam: J.C. Gieben.

Aleshire, S.B. 1991. *Asklepios at Athens: Epigraphic and Prosopographic Essays on the Athenian Healing Cults*. Amsterdam: J.C. Gieben.

Berve, H. 1966. *Gestaltende Kräfte der Antike. Aufsätze zur griechischen und römischen Geschichte*. Munich: C.H. Beck.

Beschi, L. 1967-68 [1969]. "Il monumento di Telemachos: fondatore dell'Asclepieion ateniese." *ASAtene* 45-46 (n.s. 29-30): 381-436.

Beschi, L. 1982. "Il rilievo di Telemachos ricompletato." *AAA* 15: 31-43.

Beschi, L. 2002 [2003]. "Culti Stranieri e fondazioni private nell'Attica Classica: alcuni case." *ASAtene* 80 (n.s. 3.2): 13-42.

Birge, D.E. 1982. "Sacred Groves in the Ancient Greek World." Ph.D. diss., University of California, Berkeley.

Birge, D.E. 1992. "The Sacred Square." In *Excavations at Nemea I. Topographical and Architectural Studies: the Sacred Square, the Xenon, and the Bath*, edited by D.E. Birge, L.H. Kraynak & S. Miller, 85-98. Berkeley, Los Angeles, & Oxford: University of California Press.

Blegen, C.W. 1927. "Excavations at Nemea 1926." *AJA* 31: 421-40.

Bruskari, M. 1984. "Bemerkungen über die vierte und fünfte Karyatide des Erechtheion." *ÖJh* 55: 55-62.

Burkert, W. 1977. *Griechische Religion der archaischen und klassischen Epoche*. Stuttgart: Kohlhammer.

Burn, L. 1988. *The Meidias Painter*. Oxford: Oxford University Press.

Burr Thompson, D. & R.E. Griswold. 1963. *Garden Lore of Ancient Athens*. AgoraPicBk 8. Princeton: The American School of Classical Studies at Athens.

Camp, J.McK., II. 1986. *The Athenian Agora: Excavations in the Heart of Classical Athens*. New York & London: Thames & Hudson.

Clinton, K. 1994. "The Epidauria and the Arrival of Asclepius in Athens." In *Ancient Greek Cult Practice from the Epigraphical Evidence, Proceedings of the Second International Seminar on Ancient Greek Cult, Athens, 1991*, edited by R. Hägg, 17-34. SkrAth 8°, 13. Stockholm: Svenska Institutet i Athen, distribution Paul Åströms Förlag.

Cohn-Haft, L. 1956. *The Public Physicians of Ancient. Greece*, Smith College Studies in History 42. Northampton, MA: Department of History of Smith College.

Connolly, A. 1998. "Was Sophocles heroised as Dexion?" *JHS* 118: 1-21.

De Waele, F.J. 1933. "The Sanctuary of Asklepios and Hygieia at Corinth." *JA* 37: 417-51.

Eckroth, G. 2002. *The Sacrificial Rituals of Greek Hero-Cults in the Archaic to the Hellenistic Periods*. Kernos Suppl. 12. Liège: Centre Internationale d'Étude de la Religion Grecque Antique.

Edelstein, E.J. & L. Edelstein. 1945. *Asclepius: A Collection and Interpretation of the Testimonies*. 2 vols. Repr. 1998. Baltimore: Johns Hopkins University Press.

Étienne, R. 1992. "Autels et Sacrifices." In *Le sanctuaire grec*, edited by A. Schachter & J. Bingen, 291-316. Entretiens sur l'antiquité classique 37. Vandœuvres-Genève: Fondation Hardt.

Girard, P. 1881. *L'Asclépieion d'Athènes après de recentes découvertes. BÉFAR* 23. Paris: Ernest Thorin.

Graf, F. 1992. "Heiligtum und Ritual. Das Beispiel der griechisch-römischen Asklepieia." In *Le sanctuaire grec*, edited by A. Schachter & J. Bingen, 159-99. Entretiens sur l'antiquité classique 37. Vandœuvres-Genève: Fondation Hardt.

Herzog, R. 1928. *Heilige Gesetze von Kos. Abhandlungen der Preußischen Akademie der Wissenschaften, Philosophisch-Historische Klasse* 6. Berlin: Akademie der Wissenschaften, distribution Walter de Gruyter und Co.

Iliakis, K. 1992-98. "Πρόταση για τη μορφή του αναθήματος του Τηλεμάχου Αχαρνέως." *Horos* 10-12: 73-6.

Köhler, U. 1877. "Der Südabhang der Akropolis zu Athen nach den Ausgrabungen der archäologischen Gesellschaft." *AM* 2: 171-86 + 229-60.

Korrés, M. 1996. "Ein Beitrag zur Kenntnis der attisch-ionischen Architektur." In *Säule und Gebälk. Zu Struktur und Wandlungsprozeß griechisch-römischer Architektur, DiskAB* 6, edited by E.-L. Schwandner, 90-113. Mainz am Rhein: Deutsches Archäologisches Institut – Wasmuth, distribution Philipp von Zabern.

Koumanoudis, S. 1876. *Prakt*, 14-35.

Koumanoudis, S. 1877a. "Ἐπιγραφαὶ ἐκ τῶν περὶ τὸ Ἀσκληπιεῖον τόπων." *Athenaion* 6: 127-48.

Koumanoudis, S. 1877b. *Prakt*, 6-12.

Kutsch, F. 1913. *Attische Heilgötter und Heilheroen. Religionsgeschichtliche Versuche und Vorarbeiten* 12:3. Gießen: Alfred Töpelmann.

Lambert, M. 1877. "Plan des fouilles faites par la Société Archéologique sur le versant méridional de l'Acropole." *BCH* 1: 169-70.

Mitropoulou, E. 1975. *A New Interpretation of the Telemachos Monument*. Athens: Pyli.

Moore, M.B. 1997. *Attic Red-Figured and White-Ground Pottery. Agora* 30. Princeton: The American School of Classical Studies at Athens.

Oliver, J.H. 1936. "The Sarapion Monument and the Paean of Sophocles." *Hesperia* 5: 91-122.

Paton, J.M., L.D. Caskey, H.N. Fowler & G.P. Stevens. 1927. *The Erechtheum*. Cambridge, MA: Harvard University Press.

Platon, N. 1963. "Ἐργασίαι διαμορφώσεως Ἀσκληπιείου." *ArchDelt* 18, *Chron.* 1: 18-22.

Riethmüller, J.W. 1999. "Bothros and Tetrastyle: The Heroon of Asclepius at Athens." In *Ancient Greek Hero Cult, Proceeding of the Fifth International Classical Archaeology and Ancient History*, edited by R. Hägg, 123-43.

SkrAth 8°, 16. Stockholm: Svenska Institutet i Athen, distribution Paul Åströms Förlag.

Robert, F. 1939. *Thymélè. Recherches sur la signification et la destination des monuments circulaires dans l'architecture religieuse de la Grèce.* Paris: de Boccard.

Roebuck, C. 1951. *The Asklepieion and Lerna: Based on the Excavations and Preliminary Studies by F.J. De Waele. Corinth* 14. Princeton: The American School of Classical Studies at Athens.

Şahin, M.C. 1972. *Die Entwicklung der griechischen Monumentalaltäre,* Bonn: Rudolf Habelt.

Sparkes, B.A. & L. Talcott. 1970. *Black and Plain Pottery of the 6th, 5th and 4th centuries B.C. Agora* 12. Princeton: The American School of Classical Studies at Athens.

Stillwell, R. 1933. "Architectural Studies." *Hesperia* 2: 110-48.

Svoronos, J.N. 1908-37. *Das Athener Nationalmuseum.* Translated by W. Barth. Athens: Eleftheroudakis.

Thompson, H.A. 1952. "The Altar of Pity in the Athenian Agora," *Hesperia* 21: 47-82.

Thompson, H.A. & R.L. Scranton. 1943. "Stoas and City Walls on the Pnyx." *Hesperia* 12: 269-383.

Thompson, H.A. & R.E. Wycherley. 1972. *The Agora of Athens: the History, the sharpe and use of an Ancient City. Agora* 14. Princeton: The American School of Classical Studies at Athens.

Townsend, R.F. 1982. "Aspects of Athenian Architectural Activity in the Second Half of the Fourth Century B.C." Ph.D. diss., University of North Carolina, Chapel Hill.

Travlos, J.N. 1939-41. "Ἡ παλαιοχριστιανικὴ βασιλικὴ τοῦ Ἀσκληπιείου τῶν Ἀθηνῶν." *ArchEph*, 35-68.

Travlos, J.N. 1971. *Bildlexikon zur Topographie des Athen.* Tübingen: Ernst Wasmuth.

Verbanck-Piérard, A. 2000. "Les Héros guérisseurs: des dieux comme les autres! À propos des cultes médicaux dans l'Attique classique." In *Héros et Héroïnes dans les mythes et les cultes grecs,* edited by V. Pirenne-Delforge & E. Suárez de la Torre, 281-332. Kernos Suppl. 10, Liège: Centre Internationale d'Étude de la Religion Grecque Antique.

Versakis, F. 1908. "Ἀρχιτεκτονικὰ μνημεῖα τοῦ ἐν Ἀθήναις Ἀσκληπιείου." *ArchEph*, 255-84.

Vikela, E. 1997. "Attische Weihreliefs und die Kulttopographie Attikas." *AM* 112: 167-246.

Walter, O. 1930. "Ein neugewonnenes Athener Doppelrelief." *ÖJh* 26: 75-104.

Walter, O. 1953. "Das Priestertum des Sophokles." in *Γέρας Ἀντωνίου Κεραμοπούλλου. Ἐπιστημονικαὶ πραγματεῖαι. Σειρά φιλολογικὴ καὶ θεολογικὴ* 9. Athens: Myrtidi, 469-79.

Wegener, S. 1985. *Funktion und Bedeutung landschaftlicher Elemente in der griechischen Reliefkunst archaischer bis hellenistischer Zeit.* European University Studies Series 38, Archaeology vol. 6. Frankfurt am Main, Bern & New York: Peter Lang.

Winter, N.A. (ed.). 1994. *International Conference on Greek Architectural Terracottas of the Classical and Hellenistic Periods. Hesperia Suppl.* 27. Princeton: The American School of Classical Studies at Athens.

Yavis, C.G. 1949. *Greek Altars: Origins and Typology including the Minoan-Mycenaean Offertory Apparatus. An Archeological Study in the History of Religion.* Saint Louis University studies, Monograph series, Humanities 1. Saint Louis, Missouri: Saint Louis University Press.

The Athenian Asklepieion on the South Slope of the Akropolis: Early Development, ca. 420-360 B.C.

Michaelis Lefantzis and Jesper Tae Jensen

Introduction

The Athenian Asklepieion was from at least 300/299 B.C. situated on the east terrace of the south slope of the Akropolis. Many questions regarding the Classical phase of the sanctuary remain unanswered since its excavation in April 1876 – June 1877 by the Greek Archeological Society.[1] Where exactly on the south slope was the original Asklepieion, founded by the private citizen Telemachos on the 17th or 18th Boedromion in 420 B.C.?[2] Did it stand on the middle terrace or was it on the east terrace? What subsequently happened to the first temple and the altar of the Telemachos sanctuary? And finally, how large was the sacred area of the Asklepieion and how, exactly, was it designed?

In this article, it will be demonstrated that the original Asklepieion of Telemachos was founded on the east terrace, as was suggested before this study without conclusive evidence by Ulrich Köhler, John Nikolas Travlos, Luigi Beschi, Sarah B. Aleshire, Jeffrey Hurwit and Jürgen W. Riethmüller.[3] One of the keys to unlocking this puzzle is a structure in the Asklepieion currently labeled a *bomos* that, until now, has been assumed to be the altar of Asklepios from at least ca. 300/299 B.C. when the Asklepieion's Doric stoa was constructed.[4] It will be demonstrated that the chronology of this very important monument begins about 418/7-416/5 B.C.[5] At least four distinctive construction phases detected in the bedrock under and around this structure and on its blocks can be shown to belong to this monument.[6] In this article, the first two construction phases will be investigated in depth after a careful description of the foundations belonging to Phases I-IV. Furthermore, evidence pertaining to the sacred area that belonged to the early Asklepieion will be analyzed. Here we will show what great importance and centrality this monument's impact on the design of the early Asklepieion has played.

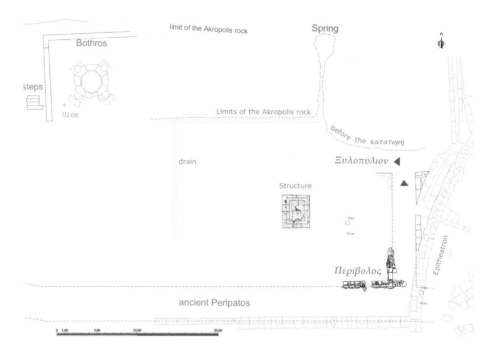

Fig. 1 Plan of the early Asklepieion with the steps west of the sacred pit, sacred pit, limit of the Akropolis rock today and a tentative suggestion of the limits of the rock before the κατατομή, the drain for the water of the spring, the spring, the tentative suggested ξυλοπύλιον with an arrow showing the cuttings in the rock for the north end of the eastern peribolos, the Classical Peripatos road, the peribolos at the southeast corner, the structure and the analemma of the epitheatron of the Theatre of Dionysos.

A presentation of the structure and its foundation

Inside the Athenian Asklepieion lies a structure approximately 16 m south of the Akropolis rock and 15 m from the analemma of the epitheatron of the Theatre of Dionysos (Fig. 1). Presently, this structure is labeled a *bomos*, both on the two general introduction posters of the sanctuary and on a limestone label block on site. The dimensions of the foundation of this structure in its latest phase (Phase IV) are 3.40 x 5.80 m (Fig. 2). All scholars have accepted the identification of this structure as a *bomos*. We prefer for now to call it a structure since we are not convinced that this was, in fact, the altar of Asklepios. In 2001 and 2002, this structure underwent cleaning and excavation. This work revealed new clues as to its function over at least four phases.[7]

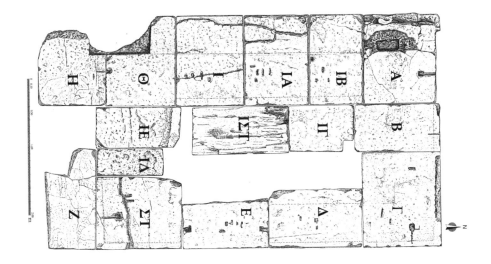

Fig. 2 Drawing of the foundation as it is restored today (Phase IV). The blocks are labeled clockwise with Greek letters.

All 15 blocks that make up the foundation of the structure's last construction phase have been labeled clockwise, beginning from the north-west corner and ending with the blocks in the middle of the foundation, also numbered clockwise (Fig. 2). The material of eleven of the blocks (**A′-Δ′, ΣΤ′-ΙΓ′**) is soft grey poros, one block is yellow poros (**E′**) from Piraeus (also called *Πειραϊκός ακτίτης*) while two blocks are Hymettian marble (**ΙΕ′** and **ΙΣΤ′**). The last block is cut from the Akropolis rock (**ΙΔ′**) (*Ακροπολίτης λίθος* or Akropolis limestone).

All twelve poros blocks (**A′-ΙΓ′**) exhibit the same tooling on their upper surface. All are finished by a combination of the tooth and the point chisel used in Phase III (Fig. 3). In addition, two specific types of pry holes are used on the blocks' upper surface. The small pry holes used in Phases I-III on seven blocks (**A′, Γ′, Δ′, ΣΤ′, Ι′, ΙΑ′** and **ΙΒ′**) clearly indicate that the blocks used in the first krepis were relatively small. The larger pry holes belong to Phase IV. Since the small pry holes do not appear to be associated with the larger ones from Phase IV, they cannot be interpreted as supplementary pry holes for the larger ones. All the dimensions of the blocks are measured from their upper surface and the dimensions given are the maximum width (w.) and length (l.). In the technical description below, we have only described the main characteristics of the treatment of the blocks. It should be noted, however, that there are many traces of additional workmanship on each block since the main parts have been re-used perhaps more than five times since their original cutting. It should also be stressed that the foundation

Fig. 3 Photo of the detail of the tool marks from the point and tooth chisel on the surface of a stone from Phases I-III. The tool marks are from Phase III.

blocks were covered with earth, thereby indicating the ancient ground level when the structure was built.

Description of the foundation blocks A′ to ΙΣΤ′ (Fig. 2)

A′
Dimensions: w. 1.14 m, l. 1.28 m
Technical description:
A smooth area 0.15 m from the south side and 0.10 m from the west side can be detected. The smooth area has been made to support a wooden post (ικρίον) but its limits are not well enough preserved to give accurate dimensions. A rectangular cutting (0.17 x 0.54 m) 0.30 m from the west side for the setting of a stele belongs to Phase II. A dowel hole (0.05 x 0.08 m) with a pour channel (l. 0.18 m) for lead can be detected on the north side 0.42 m from the west corner and belongs to Phase IV. Furthermore, the north face has a rectangular cutting (1.04 x 0.08 m) for a base. The west face has the same cutting but for a smaller base 0.72 x 0.10 m.

B′

Dimensions: w. 0.72 m, l. 1.06 m
Technical description:
A smooth rectangular area (0.20 x 0.25 m) 0.60 m from the north side and 0.15 m from the west side can be detected. The smooth area has been made by the use of a wooden post (ικρίον) from Phase III. In Phase IV, the north face of the block was re-cut with a point chisel. The north face of the rock was re-cut by Phase IV.

Γ′

Dimensions: w. 1.15 m, l. 1.35 m
Technical description:
A smooth area 0.22 m from the east side and 0.70 m from the north side can be detected. The smooth area (0.20 x 0.25 m) comes from the use of a wooden post (*ικρίον*) from Phases I-II. From Phase III, another smooth area (0.18 x 0.20 m), which also comes from the use of a wooden post, can be seen very near the first, ca. 0.69 m from the east side and 0.62 m from the north side. The block has three pry holes: from Phases I-II, one short pry hole 0.35 m from the east side and two longer pry holes from Phase IV. The first large pry hole lies 0.28 m from the east side and the second lies 0.18 m from the west side. A dowel hole (0.05 x 0.08 m) from Phase IV with main (l. 0.18 m) and secondary pour channels similar to the one used on **A′** lies 0.18 m from the east side. The north face has a cutting (0.95 x 0.08 m) for a base.

Δ′

Dimensions: w. 0.84 m, l. 1.39 m
Technical description:
The east front is dressed with the claw chisel as an external face, while the west front is roughly dressed with the point chisel as a rear surface. The dowel hole and the nearest pry hole lie exactly in the middle of the block and are used in Phases I-III. The second pry hole 0.22 m from the dowel hole is from Phase IV.

E′

Dimensions: w. 0.70 m, l. 1.24 m
Technical description:
This block belongs entirely to Phase IV with three long parallel pry holes. It was originally an ashlar block, a stretcher from a Hellenistic building probably belonging to the Asklepieion. It has a *tainia* of 0.04 m wide and traces of a small tooth chisel at its east face. Cuttings for two T-clamps can be seen at each end, as well as a dowel hole and an auxiliary dowel in the middle which were cut for its original use but served no purpose during its reuse.

ΣT′

Dimensions: w. 1.04 m, l. 1.28 m
Technical description:
From Phases I-II a smooth area (0.20 x 0.25 m) 0.50 m from the south side and 0.25 m from the east side very near the dowel hole from Phase IV can

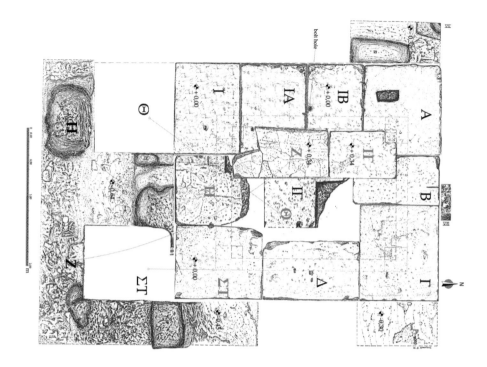

Fig. 4 Phases I-II. The movement and rotation of the blocks are shown with arrows. The entrance on the first krepis with the bolt hole for the doors is also shown.

be detected. The smooth area was made by the use of a wooden post (ικρίον). The initial position of this block was where **E′** lies today (Fig. 4). It was moved to its present position in Phase IV. Also from Phase IV, a rectangular dowel hole (0.05 x 0.08 m) with a pour channel (l. 0.18 m) can be seen at the south side with two long pry holes further to the west.

Z′

Dimensions: w. 1.46 m, l. 0.76 m
Technical description:
This block was originally placed on the first krepis in Phases I-II at the southwest corner and must have covered **IB′, Θ′, H′, I′,** and **IA′**. When the block was found by Stefanos Koumanoudis, he placed it incorrectly at the middle of the south side of the foundation (Fig. 5).[8] As can be seen from the plan (Fig. 2), the stone is today placed at the southeast corner, where it belongs in Phase IV. In an intermediate repair phase between Phases III and

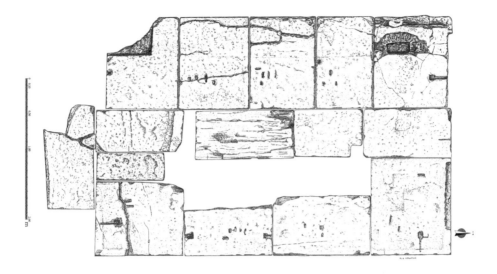

Fig. 5 The structure as it was found by Koumanoudis in 1877 until 2001.

IV, there is evidence for the stone having been rotated 90 degrees and placed upside down in the internal south side of the first krepis.

H′ and Θ′

Dimensions: **H′**: w. 1.30 m, l. 1.10 m; **Θ′**: w. 1.31 m, l. 1.02 m
Technical description:
The positions of both blocks today belong to Phase IV. They were originally placed in the internal gap of the small rectangular foundation of Phases I-III (Fig. 4). **H′** was placed between **I′** and **ΣΤ′**, while **Θ′** was originally placed between **IA′** and **Δ′**. The bottom of **H′** has a large curved area for a drain (Fig. 6), while **Θ′** has a smaller cutting for the same drain; both these features are from Phases I-III. From Phase IV, a rectangular cutting from **Θ′** (0.65 x 0.58 m) extends to block **H′** (0.25 m x 0.32 m). On the foundation the dimensions of the cutting are 0.90 x 0.58 m. The cutting for the base continues on the west side. **H′** also has a smooth band (l. 0.14 m) on the north side that indicates the position of the Phase IV krepis. 0.48 m from the east side is the dowel hole (0.05 x 0.08 m) of **Θ′** corresponding with the pour channel (l. 0.18 m) on **H′**. A large pry hole can also be seen on **H′** from Phase IV.

*Fig. 6 Axonometric view from south of the foundation with the drain on **H′***.

drain on block H′

I′-IB′

Dimensions: **I′**: w. 1.30 m, l. 0.99 m; **IA′**: w. 1.30 m, l. 0.96 m; **IB′**: w. 1.30 m, l. 0.82 m

Technical description:

These blocks are threshold blocks since their upper surface has a 0.54 m broad band showing footwear. From Phases I-III, four small pry holes lie on-line 0.30 m from the east side (**I′** and **IA′** have one pry hole, while **IB′** has two pry holes). A small circular hole (diameter 0.06 m) 0.65 m from the east side can be seen between **IA′** and **IB′**. This hole is the bolt hole for the doors (Figs. 4, 7). A pry hole on **IA′** 0.73 m from the west side belongs to Phase III. From Phase IV, seven large pry holes lie on-line ca. 0.44 m from the east side (**I′** and **IA′** have three pry holes, while **IB′** has one pry hole).

IΓ′

Dimensions: w. 0.66 m, l. 0.96 m

Technical description:

Its current position belongs to Phase IV. Originally this block belonged to the first krepis of Phases I-II and was placed at the northwest corner on top of **A′**, **B′**, **Θ′**, and **IB′**. At its northwest side, a square area (0.16 x 0.16 m) is cut away for the wooden post (*ικρίον*) on top of **A′**. In Phase III, the block was turned upside down, and the square area was then on top of **B′** with the block still laying on top of **A′**, **B′**, **Θ′**, and **IB′**.

Fig. 7 Photo of the bolt hole on **IA**′ *and* **IB**′.

IΔ′

Dimensions: w. 0.38 m, l. 0.39 m
Technical description:
This block had been placed in this position during Phase IV. Its original position may have been on the east side near the wooden post on the first krepis of Phases I-II. In Phase III, the block could have been placed in the internal part of the first or second krepis.

IE′

Dimensions: w. 0.61 m, l. 1.24 m
Technical description:
The block was placed in this position in Phase IV. All four side faces of this block are roughly dressed by the point and were reused from Phase III's krepis.

IΣT′

Dimensions: w. 0.71 m, l. 1.40 m
Technical description:
The block was placed in this position in Phase IV. The upper surface has been re-cut, but the state of preservation does not allow us to determine which tool was used. All four faces have been roughly cut as a rear surface. This means that **IΣT′** was previously used as an internal block of a krepis, from Phase III's krepis.

Analysis of the blocks and the holes adjacent to the structure

Construction phase I

The cleaning and excavation around the structure revealed nine man-made holes that are numbered with Roman numerals, as seen on Fig. 8.[9] Some were believed to be holes for trees or plants like the ones used at the north, south and west sides of the Hephaisteion on the Kolonos Agoraios during the third century B.C.[10] It has even been suggested that the holes were made for the very trees planted under the archonship of Kleokritos in 413/12 B.C., described in the inscription on the Telemachos Monument.[11] Potsherds found in the holes have been dated to the late fifth century. The date for the construction proposed below suggests that the circular holes III and IV were in use before the foundation of the Asklepieion. The rectangular hole V is cut for a foundation block pre-dating the Asklepieion, while too little has been excavated of holes VII and VIII to come to any conclusions about their function.

As can be seen on the plan in Fig. 8, the form of the holes numbered I, II, VI and IX is rectangular. A line can be drawn around the outer front of the holes, as can be seen in Fig. 9. These holes form an exact rectangle, which indicate that the holes in the bedrock were cut to hold foundation blocks. The structure is rather small and its foundation measures 3.10 m at the west side and is at least 3.00 m at the north and south sides (the east side of holes I and II is unknown). It must have been less than 3.55 m because hole V's west side is known and holes V and II do not have any relation to each other.

Fortunately, the sherds found from the holes strongly suggest that these holes were in use at the end of the fifth century B.C.[12] The date for the structure must therefore be set before ca. 400 B.C. but not earlier than 418/7 B.C., a fact that will be made clear after a careful reading of the Telemachos inscription below.

Construction phase II

Our discovery becomes more exciting when we reconstruct the second phase of the structure. The foundation is made of ten poros blocks (A′, B′, Γ′, Δ′, ΣΤ′, H′, I′, IA′, IB′, and Θ′), where seven of the blocks were found in situ (A′, B′, Γ′, Δ′, I′, IA′, and IB′). The ten blocks have the same surface treatment (A′-Δ′, ΣΤ′, H′, I′-IB′, and Θ′) and show no trace of dowel holes or pour channels. Three of the blocks have a smooth surface for wooden posts (A′, Γ′ and ΣΤ′), and five of the blocks have identical pry holes (Γ′, Δ′, I′, IA′, and IB′). Furthermore, the foundation has the exact dimensions on the west and east sides as the rectangular plan from Phase I. Its north and south sides measure 3.40 m and are thus smaller than the absolute maximum width (3.55 m) of the foundation from Phase I. The coincidence is too striking. We thereby conclude that this foundation has been reused from Phase I.

Fig. 8 Drawing of the foun-dation as it is restored today (Phase IV) with the excava-tion holes in the bedrock. The holes are numbered with Roman numerals. Two sec-tions of the foundation with the burned layer.

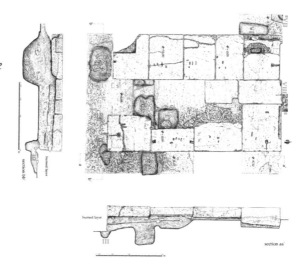

Fig. 9 Drawing of the move-ment of the foundation of Phases I and II. Phase I: Red color with the area of the first krepis indicated with hatches; Phase II: Blue color with the area of the first krepis indicat-ed with hatches.

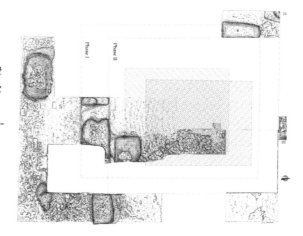

The building was moved 0.45 m to the north and 0.35 m to the east as can be seen in Fig. 9. The movement cannot be fully explained, but perhaps took place after a fire since ca. 0.10 m below the foundation of Phase II the earth shows traces of burning. The burned layer can clearly be seen on the section of the structure in Fig. 8.

Krepis

The traces of the first krepis can be seen on the foundation's top surface (Fig. 10) and measure 3.14 m wide, 2.95 m long, 0.22 m high. The remains of the blocks from the krepis that we have been able to identify so far are:

Fig. 10 Phase II. Drawing of the foundation with the blocks of the first krepis. The red line shows the area of the first krepis. The blue line shows the internal part of the poros blocks with the band between the two lines.

ΙΓ΄, Ζ΄, and ΙΔ΄. The corner of the krepis is made by wooden posts since the traces of these can be detected on Α΄, Γ΄, and ΣΤ΄, while no remains of a smooth area for the last wooden post has been preserved on the southwest corner block Ι΄.

The whole west side of the krepis consists of two blocks. ΙΓ΄ belongs to the northwest corner, while Ζ΄ belongs to the southwest corner. Running around the west front of ΙΓ΄ and Ζ΄ and the north front of ΙΓ΄ to the traces of the ending of the first step is a band 0.16 m wide. We believe that this band was covered by a finer stone than the poros blocks, and we suggest that the stone used could be the red Ακροπολίτης λίθος. It also seems that the block in Ακροπολίτης λίθος, ΙΔ΄, belongs between the posts on the east side. The width of ΙΔ΄ is exactly the same as the wooden posts, which strengthens our suggested placement of this stone.

The dowel hole placed exactly in the middle on the east side of block Δ΄ corresponds with the bolt hole for the doors set between blocks ΙΑ΄ and ΙΒ΄ on the middle of the west side of the foundation. This shows the very careful geometric planning of the monument with a strong focus on the front. Furthermore, the cuttings for a stele on block Α΄ clearly influenced the planning of the monument's construction. Since we do not have other blocks with the same surface treatment, the superstructure cannot be re-constructed, but we believe that it was made entirely of wood. The date of the construction of the structure can be set to around the end of the fifth century B.C., when the foundation was moved. The end of the structure's second phase can be dated to ca. 360-350 B.C., when the third construction phase was begun. The date of the third construction phase will be discussed in a future article.

The inscription of the Telemachos Monument

Luigi Beschi first reconstructed the Telemachos Monument correctly from *membra disiecta*.[13] Thanks to his work, we are now able to explain more of the architectural development of the early Asklepieion. It is not our intent to treat in detail the Telemachos Monument here. Rather we will repeat in translation the section of the inscription that deals with the architectural development of the sanctuary.[14] According to the chronicle of the Telemachos Monument, the following events took place in the Asklepios sanctuary during the first nine/eight years:

420 B.C.	Telemachos first set up the sanctuary and altar to Asklepios, and to Hygieia, and the Asklepiadai and the daughters of Asklepios…And thus this whole sanctuary was established when Astyphilos of Kudantidai was archon
419/8 B.C.	When Archeas was archon, the Kerykes disputed the land and hindered some actions[15]
418/7 B.C.	When Antiphon was archon (lost in a lacuna)
417/6 B.C.	When Euphemos was archon (lost in a lacuna)
416/5 B.C.	(lost in a lacuna)
415/4 B.C.	When Karias was archon, a peribolos was built apart from the wooden gateway
414/3 B.C.	When Teisandras was archon, the wooden gateways[16] were rebuilt and the rest of the sanctuary was set up in addition
413/2 B.C.	When Kleokritos was archon, the sanctuary was planted and he arranged and adorned the whole sanctuary
412/1 B.C.	When Kallias of Skambonidai was archon (lost in a lacuna)

The altar was set up by Telemachos when the sanctuary was founded in 420 B.C. A wooden gateway was built in 415/4 B.C. when the peribolos was built, but it had to be repaired in 414/3 B.C. together with another wooden gateway.[17] Although it is not certain what happened between 418/7 B.C. and 416/5 B.C., the temple must have been built during these years since it is not mentioned later in the inscription.[18] Since such an important structure would surely have received mention somewhere in the inscription, a temple must have been erected to house the cult statue in 414/3 B.C. By 414/3 B.C., the main buildings of the sanctuary were in place and only secondary decoration of the sanctuary remained to be completed, such as planting trees the coming year. Our structure's first construction phase should therefore be placed under one of the archon names from 418/7 to 416/5 B.C.

Fig. 11 Panoramic view of the southeast corner of the Asklepieion with the peribolos.

Fig. 12 Photo of the southeast corner of the peribolos.

The peribolos of the early Asklepieion

At the southeast corner of the Asklepieion, 2.44 m from the analemma of the epitheatron of the Theatre of Dionysos stand the remaining courses of the sanctuary's early peribolos in stone (Figs. 1, 11-8). Today, 6.19 m of the south side and 4.66 m of the east side of the wall are preserved. The material of the wall is Ἀκροπολίτης λίθος.

The south wall is divided in two courses, where the lower course is the socle for the wall. The wall is constructed of triangular and trapezoidal blocks in the polygonal technique (Fig. 13). The surface of these blocks is rough but an elaborated band ca. 0.06-0.08 m from the top on the south face of the blocks can be detected (Fig. 14). This band marks the beginning of the ancient ground level of the peribolos facing the ancient Peripatos road. The second course of the wall is constructed of trapezoidal and rectangular orthostates. At the east end a corner orthostate clearly indicates the southeast corner.

Fig. 13 Photo of south peribolos west of the "opening."

Elaborated band

Fig. 14 Photo of the south peribolos with the elaborated band ca. 0.06-0.08 m from the top on the south face of the blocks.

The orthostates are 0.64 m high and 0.90-1.12 m long, with a width of 0.29 m at the bottom and 0.22 m at the top. Their south face has the characteristics of a common peribolos with long vertical parallel cuttings also known as "furrowed work" (Fig. 15), but the proportions of these cuttings and their small scale are unique in the history of architecture.[19] They have 15 rows of cuttings, each cutting being 0.03 m high with a 0.02 m distance between them. There are more than 20 blocks of these orthostates spread throughout the Asklepieion.

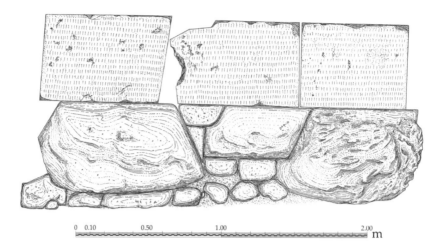

Fig. 15 Drawing of the south peribolos with the cuttings on the south face of the blocks.

Fig. 16 Photo of the south side of the peribolos with the 0.85 m long opening from the Christian Basilica.

The preserved south side of the wall has a 0.85 m "opening" beginning 2.49 m from the southeast corner of the wall (Fig. 16). Travlos interpreted this "opening," or rather entrance, as a propylon for the Asklepieion used by the staff of the sanctuary.[20] The ground level at the early Asklepieion until the end of the fifth century A.D. makes it impossible to accept this opening in the wall as a propylon for the sanctuary. The ground level at the Asklepieion was 1.40 m higher than the ground level for the opening, and this entrance was probably made during the construction of the Christian Basilica, when the ground level for the whole area was lowered.

Fig. 17 Photo of the cuttings in the east peribolos for the orthostates, illustrated with a red line.

Fig. 18 Photo of the east peribolos' north end with the cuttings in the rock illustrated with a red line.

The east side of the peribolos is built in the same polygonal style as the south wall, but due to the rising of the bedrock going from south to north, the orthostates were laid directly on the rock behind the preserved wall (4.66 m) since we can detect the cuttings for the stones (Fig. 17). We can also determine the exact length of the east wall to 13.72 m because there is a cutting in the rock at its north end (Fig. 18). It is between this end of the wall and the Akropolis rock (that had not yet been cut back to give space for the construction of the Doric stoa in 300/299 B.C.) that we believe the main propylon of the Asklepieion stood until the construction of the analemma of the epitheatron of the Theatre of Dionysos in ca. 370-360 B.C. (Fig. 1).[21]

The level measured on the top of the orthostates of the peribolos is 107.14 m above sea level. Since the level of the upper surface of our structure is 107.12 m above sea level they lie on the same ground level, which clearly suggests that the peribolos also functioned as a retaining wall for the ground of the sanctuary at this position, while the level of the ancient Peripatos at the south side of the peribolos was 0.80 m below the sanctuary's ground level.[22] It is thus fairly safe to assume that the peribolos had at least one more course with the same surface elaboration as the orthostates of the second course.[23]

The date of the peribolos

The peribolos has been dated by Walther Wrede by way of comparison to the wall south of the Byzantine cistern and its neighboring east wall.[24] These walls have been dated to the late 5th century B.C. based on the letterforms of the boundary stone (*IG* I² 874) that was found in the spring on the middle terrace behind the small temple of Themis.[25] The *hόρος κρένες* boundary stone was found by Koumanoudis in 1877 and the same stone seems to have been found again by Nikolaos Platon in 1964.[26] Even though the stone was found in this wall, Platon clearly states that this boundary stone was placed there as a filling stone. Thereby its original function as a boundary stone was not at this wall and it cannot be used to date this and the Asklepieion's peribolos to the late 5th century B.C. Platon also dates the wall to the Archaic period but does not give any evidence for this date.[27]

Riethmüller dates the peribolos together with the *sacred pit's* polygonal masonry to the late 5th century B.C. The comparison is correct since they are built in the same technique and have the same small-scale proportions, but he bases his dates for the two structures according to Wrede's dating, but as has been shown above, Wrede's date is not correct.[28] We, like Beschi and now also Riethmüller, think that the preserved peribolos is the one "mentioned" in the Telemachos inscription, which means that the wall was built in 415/4 B.C.[29] The first two propylons were made of wood but that would hardly exclude a wall built in stone. The Telemachos inscription also states that the peribolos was built out from the wooden propylon. This makes perfect sense since they must have begun construction on the peribolos from the proposed propylon at the northeast corner and then worked their way around the sanctuary (Fig. 1).

The design of the sanctuary

The structure and the *sacred pit* define the core buildings of the early Asklepieion. Together with the peribolos they form a unified design, as will be shown below. In 2000, the whole South Slope was surveyed very carefully by the excellent surveyor Dimitrios Prokakis and his team, which made it possible for us to integrate the buildings of the Asklepieion into a grid system in order to investigate whether the design of the Asklepieion had been made using a module (Fig. 19).[30] The structure has proven to be the key element in finding a unified modular, and it is from this monument that we can lay down two basic modules in the Classical period (and one more in the Roman period) that were used in the design of the Asklepieion. The whole area of the Asklepieion is, of course, measured from the external face of the peribolos.

The modules are:
α (3.40 m): The width of the structure's foundation
β (2.85 m): The width of the krepis of *Construction Phases I-II*

To elaborate on the modular units, the following examples are given:

The peribolos
Distance of the east side of the structure's foundation to the east face of the peribolos: **3α**
Distance of the south side of the structure's foundation to the south face of peribolos: **2β**
Distance of the north side of the structure's foundation to the northeast corner cuttings of the peribolos: **3α**
Distance of the east face of the peribolos to the west face of the earlier foundation of the analemma of the epitheatron of the Theatre of Dionysos: **1β**

The sacred pit
Distance of the west side of the structure's foundation to the geometrical center of the *sacred pit*: **5β**
Diameter of the internal sides of the *sacred pit*: **1β**
Intercolumnial distance of the four columns' bases: **1α**

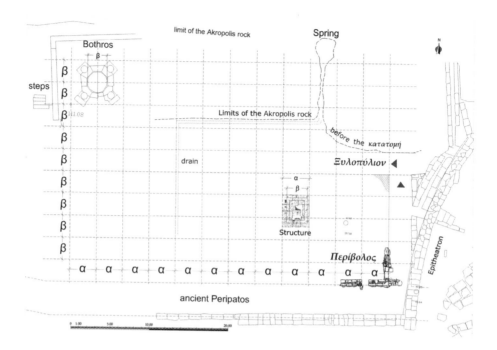

Fig. 19 Plan of the early Asklepieion with the grid. The α modular at the east-west axis and the β modular at the north-south axis.

The date of the design

It has been explained above that the structure was moved at the end of the 5th century B.C. and that one of the reasons for this movement might have been a fire. We believe that the grid system was applied to the sanctuary when the peribolos was built in 415/4 B.C. The architect responsible for the design of the sanctuary decided to use the two modules α and β from the side of the temple when he planned the sanctuary. But since the structure had already been built it did not fit correctly into the grid system. The fire, however, made it possible to move the structure so as to fit into the grid system with exactly 3α between the back of the structure and the east side of the peribolos. As Architect of the Athenian Agora, Richard Anderson has pointed out, the people responsible for the design of the Asklepieion must have been obsessed with numbers.[31]

The western limits of the peribolos

So far, we have not been able to detect any remains of the Asklepieion's early western peribolos. The remains of a wall and cuttings in the rock from the

western side of the Doric stoa extending south are all from the Roman period and theoretically this wall might have replaced the early peribolos.[32]
Since the Telemachos inscription mentions a peribolos,[33] we believe that the
western limit of the sanctuary could not have been marked out by boundary
stones as indicated by Riethmüller, but by a wall.[34] Furthermore, we believe
the *sacred pit* was part of the Asklepieion from the very beginning and stairs
cut in the rock are located at its western end (Figs. 1 and 19). This strongly
suggests that the arrangement of the western peribolos of the Asklepieion
might not have been placed at the west end of the *sacred pit* since that would
contradict the placement of the stairs. Marta Saporiti has pointed out that
we do not know the full arrangement of the *sacred pit* before the κατατομή
for the Doric stoa.[35] Maybe there were also stairs cut in the rock at its right
side or even a ramp at its front as can be seen on the plan suggested (without any architectural evidence) by Roland Martin and Henry Metzger.[36] The
proportions of the blocks from the peribolos and their small scale also strongly indicate that the peribolos belonged to a very small sanctuary and that
the wall was not very high. This means that the peribolos might not have
included the *sacred pit* at the beginning of its construction in 415/4 B.C. If we
follow the grid system a conjecture for the western limits of the early
Asklepieion could be placed along the drain for the water of the spring as
shown on the Figs. 1 and 19.[37] This will be exactly 8α between the east and
west peribolos and fits well into the design of the early Asklepieion.

The date of the *sacred pit* and its connection to the early Asklepieion are
controversial. Judith Binder has pointed out that the lip of the *sacred pit* is
dated not earlier than 350 B.C. because of the Ἀκροπολίτης λίθος used together with the tanto-orange conglomerate stone.[38] This stone is used in the
analemma of the epitheatron of the Theatre of Dionysos. The beginning of
the construction is now dated to ca. 370-360 B.C.[39] But the polygonal masonry used for the inner facing of the *sacred pit* was made around the same
date as the peribolos, which provides a date around 415/4 B.C., thereby con-
necting it to the Asklepieion. The tetrastyle of the *sacred pit* must therefore
have been changed together with the lip of the *sacred pit* around 350 B.C. It
seems that most scholars believe the *sacred pit* is very old and was made
before the establishment of the Asklepieion, but because the inner diameter
is exactly 1β it must have been planned around the same period as the
structure and the peribolos.[40] That the *sacred pit* had a tetrastyle before 350
B.C. is known. Clear evidence shows that the *sacred pit* was part of the
Asklepieion from at least the first quarter of the fourth century B.C.[41] It is
depicted with a tetrastyle together with Asklepios and one of his daughters
on a votive relief found at the Asklepieion (NM 2417, Fig. 20).[42] For cultic
reasons, Asklepios needed a *sacred pit* for his chthonic character, like the one
inside the *thymele* in Epidauros, and that makes it almost certain that it must
have belonged to the early Asklepieion.[43] One final point must be stressed:

Fig. 20 Photo of votive relief NM 2417.

it is not the architecture that defines the cult -- it is the cult and its rituals that define the architecture.

Acknowledgements:

This paper is the first of a series of articles that will attempt to elucidate the architectural development of the Athenian Asklepieion on the South Slope of Akropolis. The authors would like to express their deepest gratitude to Dr. Petros Kalligas, former president of the Committee for the Monuments of the South Slope of the Akropolis, and the Honorable Director of the 1st Ephorate of Prehistoric and Classical Archaeology. It was under his supervision in 2001 and 2002 that Michaelis Lefantzis and Vanda Papaefthimiou began their initial study of the altar. We would also like to thank former Director, Dr. Alkestis Choremi-Spetsieri, 1st Ephorate of Prehistoric and Classical Archaeology, and especially Director, Dr. Alexandros Mantis, 1st Ephorate of Prehistoric and Classical Archaeology and president of the Committee of the Theatre of Dionysos and the Asklepieion at the South Slope of Akropolis for their permission to publish this study. We would also like to express our gratitude to the late Professor Emeritus, Dr. Georgios Lavvas,

Member of the Academy of Athens. The two chief technicians that have worked for a lifetime at the Asklepeieion, Mr. Vasilis Anastasias, still working at the Asklepieion and Mr. Elias Dimitropoulos, currently working at the Stoa of Eumenes II, were also of great help. We are also very grateful to Richard Anderson, Judith Binder, George Hinge, David Scahill, Peter Schultz and Bronwen Wickkiser for taking so much of their time to discuss the contents of this article, and for their many comments and suggestions that have improved it tremendously. Furthermore, many thanks to our friends and colleagues who discussed and shared their ideas and provided very useful information: Anne Marie Carstens, Lisbeth Bredholt Christensen, Anastasia Christophilopoulou, Antonio Corso, Søren Dietz, Hedda von Ehrenheim, Richard Hamilton, Niels and Lise Hannestad, Jakob Munk Højte, Mark Wilson Jones, Dorte Sidelmann Jørgensen, Dorothy King, Jens Krasilnikoff, Carol L. Lawton, Tore Tvanø Lind, Astrid Lindenlauf, John Lund, Eri Papatheodorou, Poul Pedersen, Brunilde Sismondo Ridgway, Molly Richardson, Marta Saporiti, Kris Seaman, Ying Shen, Andrew Stewart, Esko Tikkala, Evgenia Vikela, Steven Tracy, Lambrini Vasilakopoulou, Bonna Daix Wescoat, and not least Lise Barlach, as well as the participants at the conference *Aspects of Ancient Greek Cult*, held at the University of Aarhus, for their helpful comments and suggestions. All mistakes are our own.

Notes

1 For the excavation, see Koumanoudis 1876, 14-35; 1877, 6-12; Köhler 1877, 171-2. For an overview of Asklepieions in general, see Riethmüller 2005, the brilliant study by Evgenia Vikela (2006), and Melfi 2003; 2007.

2 Bronwen Wickkiser points out the possibility that Telemachos could have been a fictive character; see Wickkiser 2003, 120 n. 412. For the date of the foundation as the 17th Boedromion, see Clinton 1994, 17-8, 29; Riethmüller 1999, 126; Hurwit 2004, 218 (a revised view from 1999); Riethmüller 2005, 245. For the 18th Boedromion, see Kutsch 1913, 18, 24; Parker 1996, 175, 179; Hurwit 1999, 219.

3 Köhler 1877, 255-60; Beschi 1967/1968b, 514; Travlos 1939-41, 60; Travlos 1971, 127; Aleshire 1989, 32, 34; Townsend 1982, 42 n. 5; Hurwit 1999, 220; Riethmüller 1999, 128; Hurwit 2004, 222. For an excellent discussion of all the arguments for or against either the middle or the east terrace as the location of the original Asklepieion, see Aleshire 1989, 24-32 and lately Riethmüller 2005, 255-9.

4 Dated after *IG* II² 1685. See Scranton 1960, 172; Townsend 1982, 71, 76, 286, 288; Aleshire 1989, 15, 27-8, 34-5; Aleshire 1991, 13-32; Hintzen-Bohlen 1997, 70; Riethmüller 1999, 131; 2005, 267. For a mid-fourth century B.C. date, see Coulton 1976, 46, 52, 225, who do not take *IG* II² 1685 into consideration.

5 In a future article, Lefantzis and I will demonstrate that this structure was used throughout the Roman period and may have been in use until the middle of the fifth century A.D. when the first Christian Basilica was built. For the excavation of the basilica, see Koumanoudis 1876, 20-1. For the date of the basilica, see Travlos 1939-41, 64; Aleshire 1989, 19-20, 35. For the re-use of the "altar"

as pavement in the basilica, see Travlos 1939-41, 42 n. 1. For the construction of the Basilica, see Xyngopoulos 1915; Travlos 1939-41; Martin 1944/45, 435. It must be stressed, as Travlos (1939-41, 48) also points out, that the three apses on the plan by Lambert (1877, 169-70) are incorrect.

6 For another opinion, see Riethmüller 1999, 128, where he sees two different building phases.

7 See the contribution by Papaefthimiou in this volume, esp. 73-4.

8 The stone can clearly be seen at the south side of the structure on the plan in Koumanoudis 1877, pl. 1 (see Fig. 5).

9 For the excavation of the holes and the dimensions of two holes, see Papaefthimiou, 73, in this volume.

10 For the plants at the Hephaisteion, see Burr Thompson 1937; Burr Thompson and Griswold 1963, 9-11, figs. 11-4; Thompson and Wycherley 1972, 149, pl. 76; Camp 1986, 87, fig. 64; Camp 2001, 103, fig. 95.

11 See Papaefthimiou, 74-7, in this volume. Telemachos Monument inscription: *IG* II² 4960/4961+4963 = *SEG* 25.226/47.232 lines 38-42.

12 See Papaefthimiou, 74, in this volume.

13 A selective bibliography for the Telemachos Monument: Köhler 1877, 241 n. 2; Körte 1893, 246; Preuner 1894, 313-5; Körte 1896, 313-21; Walter 1930; Wilamowitz-Moellendorff 1932, 223, 223 n. 1; Keramopoullos 1934/1935, 92; Schlaifer 1940, 240; Hausmann 1948, 76 and n. 307, 101, 172 no. 78; Hill 1953, 130-1; Walter 1953, 469 n. 4; Scranton 1960, 181-2; Beschi 1967-1968a; 1967-1968b, 511-4; 1969-1970, 100; Berger 1970, 67, 81-4, 103-6, fig. 77; Mitropoulou 1975; Ghedini 1980, 15-8 no. 1; Ridgway 1981, 136; Ritti 1981, 51 no. 18; Beschi 1982; Ridgway 1983, 199-201, figs. 13.6-13.7; *LIMC* 2 (1984), s.v. Asklepios, no. 394; Carroll-Spillecke 1985, 67-8 and ns. 129-32, 70 n. 164; Krug 1985, 148-50; Wegener 1985, 133-5, 301 no. 122; Aleshire 1989, 7, 11, 34; *LIMC* 5 (1990), s.v. Hygieia, no. 4, 569; Iliakis 1992-98; Foucart 1992, 297, 317-23; Garland 1992, 118-21, fig. 12; Graf 1992, 202-3; Van Straten 1993, 259; Clinton 1994, 17-34; Güntner 1994, 34-5, 42, 45-7, 48, 146-7 C 53, pl. 25; van Straten 1995, 70-1; Riethmüller 1996, 107; Ridgway 1997, 200; Vikela 1997, 170, 190-2, 194, 197, 239, fig. 3; Robertson, 1998, 294-5; Verbanck-Piérard 2000, 288 n. 28, 302-5, 308 n. 113, 311 n. 135; Camp 2001, 122; Beschi 2002, 20-1; Comella 2002, 47, 50-3, 181, 201 no. Atene 135, figs. 37-9; Leventi 2003, 50-1, 69, 78, 94 n. 48, 112-3, 134-5 R 14, pl. 15; Wickkiser 2003, 112-31; Aston 2004, 21; Camp 2004, 132; Goette and Hammerstadt 2004, 198-9; Despinis 2005, 260; Riethmüller 2005, 241-50, 255, 258, 262, 264-5, 265 n. 128, fig. 34, Wickkiser 2006, 33; 2008, ch. 4.

14 In an article in preparation, we analyze the double relief on the Telemachos Monument. Of interest here, the so-called B-side or rear-side with the *propylon* of the Athenian Asklepieion depicted on the large double relief is re-interpreted. We strongly argue that this is indeed the A-side of the double relief since the building depicted is not a *propylon* but rather the old temple of the Athenian Asklepieion. We have based our translation of the inscription upon that of Wickkiser 2003, 118-9. For the archon names, see the convincing reconstruction by Beschi 1967/1968a, 412-3.

15 *IG* II² 4960/4961+4963 = *SEG* 25.226/47.232, lines 20-3. We do not believe that the intervention by the Eleusinian priesthood, the Kerykes, was negative as all other experts of the Telemachos Monument have argued so far (with the excep-

tion of Wickkiser 2003, 128), see for instance Versakis 1912, 58 (Riethmüller (2005, 246 n. 28) cites page 59 which must be a printing error); Körte 1896, 319-32, esp. 319-20, 331-2 (why Riethmüller (2005, 246 n. 28) only cites page 329 is for us a mystery); Kutsch 1913, 19, 21-2, 24; Wilamowitz-Moellendorff 1932, 223 n. 1; Keramopoullos 1934/1935, 92-3 (not 90ff as stated by Riethmüller (2005, 246 n. 28)); Travlos 1939-41, 60 (Riethmüller (2005, 246 n. 28) cites page 59 which must be a printing error); Schlaifer 1940, 240 n. 2; Hill 1953, 131; Beschi 1967/1968a, 392-3; Beschi 1967/1968b, 514; Travlos 1971, 127; Krug 1985, 148; Aleshire 1989, 8-9; Foucart 1992, 320; Garland 1992, 126-7; Clinton 1994, 28-9; Güntner 1994, 34; Parker 1996, 180; Hurwit 1999, 220; Beschi 2002, 20; Riethmüller 2005, 246, 246 n. 28; Robertson 2005, 85. Telemachos and the people that set up the stele would not offend the powerful Eleusinian priesthood, the Kerykes, in an official document written in stone and placed on the terrace below the Parthenon. There is a strong connection between the Eleusinian deities and Asklepios, and we believe that the Kerykes in some sense helped the people involved in founding the Asklepieion. One has to remember that no deity other than Herakles (see Burkert 1983, 254 n. 26) and Asklepios (see Parker 1996, 179 n. 93) were initiated into the Eleusinian mysteries and housed in the Athenian Eleusinion before he came to the Asklepieion. Furthermore, his arrival to Athens must have been planned very carefully with the Kerykes in order to coincide with the Great festival of Demeter and Kore. Later, one of the festival days was even named the Epidauria which further stressed the close connection between Asklepios or rather the Epidaurian and the Eleusinian priesthood. For the Epidauria, see Köhler 1877, 244-5; Körte 1896, 315; Deubner 1956, 72-92, esp. 72-3, 78; Parke 1977, 64-5, 186; Clinton 1988, 69 (Riethmüller (2005, 245 n. 25) cites page 68 which must be a printing error); Foucart 1992, 317-23; Garland 1992, 123-4; Clinton 1994; Parker 1996, 8 n. 27, 179, 181; Riethmüller 1996; 97; Edelstein and Edelstein 1998, T.556-63; Lawton 1999, 233; Riethmüller 1999, 139 n. 79; *DNP* 8 (2000), s.v. Mysteria, 611-5, esp. 614; Riethmüller 2005, 245-8, 251, 270.

16 We agree with Beschi's reconstruction ξυλοπύλια since the reconstructed ancient Greek word has to be plural with the article τά, see Beschi 1967/1968a, 415. Robertson (1998, 294 n. 58) states that the reconstruction by Beschi is a conjecture. We warmly thank Molly Richardson and George Hinge for helping us in this matter and for saving us from many errors. For propylons in the Classical period, see the study by Papatheodorou (forthcoming). We thank Eri Papatheodorou for sharing her knowledge on propylons in general with us.

17 It is Beschi (1967/1968a, 415) who convincingly suggested the word περίβολον. Robertson (1998, 294) suggests that an area for the sanctuary may only have been marked out and that Beschi's reconstruction again is a conjecture.

18 Beschi (1967/1968a, 414) not only believes that a temple was built during these years but also a βωμός, and a stoa for incubation, which would make perfect sense since these buildings normally belong in an Asklepieion. Also Riethmüller (2005, 246, 258 n. 93) believes a temple was built during these years.

19 The proportion of these cuttings is for a small scale peribolos. We have not been able to find any wall with cuttings like the one described above. Rhys F. Townsend states: "...there are many fourth-century parallels for this technique" but not one of those walls in the list given by Biers and Boyd (1982, 8 n. 16)

and those suggested by Townsend looks exactly like the one at the Asklepieion; see Townsend 1982, 70 n. 84.

20 Travlos 1939-41, 62.

21 Both Versakis (1912, 55) and Beschi (1967/1968b, 512; 2002, 25) also believe that the propylon should be placed at the east side of the Asklepieion but do not state where. Girard (1882, 8, 12) believes there were two propylons; one placed in front of the new temple (the one in the Asklepieion) and one somewhere around the old temple (the temple of Themis). Many scholars have proposed that a propylon stood at the western side of the Asklepieion because there are remains of a peribolos in poros; see Köhler 1877, 253; Tomlinson 1969, 112-3; Travlos 1971, 127; Townsend 1982, 44; Aleshire 1989, 33-4; Riethmüller 1999, 128; 2005, 258. This wall begins at the west end of the Doric stoa extending south where it continues in a right angle to the east after 7.29 m. The cuttings in the rock parallel on the south side suggest a propylon. This peribolos with its propylon is clearly from the Roman period. Robertson (1998, 295) also places a propylon at this Roman western peribolos of the Asklepieion since he can see a short break near the south end, though not right at the corner. We can not follow his description, but Robertson might refer to the cutting in the rock for the south side of the Roman propylon as do Riethmüller (2005, 258). Beschi (1967/1968b, 512) places the propylon built in 413/2 B.C. at the west side of the Asklepieon but does not state where. There is no architectural evidence for placing a propylon at the south end of the corridor between the middle and east terraces as suggested by Versakis 1912, 55; Travlos 1971, 128; Beschi 1969, 388-97. According to the Telemachos inscription, there were two propylons; see 103. We have suggested the placement for the main propylon but for the second one only conjectures can be made since we have not been able to find the cuttings in the rock for its placement. For the date of the construction of the analemma, see Goette and Hammerstadt 2004, 176. We owe this reference to Judith Binder. Mrs. Binder has also pointed out that when it rains in Athens, it is possible to observe how the water comes out through a small cavity of the Akropolis rock above the Doric stoa's east end. Since the water runs down near this end, a propylon at that place would not be suitable, especially since the propylon at the early Asklepieion was made of wood as the inscription from the Telemachos Monument states. We believe that the water was collected in a drain and thereby the water would not have damaged the wooden gateway or hindered people going into the Asklepieion. We warmly thank Judith Binder again for sharing her views with us and for stimulating and fruitful discussion about the topography of the Asklepieion in general.

22 Köhler (1877, 180-1); Judeich (1931, 320-1); Wrede (1933, 56); and Riethmüller (1999, 134; 2005, 254), together with Versakis, also believed that the wall functioned as a retaining wall; however, Versakis was convinced that the south peribolos of the Asklepieion continued and was unified with the south wall at the middle terrace. See Versakis (1912, 54-5, 57 and pl. 5,) where he establishes the early Asklepieion on the western terrace.

23 Running parallel with the east peribolos of the Asklepieion ca. 2.95 m stands a wall with stones in Ἀκροπολίτης λίθος and built in the same polygonal technique as the *sacred pit* and the peribolos (see Fig. 1). This wall somehow relates to the Asklepieion and may have formed some sort of a corridor to-

gether with the east peribolos of the Asklepieion. Only an excavation might help to solve this problem in explaining this corridor and its relation to the Asklepieion.

24 Wrede (1933, 30-1, 56) correctly states that the walls cannot be dated by the inscription of the boundary stone if the latter came from another place.

25 For a photo of the wall with the *hόρος κρένες* boundary stone, see Travlos 1971, 139, fig. 187. For the area around the temple of Themis, see Walker 1979.

26 See Koumanoudis 1877, 25; Köhler 1877, 183; Platon 1964, 29.

27 Platon 1964, 29. Beschi (1967/1968b, 512) also dates the wall to the Archaic period, but does not describe the evidence for his dating.

28 Riethmüller 1999, 134, 134 n. 43; 2005, 255, 259. For photos of the *sacred pit*, see Travlos 1971, 134, fig. 180; Riethmüller 1999, 134, figs. 7-8. The *sacred pit* together with the temple near the Doric stoa are currently under study by Architect Rosalia Christodoulopoulou.

29 Riethmüller (2005, 259) also believe this statement, but still uses Wrede's date for the wall with the *hόρος κρένες* boundary stone to connect it with the peribolos mentioned in the Telemachos inscription, see the discussion above. For a comparison with peribolos walls in rural sanctuaries, see Baumer 2004, 51-3. We owe this reference to Astrid Lindenlauf and thank her for sharing her knowledge on peribolos walls in general with us.

30 For module units used in Doric temples, see Wilson Jones 2000b, 90; Wilson Jones 2001. For modules used in Roman architecture, see the excellent study also by Wilson Jones 2000a.

31 Personal communication. It is mainly due to Richard Anderson that we might explain the reason for the movement of this structure.

32 For a description of the Roman peribolos, see Martin and Metzger 1949, 342; Aleshire 1989, 22-3; Riethmüller 2005, 258.

33 *IG* II² 4960/4961+4963 = *SEG* 25.226/47.232, line 33.

34 We are well aware of the limits of the inscription and that is does not mention the length and the placement of the peribolos. Also, we do not believe that the *hόρος* (*IG* I² 861) found by Koumanoudis (1876, 28), belongs to the Asklepieion. Riethmüller (1999, 128; 2005, 259) uses this *hόρος* as the final evidence for the Asklepieion's western limit since the *hόρος* states: Hόρο[ς] το τ[ε]μένο[υς], but it does not mention the Asklepieion specifically. This *hόρος* could belong to any of the many sanctuaries on the south slope; see also Judeich 1931, 320 n. 3. Furthermore, we can not follow Riethmüller's description of a block at the southwestern angle of the Doric stoa belonging to a possible west peribolos. He further states that it is possible that this block might belong to an incubation hall that is connected to the *sacred pit* and dates to the late fifth century B.C., see Riethmüller 1999, 134.

35 Personal communication. we thank Marta Saporiti for her time and for sharing her keen insight into the matters of cult and the arrangement of space in Greek sanctuaries.

36 Martin and Metzger 1949, 331, fig. 8.

37 Beschi (1968, 512, 514) concludes that the spring at the eastern terrace in the Asklepieion was not known and in use before the construction of the Doric stoa. This conclusion is not geologically possible. The water has to come out somewhere and we believe that one of the main reasons for founding the

Asklepieion at the east terrace was access to water. Robertson (2005, 81) believes that before the Doric stoa, the spring must have been inside a cave of some sort. For the uses of water in Greek sanctuaries, see Cole 1988.

38 Letter to J.T. Jensen, dated 18 December 2003.

39 For the date of the analemma, see supra n. 23. There is, of course, also the possibility of the existence of an earlier small pit, which was made larger to fit the design of the Asklepieion.

40 Leventi 2003, 78.

41 It is dated by Leventi (2003, 122, 137) between 400-390 B.C., which strengthens our point.

42 The presence of the tetrastyle is demonstrated by Riethmüller 1999, 143. David Scahill is currently finishing a study of tetrastyle buildings connected to hero cult and we thank him for sharing his insight into this building type. See also his forthcoming article about the tetrastyle and the origin of the Korinthian capital; Scahill (forthcoming). Bibliography for NM 2417: Duhn 1877a, 150-1 no. 27; Koepp 1885, 264 n. 2; Svoronos 1908-37, 641 no. 375, pl. CL 1; Walter 1923, 48, 121, 137; 1930, 82 n. 14, 100 n. 59; Hausmann 1948, 176 no. 130; Beschi 1967-68b, 516; Beschi 1969-70, 99, 107 n. 7; *LIMC* 2 (1984), s.v. Asklepios, no. 93; *LIMC* 3 (1986), s.v. Epione, no. 7; *LIMC* 5 (1990), s.v. Hygieia, no. 57, 569; Sobel 1990, 81 no. II. 49; Leventi 2003, 78, 122, 137 R 18, pl. 18; Riethmüller 1999, 143, fig. 11; Riethmüller 2005, 272, pl. 10.

43 For the double nature of Asklepios, see Petropoulou 1991, 31; Riethmüller 1996; 97-108; 1999, 141-2; 2005, 270-3. For the latest discussion of the nature of Asklepios as a god or hero, see the excellent study by Aston 2004, 23-30.

Bibliography

Aleshire, S.B. 1989. *The Athenian Asklepieion: the People, their Dedications, and the Inventories.* Amsterdam: J.C. Gieben.

Aleshire, S.B. 1991. *Asklepios at Athens: Epigraphic and Prosopographic Essays on the Athenian Healing Cults.* Amsterdam: J.C. Gieben.

Aston, E. 2004. "Asclepius and the Legacy of Thessaly." *CQ* 54, 18-32.

Baumer, L.E. 2004. *Kult im Kleinen. Ländliche Heiligtümer spätarchaischer bis hellenistischer Zeit. Attika – Arkadien – Argolis – Kynouria.* Internationale Archäologie 81. Rahden: Marie Leidorf.

Berger, E. 1970. *Das Basler Arztrelief. Studien zum griechischen Grab- und Votivrelief um 500 v. Chr. und zur vorhippokratischen Medizin.* Basel: Archäologischer Verlag in Basel AG.

Beschi, L. 1967-68a [1969]. "Il monumento di Telemachos: fondatore dell'Asclepieion ateniese." *ASAtene* 45-46 (n.s. 29-30): 381-436.

Beschi, L. 1967-68b [1969]. "Contributi di topografia ateniese." *ASAtene* 45-46 (n.s. 29-30): 511-36.

Beschi, L. 1969-70 [1972]. "Rilievi votivi attici ricomposti." *ASAtene* 47-48 (n.s. 31-32): 85-132.

Beschi, L. 1982. "Il rilievo di Telemachos ricompletato." *AAA* 15: 31-43.

Beschi, L. 2002 [2003]. "Culti Stranieri e fondazioni private nell'Attica Classica: alcuni case." *ASAtene* 80 (n.s. 3.2): 13-42.

Biers, W.R. & T.D. Boyd. 1982. "Ikarion in Attica." *Hesperia* 51: 1-18.

Burkert, W. 1983. *Homo Necans. The Anthropology of Ancient Greek Sacrificial Ritual and Myth*. Translated by Peter Bing. Berkeley, Los Angeles, & London: University of California Press. Original edition, Berlin: Walter de Gruyter, 1972.

Burr Thompson, D. 1937. "The Garden of Hephaistos." *Hesperia* 6: 396-425.

Burr Thompson, D. & R.E. Griswold. 1963. *Garden Lore of Ancient Athens*. *AgoraPicBk* 8. Princeton: The American School of Classical Studies at Athens.

Camp, J.McK., II 1986. *The Athenian Agora: Excavations in the Heart of Classical Athens*. New York & London: Thames & Hudson.

Camp, J.McK., II 2001. *The Archaeology of Athens*. New Haven & London: Yale University Press.

Camp, J.McK., II 2004. "Athenian Cobblers and Heroes." In *Greek Art in View. Studies in Honour of Brian Sparkes*, edited by S. Keay & S. Moser. Oxford: Oxbow Books.

Carroll-Spillecke, M. 1985. *Landscape Depictions in Greek Relief Sculpture: Development and Conventionalization*. European University Studies Series 38, Archaeology 11. Frankfurt am Main, Bern, & New York: Peter Lang.

Clinton, K. 1988. "Sacrifice at the Eleusinian Mysteries." In *Early Greek Cult Practice, Proceedings of the Fifth International Symposium at the Swedish Institute at Athens, 26-29 June 1986*, edited by R. Hägg, N. Marinatos, & G.C. Nordquist, 69-80. SkrAth 4°, 38. Stockholm: Svenska Institutet i Athen, distribution Paul Åströms Förlag.

Clinton, K. 1994. "The Epidauria and the Arrival of Asclepius in Athens." In *Ancient Greek Cult Practice from the Epigraphical Evidence, Proceedings of the Second International Seminar on Ancient Greek Cult, Athens, 1991*, edited by R. Hägg, 17-34. SkrAth 8°, 13. Stockholm: Svenska Institutet i Athen, distribution Paul Åströms Förlag,

Cole, S.G. 1988. "The Uses of Water in Greek Sanctuaries." In *Early Greek Cult Practice, Proceedings of the Fifth International Symposium at the Swedish Institute at Athens, 26-29 June 1986*, edited by R. Hägg, N. Marinatos, & G.C. Nordquist, 160-5. SkrAth 4°, 38. Stockholm: Svenska Institutet i Athen, distribution Paul Åströms Förlag.

Comella, A. 2002. *I rilievi votivi Greci di periodo Arcaico e Classico. Diffusione, ideologia, committenza*. Bibliotheca Archaeologica. Bari: Edipuglia.

Coulton, J.J. 1976. *The Architectural Development of the Greek Stoa*. Oxford Monographs on Classical Archaeology. Oxford: Oxford University Press, Clarendon Press.

Croissant, F. 1986. "Epione." *LIMC* 3: 807-9.

Croissant, F. 1990. "Hygieia." *LIMC* 5: 554-72.

Deubner, L. 1956. Reprint. *Attische Feste*. Berlin: Akademie Verlag. Original edition, Berlin: Heinrich Keller, 1932.

Despinis, I.G. 2005. "Iphigeneia und Orestes. Vorschläge zur Interpretation zweier Skulpturenfunde aus Brauron." *AM* 120: 241-67.

Duhn, F. 1877. "Griechische Reliefs gefunden in den Ausgrabungen der archäologischen Gesellschaft am Südfuß der Akropolis vom April 1876 bis Juni 1877. Mit einem Anhang enthaltend die Beschreibung der Votivreliefs an Asklepios in den athenischen Sammlungen." *AZ* 35: 139-75.

Edelstein, E.J. & L. Edelstein. 1998. Reprint. *Asclepius. Collection and Interpretation of the Testimonies*. 2 vols. Baltimore & London: Johns Hopkins University Press. Original edition, Baltimore: Johns Hopkins University Press, 1945.

Foucart, P. 1992. Reprint. *Les Mystères d'Éleusis*. Librairie des Archives Nationales et de la société des Chartes. Puiseaux: Éditions Parès. Original edition, Paris: Auguste Picard, 1914.

Garland, R.S.J. 1992. *Introducing New Gods: The Politics of Athenian Religion*. London: Duckworth.

Ghedini, F. 1980. *Sculture greche e romane del Museo Civico di Padova*. Rome: L'ERMA di Bretschneider.

Girard, P. 1881. *L'Asclépieion d'Athènes après de recentes decouvertes. BÉFAR* 23. Paris: Ernest Thorin.

Goette, H.R. & J. Hammerstadt. 2004. *Das Antike Athen. Ein literarischer Stadtführer*. Munich: C.H. Beck.

Graf, F. 1992. "Heiligtum und Ritual. Das Beispiel der griechisch-römischen Asklepieia." In *Le Sanctuaire Grec*, edited by A. Schachter & J. Bingen, 159-99 (200-3). Entretiens sur l'antiquité Classique 37. Vandæuvres - Genève: Fondation Hardt.

Graf, F. 2000. "Mysteria." *DNP* 8: 611-5.

Güntner, G. 1994. *Göttervereine und Götterversammlungen auf attischen Weihreliefs: Untersuchungen zur Typologie und Bedeutung*. Beiträge zur Archäologie 21. Würzburg: Konrad Triltsch Verlag.

Hausmann, U. 1948. *Kunst und Heiltum. Untersuchungen zu den griechischen Asklepios-reliefs*. Potsdam: Eduard Stichnote.

Hill, I.T. 1953. *The Ancient City of Athens. Its Topography and Monuments*. London: Methuen & Co.

Hintzen-Bohlen, B. 1997. *Die Kulturpolitik des Eubulos und des Lykurg. Die Denkmähler- und Bauprojekte in Athen zwischen 355 und 322 v. Chr.* Antike in der Moderne. Berlin: Akademie Verlag.

Holtzmann, B. 1984. "Asklepios." *LIMC* 2: 863-97.

Hurwit, J.M. 1999. *The Athenian Acropolis. History, Mythology, and Archaeology from the Neolithic Era to the Present*. Cambridge & New York: Cambridge University Press.

Hurwit, J.M. 2004. *The Acropolis in the Age of Pericles*. Cambridge & New York: Cambridge University Press.

Iliakis, K.M. 1992-98. "Πρόταση για τη μορφή του αναθήματος του Τηλεμάχου Ἀχαρνέως." *Horos* 10-12: 73-6.

Judeich, W. 1931. *Topographie von Athen*. 2nd ed. Munich: C.H. Beck.

Keramopoullos, A. 1934/5. "Τὸ Πελαργικὸν, τὸ Ἀκληπιεῖον, αἱ ὁδοὶ αἱ ἀνάγουσαι πρὸς τὰ Προπύλαια." *ArchEph*: 85-116.

Koepp, Fr. 1885. "Die attische Hygieia." *AM* 10: 255-71.

Köhler, U. 1877. "Der Südabhang der Akropolis zu Athen nach den Ausgrabungen der archäologischen Gesellschaft." *AM* 2: 171-86 + 229-60.

Körte, A. 1893. "Bezirk eines Heilgottes." *AM* 18: 231-56.

Körte, A. 1896. "Die Ausgrabungen am Westabhange der Akropolis. III. Funde im Gebiete des Dionysion." *AM* 21: 265-332.

Koumanoudis, S. 1876. *Prakt*, 14-35.

Koumanoudis, S. 1877. *Prakt*, 6-12.

Krug, A. 1985. *Heilkunst und Heilkult. Medizin in der Antike*. Beck's Archäologische Bibliothek. Munich: C.H. Beck.

Kutsch, F. 1913. *Attische Heilgötter und Heilheroen*. Religionsgeschichtliche Versuche und Vorarbeiten 12:3. Gießen: Alfred Töpelmann.

Lambert, M. 1877. "Plan des fouilles faites par la Société Archéologique sur le versant méridional de l'Acropole." *BCH* 1: 169-70.

Lawton, C. 1999 "Votive Reliefs and Popular Religion in the Athenian Agora: The Case of Asklepios and Hygieia." In *Classical Archaeology towards the Third Millennium: Reflections and Perspectives: Proceedings of the XVth International Congress of Classical Archaeology, Amsterdam, July 12-17, 1998*, edited by R.F. Docter & E.M. Moormann, 232-4. Allard Pierson Series, Studies in Ancient Civilization 12. Amsterdam: Allard Pierson Museum.

Leventi, I. 2003. *Hygieia in Classical Greek Art*. Archaiognosia, Suppl. 2. Athens: University of Athens, Faculty of Philosophy, distribution Kardamitsa Editions.

Martin, R. 1944-45. "Seconde partie. Travaux de l'École Française. Asclépieion d'Athènes." *BCH* 48-49: 434-8.

Martin, R. & H. Metzger. 1949. "Recherches d'architecture et de topographie à l'Asclépiéion d'Athènes." *BCH* 73: 316-50.

Melfi, M. 2003. "I santuari di Asclepio in Grecia." Ph.D. diss.: University of Messina.

Melfi, M. 2007. *I santuari di Asclepio in Grecia. I. StArch* 157. Roma: L'Erma di Bretschneider.

Mitropoulou, E. 1975. *A New Interpretation of the Telemachos Monument*. Athens: Pyli Editions.

Papatheodorou, E. Forthcoming. "Die Nord-Propyläen des Asklepieion von Epidaurus. Die Entwicklung des Propylons in Griechenland von archaischen bis hellenistischen Zeit." Ph.D. diss., Justus-Liebig-Universität Gießen.

Parke, H.W. 1977. *Festivals of the Athenians*. Aspect of Greek and Roman Life. London: Thames & Hudson.

Parker, R. 1996. *Athenian Religion: A History*. Oxford: Oxford University Press, Clarendon Press.

Petropoulou, P. 1991. "Prothysis and Altar: A Case Study." In *L'espace sacrificial dans les civilisations méditerranéennes de l'Antiquité*, edited by R. Étienne & M.-T. Le Dinahet, 25-31. Paris: de Boccard.

Platon, N. 1963. "Ἐργασίαι διαμορώσεως Ἀσκληπιείου." *ArchDelt* 18, Chron. 1: 18-22.

Platon, N. 1964. "Ἀρχαιότητες καὶ μνημεῖα Ἀθηνῶν Ἀττικῆς: II. Ἐργασίαι διαμορφώσεως καὶ τακτοποιήσεως τοῦ ἀρχαιολογικοῦ χώρου Ἀκροπόλεως." *ArchDelt* 19, Chron. 2: 21-38.

Preuner, E. 1894. "Zur Einführung des Asklepios-Kultes in Athen." *RhM* 49: 313-6.

Ridgway, B.S. 1981. *Fifth Century Styles in Greek Sculpture*. Princeton: Princeton University Press.

Ridgway, B.S. 1983. "Painterly and Pictorial in Greek Relief Sculpture." In *Ancient Greek Art and Iconography*, edited by W.G. Moon, 193-208. Madison: The University of Wisconsin Press.

Ridgway, B.S. 1997. *Fourth-Century Styles in Greek Sculpture*. Madison: The University of Wisconsin Press.

Riethmüller, J.W. 1996. "Die Tholos und das Ei. Zur Deutung der Thymele von Epidauros." *Nikephoros* 9, 71-109.

Riethmüller, J.W. 1999. "Bothros and Tetrastyle: The Heroon of Asclepius at Athens." In *Ancient Greek Hero Cult, Proceedings of the Fifth International Classical Archaeology and Ancient History*, edited by R. Hägg, 123-43. SkrAth 8°, 16. Stockholm: Svenska Institutet i Athen, distribution Paul Åströms Förlag.

Riethmüller, J. 2005. *Asklepios: Heiligtümer und Kulte*. Studien zu antiken Heiligtümern. 2 vols. Heidelberg: Archäologie und Geschichte.

Ritti, T. 1981. *Iscrizioni e rilievi greci nel Museo Maffeiano di Verona*. Rome: L'ERMA di Bretschneider.

Robertson, N. 1998. "The City of Archaic Athens." *Hesperia* 67: 283-302.

Robertson, N. 2005. "Athenian Shrines of Aphrodite, and the Early Development of the City." In *Teseo e Romolo. Le origini di Atene e Roma a confronto*, edited by E. Greco, 43-112. Scuola Archeologica Italiana di Atene Tripodes 1. Athens: Scuola Archeologica Italiano di Atene, distribution L'ERMA di Bretschneider.

Scahill, D. Forthcoming. "The Origins of the Corinthian Capital: The Case for Metal Attachment and Tetrastyla." In *Structure, Image, Ornament:*

Architectural Sculpture of the Greek World, edited by R. von den Hoff & P. Schultz.

Schlaifer, R. 1940. "Notes on Athenian Public Cults." *HSCP* 51: 233-60.

Scranton, R.L. 1960. "Greek Architectural Inscriptions as Documents." *Harvard Library Bulletin* 14: 159-82.

Sobel, H. 1990. *Hygieia: Die Göttin der Gesundheit*. Darmstadt: Wissenschaftliche Buchgesellschaft.

Svoronos, J.N. 1908-37. *Das Athener Nationalmuseum*. Translated by W. Barth. Athens: Eleftheroudakis.

Thompson, H.A. & R.E. Wycherley. 1972. *The Agora of Athens: The History, the Shape and Use of an Ancient City. Agora* 14. Princeton: The American School of Classical Studies at Athens.

Tomlinson, R.A. 1969. "Two Buildings in Sanctuaries of Asklepios." *JHS* 89: 106-17.

Townsend, R.F. 1982. "Aspects of Athenian Architectural Activity in the Second Half of the Fourth Century B.C." Ph.D. diss., University of North Carolina, Chapel Hill.

Travlos, J.N. 1939-41. "Ἡ παλαιοχριστιανικὴ Βασιλικὴ τοῦ Ἀσκληπιείου τῶν Ἀθηνῶν." *ArchEph*: 35-68.

Travlos, J.N. 1971. *Bildlexikon zur Topographie des Athen*. Tübingen: Ernst Wasmuth.

Van Straten, F.T. 1993. "Image of Gods and Men in a Changing Society: Self-Identity in Hellenistic Religion." In *Images and Ideologies: Self-Definition in the Hellenistic World*, edited by A.W. Bulloch, E.S. Gruen, A.A. Long & A. Stewart, 248-64. Hellenistic Culture and Society 12. Berkeley, Los Angeles & London: University of California Press.

Van Straten, F.T. 1995. *Hiera Kala. Images of Animal Sacrifice in Archaic and Classical Greece*. Religions in the Graeco-Roman World 127. Leiden, New York & Köln: E.J. Brill.

Verbanck-Piérard, A. 2000. "Les Héros guérisseurs: des dieux comme les autres! À propos des cultes médicaux dans l'Attique classique." In *Héros et Héroïnes dans les mythes et les cultes grecs*, edited by V. Pirenne-Delforge & E. Suárez de la Torre, 281-332. Kernos Suppl. 10. Liège: Centre Internationale d'Étude de la Religion Grecque Antique.

Versakis, F. 1912. "Ὁ τοῦ Ἀθήνησιν Ἀσκληπιείου περίβολος καὶ τὸ Ἐλευσίνιον." *ArchEph*: 43-59.

Vikela, E. 1997. "Attische Weihreliefs und die Kulttopographie Attikas." *AM* 112: 167-246.

Vikela, E. 2006. "Healer Gods and Healing Sanctuaries in Attica. Similarities and Differences." *ARC* 8: 41-61

Walter, O. 1923. *Beschreibung der Reliefs im kleinen Akropolismuseum in Athen*. Vienna: Österreichische Verlagsgesellschaft.

Walter, O. 1930. "Ein neugewonnenes Athener Doppelrelief." *ÖJh* 26: 75-104.

Walter, O. 1953. "Der Priestertum des Sophokles." In Γέρας Ἀντωνίου Κεραμοπούλλου. Ἐπιστημονικαὶ πραγματεῖαι. Σειρά φιλολογικὴ καὶ θεολογικὴ 9. Athens: Myrtidi, 469-79.

Walker, S. 1979. "A Sanctuary of Isis on the South Slope of the Athenian Acropolis." *BSA* 74: 243-57.

Wegener, S. 1985. *Funktion und Bedeutung landschaftlicher Elemente in der griechischen Reliefkunst archaischer bis hellenistischer Zeit.* European University Studies Series 38, Archaeology vol. 6. Frankfurt am Main, Bern, & New York: Peter Lang.

Wickkiser, B.L. 2003. "The Appeal of Asklepios and the Politics of Healing in the Greco-Roman World." Ph.D. diss., University of Texas at Austin.

Wickkiser, B.L. 2006. "Chronicles of Chronic Cases and Tools of the Trade at Asklepieia." *ARG* 8: 25-40.

Wickkiser, B.L. 2008. *Asklepios, Medicine, and the Politics of Healing in Fifth-Century Greece: Between Craft and Cult.* Baltimore: Johns Hopkins University Press.

Wilamowitz-Moellendorff, U. von, 1932. *Der Glaube der Hellenen.* Vol. 2. Berlin: Weidmannsche Buchhandlung.

Wilson Jones, M. 2000a. *Principles of Roman Architecture.* New Haven & London: Yale University Press.

Wilson Jones, M. 2000b. "Doric Measure and Architectural Design 1: The Evidence of the Relief from Samos." *AJA* 104: 73-93.

Wilson Jones, M. 2001. "Doric Measure and Architectural Design 2: A Modular Reading of the Classical Temple." *AJA* 105: 675-713.

Wrede, W. 1933. *Attische Mauern.* Athens: Deutsches Archäologisches Institut.

Xyngopoulos, A. 1915. "Χριστιανικὸν Ἀσκληπιεῖον." *ArchEph*: 52-71.

Divine Images and Royal Ideology in the Philippeion at Olympia

Peter Schultz

For Olin Storvick

The use of heroic or divine iconographies for the portraits of kings, queens and rulers is one of the most well-known aspects of Hellenistic visual culture.[1] In paintings, statues and coins, Hellenistic monarchs consistently elevated themselves above those they ruled with a common iconographic language that pointed directly to their own god-like power. Indeed, since divine portraits helped generate and confirm the superhuman status of the men and women that they represented, this sort of heroic iconography was seen as a fundamental aspect of a king or queen's royal persona. Following the battle of the Granikos in 334 B.C., for example, Alexander descended upon the city of Ephesos where a royal portrait was commissioned by his court painter Apelles (Plin. *HN*. 35.92). The portrait – probably reproduced by the famous Neisos gem in St. Petersburg (Fig. 1) – showed the young king holding Zeus's thunderbolt and left little doubt as to Alexander's status as the supreme overlord of Asia.[2] About twenty years later, in a famous decree of 311 B.C., the grateful city of Skepsis in the Troad awarded divine honors to Antigonos Monophthalmos, honors which included a *temenos*, an altar and – most importantly – a cult statue that would have been constructed in appropriate divine guise.[3] (Four years later in Athens, Antigonos and his son Demetrios Poliorketes were again given divine honors and, again, received heroic portraits, this time set along side the famous Eponymous Heroes in the Athenian Agora.[4]) The same concern with divine imagery dominated numismatic iconography throughout the Hellenistic age, with kings and queens using godly attributes on coin portraits that were distributed throughout their realms; the famous tetradrachms of Demetrios Poliorketes that show him with the divine horns of a bull (Fig. 2) are only the earliest and most famous example.[5]

While the roster of such divinizing or heroizing images is well known and virtually endless, the origins of this iconographic phenomenon have never been subjected to systematic analysis. Unfortunately, such a task is beyond the scope of this article. What is possible, however, is a discussion of a monument that may have served as one inspiration for the use of such

Fig. 1. Cast of a red cornelian gemstone showing Alexander the Great holding the thunderbolt of Zeus, possibly after Apelles portrait painted in 334 B.C. Inscribed ΝΕΙΣΟΥ. St. Petersburg, Hermitage, inv. 609. Ht. 4.5 cm. Ca. 300-250 B.C. (Photo after Stewart 1993, fig. 66)

Fig. 2. Silver tetradrachm of Demetrios Poliorketes showing the king with the divine horns of a bull. Reverse shows a seated Poseidon with the inscription ΒΑΣΙΛΕΩΣ ΔΗΜΗΤΡΙΟΥ. Minted in Amphiopolis ca. 290 B.C. (Photo after Smith 1988, fig. 74.8)

divine or heroic imagery in Hellenistic royal art – Leochares' Argead portraits in the Philippeion at Olympia.

In early August of 338 B.C., Philip II of Makedon destroyed the armies of Athens and Thebes on the Boiotian plain of Chaironeia and changed the Greek world forever.[6] To commemorate this spectacular triumph, the king commissioned a set of dynastic portraits from the renowned Athenian sculptor Leochares. According to Pausanias (5.17.4, 5.20.9-10), Leochares' royal portrait group was dedicated at Olympia and consisted of a portrait of Philip alongside portraits of his immediate family members: his son Alexander, his wife Olympias, his mother Eurydike and his father Amyntas. Sometime later, again according to Pausanias, the portraits of Olympias and Eurydike were separated from the group and moved to the nearby temple of Hera.[7] Two physical characteristics of Leochares' Argead dynasts seem to have made them extraordinary – even revolutionary – for their time. The first of these was that the images of Philip and his family appeared to be fashioned of ivory and gold, exceedingly precious materials most famously associated with the titantic cult images of the fifth century. The second was that the portrait group was dedicated and installed inside the sacred Altis – arguably the most revered *temenos* of the Greek mainland – in a tholos specifically designed to hold them. It was this tholos that became known as the Philippeion (Figs. 3-6).

So much is known from the traveler's famous description of the monument. But what can Pausanias tell us about the use of divine or heroic ico-

Fig. 3. Olympia. Plan showing the position of the Philippeion. (Drawing: public domain)

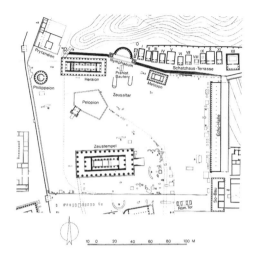

Fig. 4. Plan of the Philippeion incorporating some recent discoveries by Klaus Herrmann, Hajo van de Löcht and the author. (Drawing by David Boggs after Schlief 1944)

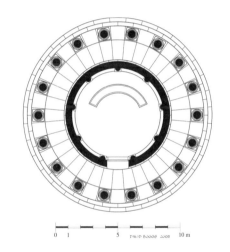

Fig. 5. Elevation of the Philippeion's eastern elevation incorporating some recent discoveries made by Klaus Herrman, Hajo van de Löcht and the author. (Drawing by David Boggs after Schlief 1944)

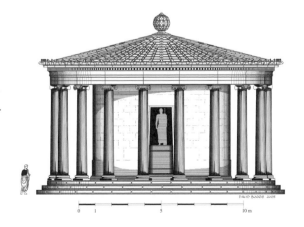

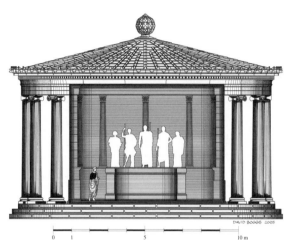

Fig. 6. Cut-away elevation of the Philippeion's interior incorporating some recent discoveries by Klaus Herrmann, Hajo van de Löcht and the author. (Drawing by David Boggs after Schlief 1944)

nography in this particular context by what was arguably the first Hellenistic royal family? While Leochares' unprecedented use of gold and ivory is very suggestive – as is the fact that the portraits were set up in their own precinct inside the Altis – can anything more concrete be said about these images and their place in the development of Hellenistic royal portraiture and its divinizing and heroizing conventions?[8]

Here, the archaeology of the site and building becomes important. Specifically, examination of the elaborate semi-circular statue base for Leochares' dynastic portraits inside the Philippeion provides important new information about Philip's dedication generally and his sculptor's possible use of heroic or divine iconography in particular. Interestingly, this statue base has never been the subject of systematic analysis or extended discussion.[9] This is a problem since study of the only piece of original physical evidence connected to Leochares' famous portraits is a basic, preliminary step towards a more nuanced and complex understanding of the Argead dynasts and their position in the history of Hellenistic portraiture, a step that has yet to be taken.

As it turns out, examination of the statue base in the Philippeion seems to clarify and/or complicate the answers to three questions that have consistently surrounded the monument.

The first is the question of patronage. Whose dedication is this exactly? While Pausanias tells us that Φιλίππῳ δὲ ἐποιήθη μετὰ τὸ ἐν Χαιρωνείᾳ τὴν Ἑλλάδα ὀλισθεῖν (5.20.10), in what sense is the dative used here? In the sense of agency, as it is normally understood – that the tholos was built "_by_ Philip" – or in the proper sense, as is sometimes suggested – that the tholos was built "_for_ Philip," with Alexander understood as the agent? Since the grammar can be read either way (and thus can support either position) and since Philip was dead by 336 B.C. (a mere two years after the building seems to have been commissioned, a point that will become important shortly) most archaeologists have opted for two distinct phases of patronage for the monument. Original sponsorship of the building is thus commonly given to Philip while the final stages of construction and the actual patronage of Leochares' portraits are given to Alexander. This question is important for understanding the early royal use of divine imagery. A loyal son's dedication of heroic, votive portraits in honor of his murdered father is quite different than a divine family commissioned by a conquering king to commemorate his overlordship of the Greek mainland. The nuances of patronage have a direct bearing on the meaning of the monument. Can examination of the statue base in the Philippeion clarify the nature of this specific and notorious problem?

The second – more important – question is the question of composition and appearance. For the last century, scholars have wrangled over the arrangement of the images. While there is no question that the semi-circular form of the statue base corresponded perfectly with the round plan of the tholos proper, how exactly were the portraits actually displayed and what did they look like? Like the question of patronage, this issue is tightly linked to the notion of heroic or divine iconography. How can it be reasonably argued that Philip and his family represent an early phase of divinizing royal imagery if we do not know what the portraits looked like? Can the statue base tell us anything about the portraits' arrangement and appearance? Were the Argead dynasts actually shown in heroic or divine guise?

Finally, there is the question of the tholos' symbolic and practical function. How can the tholos form be understood in this particular context? Did the architecture of the Philippeion suggest some sort of pan-Hellenic council house, a treasury, a heroön, simply an elaborate victory dedication, a combination of all these or is there yet another, complementary, hypothesis that can be supported by the evidence? Can discussion – or rather, a full contextualization – of the statue base allow further insight into the significance of the portraits' elaborate setting and how might this issue have effected the manner in which they were viewed? Does the tholos itself communicate something of the heroic or the divine?

Patron and sculptor

As noted, the dominant view of the Philippeion's patronage is that it was split between Philip and Alexander. Pausanias (5.20.10) notes that the tholos was constructed after the battle of Chaironeia in 338 B.C. For this reason, Philip is generally given credit for founding the building while Alexander is seen as completing the project and commissioning the portraits.[10] This conclusion is based on the notion that the twenty-two months falling between

Philip's victory at Chaironeia (August 338 B.C.) and his assassination (June 336 B.C.) were insufficient to complete the building and portraits and that the building project was thus halted and re-organized following the king's death. The questionable veracity of this assumption will be treated shortly. More significant now is the implicit claim, often made explicit in specific arguments, that the plan or composition of the monument was physically altered to accommodate Alexander's hypothetical new agenda. The most radical expressions of this popular hypothesis were given by Arnaldo Momigliano in 1934 and, more recently, by Jan Huwendiek in 1996. Momigliano thought that the portraits, but not the building, were Alexander's idea and that they were set up in 324 B.C. following the young king's move to deify his mother.[11] Huwendiek, on the other hand, argued that the original idea for the portraits was Philip's but that the king had initially intended only four portraits: himself, his new wife Kleopatra and his two parents. It was this program, according to Huwendiek, that was halted after the assassination with Alexander then commissioning a new set of portraits from Leochares at some later date.[12]

Autopsy reveals three physical characteristics of the statue base that stand against the notion of a divided plan and multiple building phases for the Philippeion.[13] To begin, the marble used for the statue base, the gutters and the floor of the Philippeion is identical. Now it has been accepted since the end of the nineteenth century that the Philippeion's floor and details were made of Parian marble. This is now supported by Klaus Herrmann's recent treatment of Parian stone at Olympia.[14] Identical marble, therefore, cannot mean Parian marble generally, since "Parian" can describe a wide range of marble types. On the contrary, the Parian marble used for the floor, details and the statue base shares identical physical and visual characteristics that are most likely explained if it was harvested from the same marble deposit within the same Parian quarry. Grain size is consistently large (ca. 2.5-4.5 millimeters) in both floor and base. Also consistent is the presence of pale silver-gray bands of varying size running parallel to the dominant planes of the base and floor.[15] In terms of luminosity, the base, the floor and details were observed in raking morning light, in direct perpendicular noon sunshine and in diffused twilight. To the naked eye, light refraction at all times was identical. While these observations prove nothing, they do represent the first step of physical analysis and suggest that the base and building could belong to the same project. Or, to reverse the argument, if marble type and quality had varied noticeably between statue base and architecture, the hypothesis that the base and portraits were late additions to the project might be said to gain a minor piece of archaeological evidence in its favor.[16] This is not the case.

In addition to similar marble, the patterns of tooling on the statue base, on the gutters and on the floor of the Philippeion are also identical. This is most clearly demonstrated by the use of a similar claw chisel on both the statue base and the marble architectural elements. The claw chisel in question was very fine and had 5 teeth every ca. 0.011 m; its bite is consistently ca. 0.001 m.[17] Traces of this tool were found on both the front and back of all base blocks and across the gutters and floor. These data, when supplemented with the discussion of marble, are significantly more telling. The chance that similar tools were used on similar stone belonging to two distinct projects is fairly small. Marble working tools were unique, handmade and often tailored to meet consistent and specific workshop criteria.[18] If Leochares' statue base had been constructed and placed in the Philippeion at some date after the construction of the building or if the base had been reworked at any time after the building was finished, this physical similarity could not exist. Similar tooling of identical stone suggests a single building cycle for both architecture and statue base.

In addition to identical marble and tooling, the pi-shaped clamps used in the statue base are identical to the pi-shaped clamps found throughout the rest of the Philippeion's architecture. Now it is important to note that "identical" here does mean that the clamps were simply the same "pi-shape," or style. This, by itself, would mean nothing since pi-shaped clamps are used throughout the history of Greek architecture. Rather, identical here means that the cuttings for these pi-shaped clamps have identical dimensions. This, in turn, suggests fast, "batch ordering" not a prolonged, multi-phased project. The clamp cuttings in the statue base consistently measure ca. 0.30-0.32 m long, ca. 0.02-0.025 m wide and ca. 0.03-0.05 m deep. Similarly, all clamp cuttings found in the epistyles, frieze backers, stylobate and euthynteria of the Philippeion itself conform to these general dimensions. It is unlikely that this is a coincidence. Even casual survey of architectural pi-clamps shows how widely these units could vary in size from building to building or even vary within the same project.[19] The range of possible clamp sizes available to the ancient architect was almost infinite.[20] The probability that identical clamps could show up in a second, unconnected building phase (in which marble and tooling is also identical) is highly unlikely. The use of pi-clamps of identical dimension in similarly tooled, identical Parian marble argues strongly for a single, uninterrupted construction cycle.

The marble, the tooling and the clamps of Leochares' statue base find direct parallels in the architecture of the Philippeion itself. If variation or discrepancy had been detected in one of these fields, reason might exist to posit a second phase of construction for the monument. (Indeed, it was exactly this sort of discrepancy that was anticipated before autopsy.) At present, however, the idea that the statue base was somehow adjusted or that it belongs to a hypothetical later or altered phase of the Philippeion's construction can be abandoned. This reading of the stones can now be combined with Dimitris Damaskos' careful demonstration that Pausanias' use of the dative in reference to the Philippeion *could* – although not necessarily *must* – be understood in the sense of agency.[21] (Of course, as noted earlier, Pausanias' prose composed five hundred years after the building's construction cannot be conclusive one way or another and can be used to sustain either position.) Barring the discovery of further evidence, it seems likely that if the Philippeion was commissioned and begun under Philip, as Pausanias' testimony suggests, then the king's original design was fulfilled.[22] At the very least, the base provides no physical data in support of the popular notion that the building was somehow altered during the course of construction or that the statue base belongs to a later, Alexandrian building phase.

But what of the old and pervasive idea that the Philippeion could not have been completed in the twenty-two months that fell between Philip's victory at Chaironeia in August of 338 and his assassination in June of 336? While nothing conclusive can be said barring the discovery of further evidence, it is worth remembering that other architectural projects funded by powerful patrons and/or committees could be finished very quickly indeed. The more complex architectural program of the Parthenon, for example, was completed in nine years (*IG* I³ 436-44) while the vast majority of the architecture of the Propylaia was completed (although the building was never fully finished) in five (*IG* I³ 462-66). All architecture and sculpture of the temple of Asklepios at Epidauros was finished in under four years and eight months.[23] With regards to Makedonian patronage specifically, Alexander's construction of the mole at Tyre in under seven months (Plut. *Vit. Alex.* 24.3-25.2; Polyainos, *Strat.* 4.3.4; Justin. 11.10.10-4) provides an instructive example and, if Diodoros (17.115.1-5) is to be trusted, then Alexander's commission for the massive and elaborate pyre of Hephaisteion seems to have been completed in only eight.[24] (Makedonian kings apparently had no patience with sluggish architects and they could afford to demand speed.) Could the Philippeion – modestly adorned with a single bronze akroterion and with lion's head water spouts and constructed (with the exception of the floor and other select details) of easily worked conglomerate and limestone – have been completed in a little under two years?

There are four reasons why this possibility should be considered. First, Philip's control and influence at Olympia was pervasive up until his death in 336 B.C. There is no reason to believe that construction would have been halted for political or economic reasons.[25] Second, limestone and conglomerate are much easier (and thus much quicker) to work than marble, perhaps requiring as little as one-fifth the effort.[26] This fact must be figured into the comparisons made with the Periklean program noted above. A limestone Propylaia could have been finished quickly indeed and the use of local conglomerate at Olympia ensured that the time spent transporting material was kept to an absolute minimum. Third, formal details, in particular the architectural moldings, show evidence of hasty execution as Lucy Shoe pointed out long ago; this, in turn, suggests a sense of urgency on the part of the builders.[27] Finally, and most importantly, an incomplete tholos in 336 B.C. would have been a straightforward embarrassment for the Makedonian king. 336 B.C. was the year of 111th Olympic games, the first festival after Philip's triumph at Chaironeia. It seems almost impossible that Philip's plan was to commission the building and then not have it ready for exhibition at the pan-Hellenic festival of the year. It is a well-known fact that the Olympic games had served as the dominant locus for Philip's propaganda for over two decades.[28] Is it conceivable that Philip – the master of pan-Hellenic propaganda and the then practical master of Olympia proper – wanted his victory monument seen as an unfinished pile of rocks, a half-finished construction site at the first games after his triumph? For anyone familiar with the king's character, the idea is bizarre at best. Indeed, one of the fundamental components of the Philippeion's impact was that the monument materialized almost overnight in the middle of the Altis for every Greek to see. The possibility that the Philippeion was finished during Philip's lifetime is real.[29] Indeed, unless compelling evidence can be given to explain Philip's specific inability to complete a hastily constructed tholos after his victory, the notion of Alexandrian patronage of the Philippeion should probably be rejected until compelling evidence can be found to substantiate it. The monument and portraits were almost surely Philip's idea and the dedication should be understood as a device by which the king – not his famous son – communicated a specific message to the Greek community.

Now even if it is likely that the Philippeion was completed in about two years, it must be admitted that the archaeologically based arguments given so far can prove nothing regarding the date of the monument. A construction period of ca. 338-336 B.C. is owed entirely to Pausanias' testimony. Even so, some tentative confirmation for this date comes from the statue base's ornament.

As most commentators have noted, the base and crown moldings of the pedestal are elaborate and quite distinct (Figs. 7-8) and Shoe pointed out that the base moldings were modeled on the intricate moldings found on the wall and column bases of the Erechtheion.[30] The most immediate parallel, however, comes from the temple of Athena Alea at Tegea, specifically the crown of the Great Altar and the interior wall moldings (Fig. 9).[31] This parallel was noted early by Carl Weickert in 1913 and Willy Zschietzschmann in 1944 but then virtually forgotten.[32] Weickert and Zschietzschmann seem to have been correct, however. The moldings from the temple of Athena are very close to those used in the Philippeion; the designer of the Philippeion base was familiar with the intricate Tegean moldings which he simply scaled down and refined to fit his base. This comparison generally supports Pausanias' date in the early 330s B.C. for the dedication of the Philippeion since it is now clear that the temple at Tegea was completed ca. 350-335 B.C.[33]

Peter Schultz

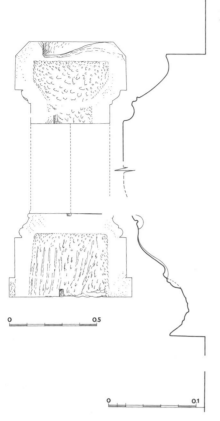

Fig. 7. Leochares' statue base in the Philippeion, molding profiles. (Drawing by Chrys Kanellopoulos)

Fig. 8. Leochares' statue base in the Philippeion, photograph of the crown (top) and base (bottom) molding. (Photograph after Schleif & Zschietzschmann 1944, pl. 20)

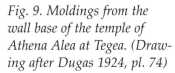

Fig. 9. Moldings from the wall base of the temple of Athena Alea at Tegea. (Drawing after Dugas 1924, pl. 74)

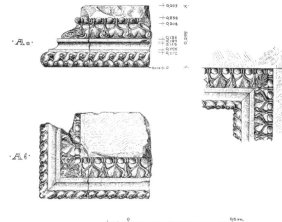

The relationship between the temple of Athena Alea and the Philippeion as suggested by the moldings, however, is more complex than simple temporal and geographical proximity. Indeed, it is well known that the team of sculptors and architects responsible for the temple of Athena Alea were intimately connected with work on the Maussolleion at Halikarnassos. This association is supported by the attested presence of Skopas at both sites (Plin. *HN.* 36.30; Paus. 8.45-7) and archaeologically confirmed by several minor monuments, the most important of which is the famous Idrieus relief found at Tegea sometime in the mid-1860s.[34] The relief shows Karian Zeus flanked by the Hekatomnid rulers Ada and Idrieus, the satrap of Karia and brother of the great Maussollos himself. In the past, this important monument has been read as a votive dedicated in Tegea by a Karian craftsman who had followed Skopas to the mainland from Halikarnassos. Geoffrey Waywell, however, showed that the stele was instead the heading for a decree set up in thanks to Ada and Idrieus for money that allowed the final completion of the Tegean temple.[35]

In this context, it is noteworthy that another parallel for the moldings on the statue base in the Philippeion comes from yet another Karian monument, this time a middle fourth century B.C. column base from Knidos drawn by Jean-Nicolas Huyot in 1820. This parallel, also, was noted early by Zschietzschmann but then ignored.[36] While it is true that the moldings of the Philippeion's statue base generally reflect the moldings from the Erechtheion – and are thus both Attic and Classicizing stylistically – Shoe's description of them as *purely* Athenian requires some modification. Indeed, the line of transmission for the moldings – Athens-Karia-Tegea-Olympia – could not be cleaner, even if it is more complex than previously allowed. This chain of influence is further supported by the radical use of dentils along with an

Ionic frieze in the Philippeion, an innovation that seems to manifest for the first time in Karia at the Maussolleion in Halikarnassos.[37] These details matter because they suggest the presence of an Athenian sculptor/architect working at the Philippeion who may also have worked in Karia before returning to the mainland in the third quarter of the fourth century B.C. This description corresponds perfectly with what is known of the career of Leochares so the archaeology independently supports Pausanias' identification of the Athenian master as the sculptor of the Argead dynasts.[38]

Even more interesting information can be squeezed from the *form* of the statue base which, like its mouldings, springs from a long and interesting tradition. In fact, because semi-circular statue bases anticipate tholoi as vehicles for dramatic sculptural display by almost a century and since Adolf Borbein and others have already pointed out that Leochares' sculptural composition was the *raison d'être* for the design of the Philippeion proper, it seems worth considering what motivated the decision to place portraits on a semi-circular base before discussing the possible significance of the tholos itself.[39] In the end, it may be that the building's design can best be understood from the inside out.

Semi-circular statue bases, while rare, were hardly revolutionary by the third quarter of the fourth century B.C. The famous semi-circular base for the portrait of the Athenian general Konon and his son Timotheos, dedicated after the triumph at Knidos in 394 B.C. and set not too far from Leochares' statues of Pandaites and his family, is only the most obvious example with which Leochares would have been familiar.[40] Moving outside Athens, the famous double semi-circles of the Argive dedications in Delphi (Fig. 10) and the semi-circular Achaian dedication in Olympia (Fig. 11), also may have influenced the composition.[41] These two famous semi-circular monuments were intimately familiar to both patron and sculptor (the extended presence of both Philip and Leochares at Olympia and Delphi is well known and indisputable), a fact that makes them good conceptual frames through which the formal significance of the semi-circular base in the Philippeion might be more clearly understood. These famous predecessors, in other words, might help explain why Philip and/or Leochares chose a semi-circular base in the first place and this knowledge, in turn, might lead to a better understanding of the form's possible meaning and possible heroic connotations.

The semi-circular dedication holding portraits of the Argive kings at Delphi (Fig. 10) may have influenced the decision to employ a semi-circular base in the Philippeion. Why? Because the Makedonian royal house claimed direct decent from Argive heroes, a piece of well known propaganda that, significantly, was first engineered at Olympia itself by the early Argead dynasts so that they might compete in the pan-Hellenic games (Hdt. 8.137-9; Thuc. 2.99).[42] Equally well documented is Alexander's own obsession with his descent from the Argive Herakleidai.[43] This idea had circulated in Pella

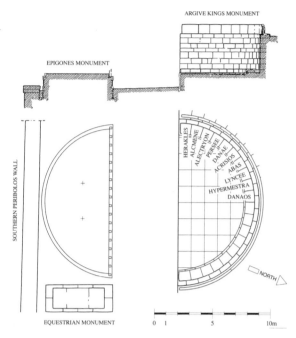

Fig. 10 Drawing of the semi-circular Argive dedications at the sanctuary of Apollon at Delphi. (Drawing by David Boggs 2006, after Bommelaer 1991, fig. 38)

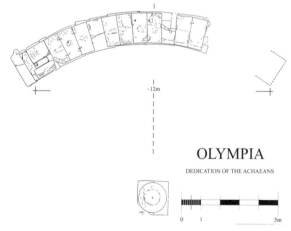

Fig. 11. Drawing of the semi-circular Achaian dedication at the sanctuary of Zeus at Olympia. (Drawing by David Boggs 2006)

ever since Isokrates (*Philippos* 105; 109-12) used the Argive Herakles as an ideal model for Philip. It was thus known to Leochares who had – at the very least – a business relationship with the Athenian orator since he was responsible for one of Isokrates' more famous portraits ([Plut.] *X orat.* 838d). The Makedonian-Argive connection was also reinforced during Philip's lifetime by Aristotle who, in his *Hymn to Excellence* (Athen. 15.696b-d), singled out Herakles (along with Achilleus and Aias) as the heroic models from whom *aretē* might best be learned.[44]

So much is known. What has not been emphasized, however, is the extent to which this perceived relationship with Argos actually influenced Makedonian policy under both Philip and Alexander. In his letter to Philip of 346 B.C., Isokrates (*Philippos* 5) included the then relatively insignificant Argos as one of the four great city states to be united by Philip in his Pan-Hellenic crusade as a nod to the king's ancestral claims.[45] Philip went to the aid of Argos in 344 B.C. with both money and mercenaries in response to pleas from his "kin" (Dem. 6.15); the Argives themselves hailed Philip as a rightful conqueror after Chaironeia (Plut. *Amat.* 760a-b) and received a major land grant from Philip for their support. It is also clear that the king had cultivated long-lasting political relationships in Argos until his death in 336 B.C. (Dem. 18.295; Polyb. 18.14).[46]

Alexander continued the family tradition. After the Granikos, the Argives, as a city contingent, were placed under the command of Pausanias as the garrison of Sardeis, the first conquered Persian capital, maybe a sign of particular trust (Arr. *Anab.* 1.17.8; Diod. Sic. 17.22.1). A year later, Alexander spared the Kilikian city of Mallos and, amazingly, remitted the tribute it had paid to Dareios purely on the basis of shared ancestral ties: the town was supposedly an Argive colony (Arr. *Anab.* 2.5.9). This fixation even seems to have penetrated the realm of the utterly mundane, with Argos being granted special powers of arbitration under the League of Korinth over minor border disputes.[47]

Now since it is certain that Philip, and later Alexander, valued and dramatized their Argive "heritage," it does not seem unreasonable to suppose that the new conqueror of Greece might have preferred a monument that recalled, at least implicitly, his Argive roots. At the very least, it seems clear that semi-circular bases and circular galleries – some of which have been associated speculatively with cults of Argive Herakles – became popular in the royal palace at Pella immediately following Philip's death.[48] More interestingly, Bonna Wescoat has recently suggested that an Argive, or at least a Peloponnesian, influence can be detected in a number of Makedonian monuments and that this stylistic trend might reflect the Argeads' obsession with their legendary Argive origins.[49] With all this in mind, is it possible that Philip, striding triumphantly into Delphi during the Pythian Festival of 338 B.C., gave a quick nod at the Argive dynasts, making his preference for his own monument known?[50] Given the historical background, this seems possible. The form of the Argive king monument might then be understood as one direct inspiration for the form of Philip's own dynastic portrait group. And if this is true, then the connection between the early Argive heroes and the Argead dynasts would be secure. The *form* of the base linked Philip and his family with the Argive kings of old and may have provided a platform – both literally and figuratively – for a set of heroic or divine images.

Now even if the Argive kings failed to impress Philip, it seems certain that the dramatic, theatrical organization of the famous Achaian dedication at Olympia – also organized in a semi-circle – influenced the sculptor Leochares (Fig. 11). Aileen Ajootian has recently demonstrated that semi-circular bases were employed since the middle fifth century B.C. with very specific narrative strategies in mind, strategies that seem to have appealed to the Athenian master's dramatic sensibilities.[51] In particular, Ajootian showed how the semi-circular base of the Achaian dedication at Olympia – sculpted and signed by the renowned Onatas of Aigina (Paus. 5.25.8-10) – was specifically designed to facilitate the viewer's entry into a narrative space that relied heavily on the visual modes of the ancient theatre. Stepping within the circular theatre that these bases inscribed – in the case of Onatas' group, the tableau showed the Achaians drawing lots from Agamemnon's helmet (held by Nestor) for the *monomachia* with Hektor (*Il.* 7.131-208) – the ancient audience immersed themselves in the heroic episodes of Homer and entered a world in which the distinction between contemporary and mythical time collapsed.[52] In the Achaian dedication, Onatas emphasized this effect by placing Nestor on a separate base several meters across from the main action. Spectators walked between the heroes and into the time of legends.

This spatially defined blurring of temporal boundaries, the blending of history and legend within a distinct theatrical precinct, seems to be a direct conceptual antecedent for Leochares' sculptural and architectural tableau. Indeed, the base in the Philippeion represents an interesting development of Onatas' original idea since, upon entering the Philippeion, the ancient viewer would have been placed in Nestor's position, set across from a new set of "Greek" heroes. All of this is in line with Florian Seiler's observation that the Philippeion was designed as the locus for the specifically *theatrical* display of the Argead dynasts, an idea rooted in the tradition of dramatic form first exemplified by the Achaian dedication at Olympia as interpreted by Ajootian.[53] Since it seems possible that the arrangement and costumes of the Argead dynasts deliberately pointed back to late fifth and early fourth century B.C. artistic models (as will be suggested below) there seems no better precedent for the theatrical mode of display witnessed in the Philippeion than Onatas' fifth century B.C. composition less than 150 meters to the east inside the Altis; the monuments were a stone's throw away from each other (Fig. 3). That the conceptual basis for such a composition was established over a century prior to the Philippeion's construction provides a glimpse into Leochares' rich art historical self-consciousness, a point to be made explicit shortly. Even more important is the fact that we have, yet again, patron and sculptor drawing on a formal pattern of arrangement that was seen as appropriate for Greek heroes.

Composition and appearance

Regarding the precise composition of the Argead portraits, autopsy of the
statue base again yields interesting information that is relevant to the present query. Schleif's early drawing of the base crowns and their plinth beddings has been the source of a great deal of speculation and confusion.
Systematic study has clarified the picture. New drawings by Chrys Kanellopoulos show the organization of the base, its correct reconstruction and,
most importantly, the shapes and sizes of the plinth cuttings (Figs. 12-15).
These data can be directly translated into results regarding the original
composition and appearance of Leochares' dynastic group.

The plinth bedding on block **C5** (Figs. 12 and 16) provides a good starting
point. The bedding cut into **C5** is trapezoidal. It is consistently ca. 0.32 m
wide with a varying length of 0.53 m at the front and 0.46 m at the rear. Most
commentators have rightly placed a heavily draped female figure on this
base.[54] In addition to being supported by innumerable other examples of
trapezoidal plinth cuttings that held draped females (the shape is very common), this conclusion is specifically confirmed by the plinth socket in the
statue base of Eurydike's portrait recently excavated at Vergina (Figs. 12 and
16) which is of identical shape and held, without doubt, a standing, draped
female figure in marble.[55] Indeed, Eurydike's plinth bedding at Vergina, at
ca. 0.59 x 0.46 m, is close in size to **C5**'s bedding and even exhibits similar
right and oblique angles.[56] This rather basic reading of the physical evidence
is confirmed by the pry mark that is cut in the rear of **C5**'s bedding. Of all
the plinth cuttings on the base's crowns only **C5** carries such a notch. This
kind of pry mark is exactly what might be expected if the image was carefully separated from its base and moved within the sanctuary (as opposed
to being hacked to pieces by metal hunters). Pausanias (5.17.4) tells us that
the two female Argeads were moved to the Heraion before his visit. His
testimony is confirmed by the physical evidence.[57] The Argead queens stood
on the ends of the base.[58]

The positions of Philip, Alexander and Amyntas have also been considered
controversial. Sometimes Philip is placed in the middle of the base, sometimes Alexander is given the prominent position but most commentators
agree that certainty is elusive. This may not be the case. Since the oblong
plinth beddings on **C2-4** have nothing in common with trapezoids that almost
always hold plinths of draped females, these beddings held portraits of men.
Of greater importance, however, are the actual and comparative sizes of the
beddings. They vary significantly and enough to justify interpretation. As
shown by Table 1, the bedding on **C2**, at 0.175 m², is noticeably smaller (just
under 15% smaller) than that on **C3** (0.202 m²) or **C4** (0.200 m²) but noticeably larger (just over 15% larger) than the bedding for the female portrait
on **C5** (0.151 m²).[59]

Fig. 12. Leochares' statue base in the Philippeion, plan of the reassembled crown. (Drawing by Chrys Kanellopoulos 2002)

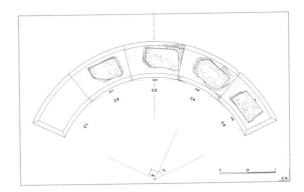

Fig. 13. Leochares' statue base in the Philippeion, plan of the reassembled base. (Drawing by Chrys Kanellopoulos 2002)

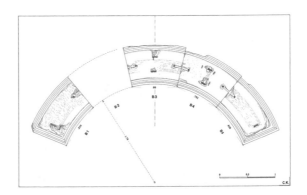

Fig. 14. Leochares' statue base in the Philippeion, crown detail C3. (Drawing by Chrys Kanellopoulos 2002)

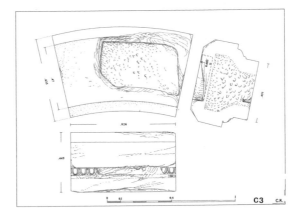

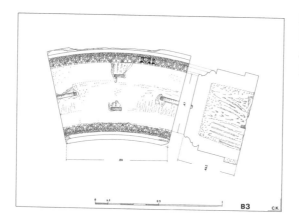

*Fig. 15. Leochares' statue base in the Philippeion, base detail **B3**. (Drawing by Chrys Kanellopoulos 2002)*

*Fig. 16. Leochares' statue base in the Philippeion, photograph of crown block **C5**. (Photograph by author)*

Table 1. Dimensions of plinth beddings, the statue base in the Philippeion

Block	Area^2
C1	missing
C2	0.175 m^2
C3	0.202 m^2
C4	0.200 m^2
C5	0.151 m^2

Now, even if it was not known that these four bases held two adult men, a youth and a woman, the size of the plinth beddings would have suggested as much. Of the three oblong beddings that held portraits of men **C2**, the smallest of the three, held Alexander. This can be stated with confidence since Alexander's age would have demanded a smaller size when placed next to his elder male relatives.[60] While a shift in pose – and thus perhaps plinth type – might be seen as the reason for the difference in bedding size, it cannot be denied that the portrait placed in the position of honor next to the central figure was conceived as spatially subordinate. This makes good sense for a portrait of the young prince set up in 338 B.C. This reading of the archaeology is confirmed by the famous Kallithea Monument which clearly shows how late fourth century B.C. Athenian, free standing, commemorative marble portraiture showed teenage sons of prominent families as slightly smaller adults when placed beside their fathers in order to communicate the precise nature of the hierarchical and familial relationship.[61] An identical phenomenon can be observed in the Daochos Monument in Delphi and there are many other examples.[62] Alexander stood at his father's right hand.

This physical evidence bears upon the question of patronage. Had he commissioned Leochares' portrait group, Alexander surely would have requested to be shown *younger* than his elder male relatives but it is unlikely that the new king would have asked to be shown *smaller* and in a subordinate position to his father with whom he consistently competed. Unless compelling reason can be given to explain this physical evidence, patronage of the portraits, and thus the monument as a whole, should probably belong to Philip – a conclusion that was already suggested and supported by independent archaeological evidence in the first part of this paper.

Once it is accepted that **C2** held the portrait of Alexander, the rest of the composition falls into place. Since Amyntas cannot have been placed in the center of the group, **C3** (which also preserves the largest plinth cutting) held the portrait of Philip. The portrait of Amyntas was placed on **C4** and his wife Eurydike was placed next to him on **C5**. Olympias should then be placed on the lost block, **C1**, next to her son. Mother and son shared the position of honor at Philip's proper right, a placement that has dramatic political and ideological ramifications.[63] From left to right then, the correct order of the portraits was Olympias (**C1**), Alexander (**C2**), Philip (**C3**), Amyntas (**C4**) and Eurydike (**C5**). Clearly, the building was called the *Philippeion* for a reason.

Now, in addition to providing some important information regarding the organization of the Argead portraits, analysis of the base also sparks a different sort of question. Namely, can the statue base suggest other information regarding the actual *appearance* of the Argead dynasts? Since the semi-circular form of the statue base is rooted in a fifth and mid-fourth century B.C. tradition and since the statue base's moldings are clearly Attic and Classicizing (even if they are strained through the filters of the Karian and Tegean monuments as noted above), one obvious question might be whether this information can be translated into anything solid regarding the *style* of the images themselves. Beyond the obviously significant Athenian ethnicity of the sculptor, is there reason to believe that the Argead portraits were stylistically Atticizing and/or retrospective?

This question would be purely rhetorical if not for the excavation of the Vergina Eurydike in 1989 by Chrysoula Saatsoglou-Paliadeli (Figs. 17-19).[64] This important middle fourth century B.C. marble portrait of Philip's mother was set up within the sanctuary of Eukleia in the Agora of ancient Vergina. The Vergina Eurydike provides the ideal – and at present the only – model for the queen's portrait in Olympia.[65] The two portraits are roughly contemporary, the plinth cuttings for both portraits are very similar in shape and size and Andronikos and Saatsoglou-Paliadeli would even make them simultaneous dedications commemorating Chaironeia (although this reading is not without serious complications).[66]

More importantly here, however, is the fact that the Vergina portrait is both Atticizing and retrospective and that these stylistic traits provided the formal armature for an iconography of heroization, a vital point in the present discussion.[67] Saatsoglou-Paliadeli has suggested that the workmanship of the Vergina portrait is Attic, an observation that is supported by the fact that the portrait is made of Pentelic marble.[68] More significant is the fact that the dress and basic pose of Eurydike's portrait in Vergina – especially the broad back-mantle, hang of the apoptygma, heavy kolpos and the columnar verticals of the lower peplos (but not the veil) – take as their immediate iconographic model Kephisodotos the Elder's famous Attic masterpiece, the statue of Eirene and Plutos set up in Athens around 370 (Fig. 19).[69] The heavy costume seems to have been particularly appropriate for traditional, matronly women and may have communicated a sense of the heroic past.[70] Sir John Boardman has noted that Eirene's peplos was specifically old-fashioned (which would make such costume in the 330s positively antique) and Olga Palagia has pointed out that the dress is worn with particular frequency by matronly, divine figures (specifically Demeter) on fourth century reliefs.[71]

Now none of this proves that Leochares' portrait of Eurydike in the Philippeion was stylistically retrospective or that she was costumed in old-fashioned or heroic dress. At the same time, it does seem logical to suppose that if Eurydike was iconographically heroized in the hinterlands of Makedon then she might have been similarly represented in the center of the Greek world during a time when her son's influence was utterly pervasive and at a site where her position as the queen mother was specifically being emphasized.[72] The other retrospective facets of the monument point firmly (and independently) towards this conclusion. This hypothesis also works well with Sheila Dillon's recent discussion of costume as a defining attribute of early Hellenistic portraits of women and with Wilfred Geominy's new demonstration that heroized portraits of the early Hellenistic period could be shown in "historical" (i.e. retrospective) costume to recall ages past.[73] By this reasoning, the possibility that Eurydike was shown in heroic guise is real. For the first time in the history of Greek sculpture, a historical (possibly living) woman was shown in the guise of a heroine.

Fig. 17a-c. Marble portrait statue of Eurydike, mother of Philip II. From the sanctuary of Eukleia, Vergina. Ca. 350-340 B.C. Restored H. 1.90 m. (Photographs by Petros Themelis)

So much can be said for Eurydike. But what of her son Philip? If what has been suggested about his mother is correct, the restoration of a heroic or divinizing Philip at the center of the dynastic ensemble seems equally possible. (Whether any solid iconographic data can be taken from this remains speculative pending the discovery of further evidence.) It is worth remembering that the Argead dynasts, Philip foremost among them, claimed direct descent from Zeus *via* Herakles and the Argive Temenids.[74] Leonhard Schumacher, among others, has also suggested a close connection between Philip and Zeus on Makedonian coins minted in the third quarter of the fourth century.[75] This interesting (but speculative) connection is made more compelling by the presence of the subtle *anastolē* in Zeus's hair witnessed on several issues (this particular hair style would, of course, become Alexander's trademark) and the fact that the head of Zeus had never appeared on Makedonian coins before those of Philip.[76]

Much more concretely, a portrait of Philip was set up inside the great temple of Artemis at Ephesos sometime before 334 B.C. (Arr. *Anab.* 1.19.11) making him a co-occupant of the Artemision. This is a critical point in the argument since later Hellenistic kings – for example, Antiochos' queen Apollonis, Attalos I, Attalos III, Antiochos III, Ariarthes V and Mithradates VI – followed Philip's lead and made specific efforts to place themselves inside other gods' temples to enhance their own royal/divine statue.[77] Also important is the fact that Philip had no qualms about commissioning his own "god-like" portrait to be carried in procession and "enthroned" with

Fig. 18. Marble portrait statue of Eury-dike, mother of Philip II. From the sanc-tuary of Eukleia, Vergina. Ca. 365-340 (?) B.C. View of head, veil is missing. (Photographs by Petros Themelis)

the twelve Olympians on the ill-fated day of his daughter's wedding that same year (Diod. Sic. 16.92.5, 16.95.1).[78] That both of these "divinizing" portraits of the king were set up immediately *after* Leochares' commission in 338 B.C. may not be a coincidence. The establishment of a cult of Zeus Philippios by the Eresians of Lesbos further shows how closely Philip was connected with Zeus and his cult, a fact that might hint at his own divine pretensions.[79]

Of even greater interest here are two pieces of neglected textual evidence. The first is a middle fourth century inscription (*SEG* 38.658) found reused as building material in Basilica A in Philippoi and published in 1988 by Pierre Ducrey.[80] While fragmentary, this inscription clearly records the sale of plots of sacred land (*temenē*) that are specifically ear-marked as the property of the gods. A *temenos* of Ares is mentioned by name (l. 9, col. 1) as are a *teme-nos* of Poseidon (l. 9, col. 2) and a *temenos* "of the heroes" (l. 9, col. 2). Of critical significance is that at least two *temenē* of Philip are also plainly dis-cussed (ll. 1 and 6). Ducrey originally argued that the existence of these *temenē* of Philip did not necessarily imply cult or divine/heroic status for the king.[81] This reading, however, was immediately challenged by Miltiades Hatzopoulos, who noted that a "*temenos*" should almost certainly be under-stood as consecrated land.[82] This opinion has now received strong support

Fig. 19. Eirene and Plutos by Kephi-sodotos. Roman copy of an original ca. 375-370 B.C. Munich, Glyptothek 216. Ht. 2.01 m. (Photograph courtesy Sta-atliche Antinkensammlungen und Glyptothek)

from Angelos Chaniotis who has suggested that this evidence represents the deciding factor in the debate over Philip's divine or heroic status.[83] What-ever the final solution to the problems presented by this particular stone, there can be no doubt that the inscription ranks Philip amongst the highest of heroes and gods. And if this idea circulated epigraphically in fourth cen-tury B.C. Makedonia, it is certain that the same notion could have been communicated iconographically by fourth century artists and sculptors. If this is true, then Philip stands as the father of the Hellenistic divine portrait convention and the nature of his image in the Philippeion should probably be considered divinizing or, at the very least, heroic.

A final piece of evidence lends strong support to this hypothesis. In an often overlooked passage from the thirty-seventh Discourse of Dion Chryso-stom (37.42), the orator relates a story in which Mummius stole a statue of Philip from Thespiai, labeled the portrait Zeus, then dedicated the image in Rome.[84] If this tale is accurate, then Damaskos must be correct when he notes that Philip's portrait should have at least resembled Zeus if Mummius could confuse the two images.[85] While this idea cannot shed any light on the problematic subject of Philip's physiognomic likeness (nothing is known with certainty), it does begin to confirm the argument regarding Philip's use of explicitly divinizing imagery.[86] That this divinizing public persona was first engineered (or maybe finally perfected?) by Leochares within the potent architectural and religious context of Zeus' sanctuary in the Altis seems likely.

Is it possible to suggest that the young general Alexander was also cast in heroic guise? Here, Andrew Stewart's famous archaeological hydra – the Alexander Doryphoros – grows a new, and potentially ugly, head.[87] The evidence for multiple versions of this important portrait of Alexander with spear is solid and very well-known. There can be no doubt regarding the existence of many fourth century B.C. versions. The question here, however, is whether one example of the Alexander Doryphoros could possibly have been sculpted by Leochares and set up in the Philippeion. The single conceptual problem with this line of inquiry – that the invention of the Alexander Doryphoros is often exclusively attributed on the authority of Plutarch (*De Alex. fort.* 335f; *De Is. et Os.* 360d) to Lysippos – has been effectively countered by Smith and Stewart.[88] Both have demonstrated that there is no reason to assume on the basis of Plutarch's text that there was one particularly famous prototype of the Alexander Doryphoros nor that this prototype must belong exclusively to Lysippos. The field of inquiry is open. Since this is so, might the invention of the type be slightly earlier than previously allowed and might an example of the type have been placed in the Philippeion? Three points ask that the possibility should be considered.

First, with regards to date. As is well known, the chronology and development of the Alexander Doryphoros is based on three series of bronze statuettes, the Stanford, Fouquet and Nelidow types.[89] Because of their various poses and scales, these images necessarily suggest a wide range of dates and prototypes. The Stanford Alexander – apparently the earliest of the three statuettes typologically and thus the only one that could plausibly be connected to a pre-334 B.C. monument – is often dated to the middle 330s B.C. (Fig. 20). This date is based on its reserved, introspective pose and the type's appearance on a rock cut relief at Myra in Lykia carved sometime after 334 B.C. when Alexander passed through the region.[90] Two things are worth remembering in this context. First, the Myra relief provides only a *terminus ante quem* for one possible original Alexander Doryphoros, nothing more. Second, and more importantly, an identical contraposto was broadly used throughout the late fifth and fourth century B.C. for portraits of athletes and soldiers as well as for heroes and deities.[91] That the Stanford Alexander might generally reflect a prototype of ca. 338-336 B.C. as opposed to ca. 334 B.C. cannot be rejected on the basis of style or typology. More to the point, even if there is no direct connection between the Stanford statuette type and Leochares' portrait of Alexander in the Philippeion, there is no question that the basic type was available for use in the middle 330s B.C.

Fig. 20. Bronze statuette of Alexander, Hellenistic/Roman copy after an original of 330 B.C. Iris & B. Gerald Cantor Center for Visual Arts at Stanford University, inv. no. 1975-47. H. 10.7 cm. (Photo: Iris & B. Gerald Cantor Center for Visual Arts at Stanford University. The Hazel Hansen Fund, neg. 19231)

Second, heads associated with the Stanford statuette can provide some useful (if still hypothetical) data as to a possible connection between the type and a possible Alexander Doryphoros in the Philippeion. Only two portrait types can be firmly associated with the Alexander Doryphoros: the Azara types and the Schwarzenberg types. The Azara-type has, for good reason, been seen as reflecting a late portrait of the king, so it cannot be realistically connected to the Stanford statuettes which reflect an early prototype.[92] This leaves the Schwarzenberg head which does seem particularly suited to the Stanford type statuette on account of the very slight tilt of the head to the proper left.[93] (This stance, incidentally, would be ideal for an Alexander placed slightly to the viewer's left on a high pedestal, just as he was placed in the Philippeion.) Of particular importance here is the apparent youth of the sitter. From the rarely photographed oblique proper right (Fig. 21), Alexander appears just as young – if not younger! – than the Akropolis Alexander that is consistently associated with Leochares' portrait.[94] His age is specifically emphasized by his boyish large ears, his thin neck and his *very* short hair. These

Fig. 21. Head of Alexander, the "Schwarzen-berg" Alexander. Roman copy (?) of an original ca. 340-330 B.C. Vienna, Collection Erkinger von Scwarzenberg. Marble. H. ca. 35.5 cm. Oblique view from the proper right. (Photograph by Andrew Stewart)

features are more than appropriate for a portrait carved when the sitter was in his late teens. The conspicuous lack of long, leonine mane, so important in later characterization of the king, is particularly telling and must be explained.[95] Also important is the fact that Erkinger Schwarzenberg showed long ago that the *anastolē* seen in this young portrait derives directly from the portrait of a man from the Maussolleion at Halikarnassos.[96] As has been shown, the link between the Philippeion and the Maussolleion is firm archaeologically and Leochares' presence is attested at both sites in the literature. While this argument does not demand that the Schwarzenberg head reflect a Leocharean original, it does seem worth pointing out that the only portrait head that can be firmly associated with an early Alexander Doryphoros can also be associated with the Attic sculptor – an interesting coincidence.[97]

Third and finally, an Alexander Doryphoros in the Philippeion makes good sense iconographically. The connection between the mighty spear-bearing Achilleus and Alexander had been cultivated in Pella since the prince was a boy (Plut. *Vit. Alex.* 2.1). There is no reason to believe that the type must be a post-334 B.C. invention. More importantly, the Philippeion was a *war* monument. With Philip divinized beyond worldly concerns and the Argead queens heroized and calm, an Alexander Doryphoros might have provided a device by which the actual occasion for the monument was subtly (or not so subtly) evoked. Certainly Alexander's position in the battle of Chaironeia as Philip's right-hand general was known throughout Greece (Plut. *Vit. Alex.* 9.4; Curtius 8.1.23) and this, too, may have inspired the use of the spear-bearing type in this particular context. The appropriation of what was still considered to be a quintessential Greek (and specifically Ar-

give) form would also have accorded perfectly with Argead propaganda and
the Makedonian quest for racial legitimacy on the mainland, a quest that
began at Olympia.[98] Also important here might be the interesting tension
between the idealized, heroic sculptural category (the *doryphoros* type generally) and the historical reality (Alexander's status as general) that made the
form viable as a realistic image of the young warrior-prince.[99] More interesting, however, is the fact that some versions of the Stanford type (and only
the Stanford type) show Alexander with his spear held point down. Among
other examples, the motif is most famously shown on the Alexander fresco
in Pompeii. Stewart has provocatively noted that women are present at this
and all other occasions in which Alexander holds his spear point-down and
that the reversal of this old military motif might have communicated the
idea that War has given way to Peace.[100] The point-down spear as a peace
sign is hardly a Roman invention, as the famous Bendis relief (329/28 B.C.)
in Copenhagen, among others, demonstrates.[101] The presence of Alexander's
mother and grandmother in the Philippeion and the particular propaganda
required by Philip for his Common Peace provide an ideal archaeological
and historical frame for this interpretation of the motif. A heroized Alexander Doryphoros, with spear held point-down, would have perfectly communicated much of the monument's message.

An interesting point is raised by the preceding arrangement and reconstruction of figures. If the dominant central figure of Leochares' group (a
divinized Philip) was, in fact, flanked by a heroic younger couple on his
proper right (Alexander/Doryphoros and Olympias/Peplophoros) and an
elderly couple on his proper left (Amyntas and Eurydike/Peplophoros), then
Leochares' sculptural composition in the Philippeion takes as its most obvious model the center of the temple of Zeus's east pediment about 120 meters
to the east as correctly restored by Herrmann, Stewart, and Boardman
(Fig. 22).[102] This blatant example of early Hellenistic *invenzione all'antica* is
not surprising. On the contrary it is quite typical of the hyper-intellectualized
fourth century B.C., quite in line with the other retrospective characteristics
of Leochares' composition and more than appropriate when Philip's long
standing patronage of the site and his strong connections to Pelops, Olympic
chariot racing and Olympian Zeus are remembered.[103] The iconographic
implications of this comparison are fairly obvious. The Makedonian royal
family is likened to the founding heroes of Olympian myth with Philip likened specifically to Zeus, an iconographic move that receives independent
confirmation from Dion Chrysostom (37.42), as noted above.

Now within this context of speculative heroizing and/or divinizing portraits, the materials that Leochares used for his heroic composition are worth
discussing again. Indeed, everything suggested so far regarding the possible
composition and appearance of the Argead dynasts is perfectly supported
by the sculptor's supposed choice of precious materials since the use of gold

Fig. 22. The east pediment of the temple of Zeus at Olympia as restored by Hermann (1972), Stewart (1990) and Boardman (1991). (Drawing by David Boggs 2006, after Boardman 1991, fig. 18)

and ivory (the material of the dynasts as reported by Pausanias) had been hitherto reserved for Classical cult images most famously constructed by the Attic school.

The problem, of course, is that one look at the plinth cuttings (Figs. 12, 14, 16) found on the Philippeion's base should be enough to convince any archaeologist that Pausanias was misinformed when he reported the materials from which the Argead portraits were fashioned. The beddings on the Philippeion's base were made to hold stone images – presumably of marble – not images of gold and ivory.

This is not a new idea. In his 1987 commentary on Pausanias, Felix Eckstein suggested that Leochares' Argead portraits were made of marble on the basis of the obvious evidence on the statue base.[104] The idea was embellished by Konrad Hitzl in 1995, who acknowledged Eckstein's hypothesis but proposed that Leochares had used a hitherto undocumented type of akrolithic technique using marble and ivory although no comparanda for a hybrid ivory/marble free standing portrait was given.[105] Eckstein's hypothesis seems like it may be the better one.[106] If these bases had been excavated without Pausanias' testimony and if the archaeologist responsible had proposed that the bases held images of ivory and gold, the excavator's proposal would have been dismissed out of hand. The physical evidence is that clean.[107] The beddings are meant to hold stone plinths.

To clarify the point, it might be useful to review how chryselephantine images were mounted. The best example comes from the Athenian temple on Delos most recently treated in detail by Kenneth Lapatin.[108] In this case, the gold and ivory statues were fashioned and mounted on wooden armatures. The support structures of these images were wooden frames like those employed for the Athena Parthenos in Athens.[109] These wooden frames were secured to their statue bases by way of square wooden posts wrapped in bronze sheet. The sockets for these posts on Delos are consistently 12-18 cm deep. This is over twice the depth of the flat beddings on the Philippeion base. If the base in the Philippeion held images of ivory and gold, the cuttings for the posts of the chryselephantine statues' wooden armature would remain as Lapatin has already pointed out.[110] They do not. Indeed, even if the plinth beddings on the Philippeion's base belonged to some hypothetical second phase – for which there is no evidence – traces of the original fastenings would still remain within the shallow beddings themselves. The Argead portraits were almost certainly made of stone.

Now there is good reason to question Pausanias' account in this particular case. The traveler also mistook the Philippeion's limestone ashlar wall for fired brick (5.20.10). This error is acknowledged by all modern commentators. The traveler does not seem to have inspected the Philippeion first hand. Indeed, since Pausanias generally prefers sacred to profane monuments, since he laments the "tragedy of Chaironeia" on five separate occasions (1.25.3, 5.20.10, 7.10.5, 9.6.2, 10.3.2) and since he specifically detested Philip (5.4.9, 8.7.5), he may have had less interest in a war monument that commemorated Philip's triumph and the ruin of Greece than modern archaeologists have assumed.[111] If this was true, then he probably just asked his guide – Aristarchos, supposedly a descendant of the great Iamos – who then gave him the usual run around. It is important to remember that Christian Habicht, Pausanias' most formidable modern defender, has explicitly noted that this same Aristarchos was responsible for the most ridiculous story in the traveler's entire work.[112] Aristarchos might also be responsible for the other errors that W.K. Pritchett and Anne Jacquemin have discussed in connection with Pausanias' description of the Altis.[113] These acknowledged errors were consistently made in connection to sculpture and architecture that the traveler did not personally inspect. Since Pausanias is very reliable elsewhere, the oversight regarding the materials from which the Argead dynasts were made should probably be attributed to his guide.[114] More important than all this, however, is the fact that the statues of Eurydike and Olympias are specifically *not* included in Pausanias' list (5.17.3) of the other chryselephantine images that he saw inside the Heraion. Instead they are added as an after thought. Indeed, since the text gives no reason to believe that he inspected these images first hand Pausanias probably depended (again) on the problematic Aristarchos for his information.

It is not difficult to speculate how this story of chryselephantine portraits may have circulated. The most likely possibility is that the images of Philip and his family were heavily gilded and/or painted either originally or at some later date.[115] This gilding, when combined with the natural aging and polishing of Parian stone, could have produced an image that appeared chryselephantine, an effect that would have been enhanced if the images were, in fact, heroizing or divinizing in appearance.[116] This idea was then fostered by local guides looking for something spectacular to say about the most historically significant monument on the site – an easy habit to get into when a tour or lecture demands a spectacular material correlate for a spectacular battle![117] The phenomenon of painting, gilding and polishing ancient marble is well known so this hypothesis is not particularly radical.[118] Praxiteles' gilded portrait of Phryne (Paus. 10.15.1) is probably the most relevant example, but certainly not the only one.[119] There may even have been something of a tradition of gilded Makedonian royal portraits upon which Philip based his decision. Alexander I set up gilded (not solid gold or chryselephantine) portraits of himself at Delphi and, more importantly, at Olympia itself.[120] Alexander III followed suit and seems to have ordered his generals to erect gilded (again, not solid gold or chryselephantine) portraits of himself at Delphi.[121] It is also worth remembering that the notion of secondary gilding is specifically attested within the context of Alexandrian portraiture when Nero had a fourth century B.C. portrait of the young king plated in gold (Plin. *NH* 34.63).[122] The use of gilding for the Argead dynasts seems to be the best one, reconciling as it does Pausanias' second-hand information, the clear evidence on the statue base and the archaeological comparanda.

This conclusion that Leochares' Argead portraits were gilded and/or heavily painted marble as opposed to gold and ivory need not affect the hypothesis that Philip and his family were shown in heroic or divine guise. Clearly, the materials from which the portraits were made represent only one factor among many in an argument for the restoration of heroizing or divinizing images. In any case, by the end of the fourth century B.C. the use of marble for portraiture may have had heroic connotations. This was certainly the case a generation later when the use of marble for portraiture (as opposed to bronze) had blatantly heroic or divine connotations.[123]

Setting

It remains only to comment briefly on the Philippeion itself. The architectural setting of Leochares' Argead portraits contributed greatly to the significance of the sculpture group.[124] At Olympia, a sanctuary in which portraits had been dedicated under the open sky for centuries, the creation of a closed, exclusive architectural zone for the display of the Argead dynasts was unique. In many ways, the significance of the Philippeion can be seen to rest in this simple fact. The elaborate venue for Leochares' images – by its very existence – divided and distinguished the Argead dynasts from the hundreds of other portraits that had been dedicated at Olympia in the past. Simply by virtue of their placement within the tholos, the portraits made a powerful statement. The significance of later galleries for other groups of heroized portraits, like the rectangular gallery that held Daochos' family at Delphi for example, can also be understood in this manner.[125] The architecture framed and emphasized the royal images, elevating them above the common throng of votive portraiture.

But even if the architecture is understood as an elite gallery, the Philippeion hardly had to be designed as a tholos. What motivated the decision to place Leochares' portraits in a *round* building? Here it is worth considering other readings that have been given for the Philippeion's architecture. To begin, there seems to be little doubt that the Philippeion could be understood as a victory dedication and thank offering to Zeus.[126] It is also possible that the Philippeion's architecture may have communicated the general idea of "treasury" (even though it now seems clear that the building's primary function was not to protect chryselephantine images) or even "pan-Hellenic headquarters" (an old idea based on false analogy with the tholos in Athens).[127] While there seems to be no unequivocal evidence for cult in connection with the building, the urge to understand the Philippeion's architecture as communicating the idea of "heroön" is also very strong, and probably correct on some level if the Argeads were shown in heroic or old-fashioned costume.[128]

While all these readings of the Philippeion are interesting, the difficulty with them is that the defining characteristic of the tholos – its *circular* plan – does not play a central role in defining the architecture's meaning. Indeed, since Townsend has now shown that the Philippeion's form as a whole must be broadly understood as a text to be decoded and unpacked, the *roundness* of the tholos should have at least something to do with the architecture's significance.[129] In this context, it is must be admitted that the Philippeion's status as a victory dedication is not uniquely communicated, or even emphasized, by the tholos form. By the same token, treasuries were consistently rectangular, not round.[130] While the Philippeion's circular architecture may have recalled a Mycenaean tholos tomb (and thus hinted at the heroic past) the vast majority of known, monumentalized heroa from the Geometric period and later were polygonal not circular.[131] In the end, the characterizations of the Philippeion as a victory monument, a treasury, or a heroön do not seem to fully explain the defining circularity of the tholos nor why this form was chosen as the appropriate locus for the presentation of the Argead dynasts.

One alternative idea that might move the discussion forward would be if the Philippeion's round architecture could be understood as a straightforward *theatron* – literally a place for seeing – or more specifically, a place for spectacle. Indeed, if other symbolic readings of the building's architecture are necessary, they could all be built on top of the practical and fairly mundane idea that by the second quarter of the fourth century B.C., tholoi (and round spaces generally) had become the ideal spaces for the spectacle and display. While the Philippeion obviously was not open to the air like a fourth century B.C. Greek theater, it was still a monumentalized orchestra and its design was based upon an identical circular geometry. All of this may have factored into the building's design. The formal significance of the Philippeion's round architecture, to come full circle, may be nothing more than a simple expression of its simple function as a space for the presentation of Leochares' votive portraits.

Now this notion of circular spaces as ideal zones for sculptural display seems to originate in the early fifth century B.C. with the invention of semi-circular statue bases and their inscribed *theatra*. As noted above, Ajootian has shown how the semi-circular base of the Achaian dedication at Olympia, and others like it, were designed to facilitate the viewer's entry into a narrative zone that was blatantly heroic and theatrical.[132] Equally important here are other important fifth and fourth century B.C. semi-circular bases that were set within their own, distinct architectural contexts. The semi-circular bases within the choregic monuments in the Dionysion at Thasos (Fig. 23) and the semi-circular statue base inside the "dynastic" Monument to the southwest of the Daochos Monument in Delphi (Fig. 24) are only the best known examples.[133] In these instances, the function and significance of the semi-circular statue bases was, as Borbein showed regarding the choregic monuments on Thasos, patently *dramatic* in the full Greek sense of the word while the buildings that framed these bases were designed to protect the sculpture from the elements and to provide a setting within which the theatrical tableau might be observed.[134] Even more important is the fact that, at least in the case of the Thasian monuments, the statues set on these semi-circular bases were not simple portraits but rather images of gods and personifications. The same might be said of the Philippeion. The building performed the same theatrical function as the galleries noted above and may have communicated the same notion of elevated status for the images set within it. The distinction between the Philippeion and other fourth and third century B.C. galleries is that the round form of the tholos, in contrast to the rectangular buildings noted above, followed the shape of the base and thus hinted at the building's function. In this sense, then, the building was designed from the inside out.

Of course, the Philippeion was not the only early Hellenistic tholos to be used as a *theatron*. The tholos on the highest terrace of Knidos – excavated by Iris C. Love in the late 1960s and early 1970s – was almost certainly designed for the specific display of Praxiteles' Knidian Aphrodite (Fig. 25).[135] While the function and date of the Knidian tholos has become somewhat (and maybe

Fig. 23. Plan of the Dionysion on Thasos showing the choregic monuments statue bases, late fourth century B.C. (Drawing by David Boggs 2006)

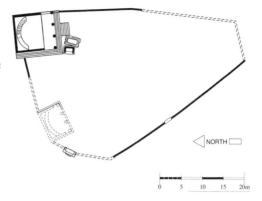

Fig. 24. Plan of the "dynastic" Monument at Delphi, ca. 325 B.C. (Drawing by David Boggs 2006)

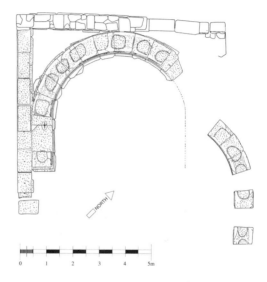

needlessly) controversial since Hansgeorg Bankel's 1997 re-study of the monument, the famous testimony of Pliny (*NH* 36.21) and Pseudo-Lukian (*Amores* 13-4) is strong, unambiguous and cannot be lightly dismissed.[136] Both authors stress the importance of the theatrical setting within which the image was placed and the manner in which the tholos specifically facilitated viewing. For Pliny (*NH* 36.21): "the whole of its small temple is open, so that the likeness ... can be seen from every side. The same wonder is provoked from every view." While for Pseudo-Lukian (*Amores* 13-4): "the temple has doors on both sides, for those who want to see the goddess in detail from the back, in order that no part of her be wondered at. So it is easy for men entering at the other door to examine the beautiful form from behind." The Knidian tholos was a *theatron* – it was a display space.[137] (Interestingly, Giorgio Ortolani has now shown that an identical concern dictated the design of the Roman copy of the

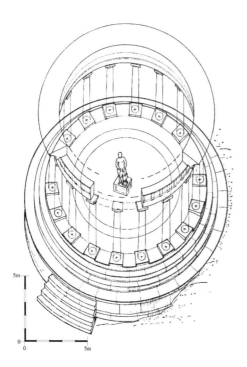

Fig. 25. Reconstuction of the temple of Aphrodite Euploia on Knidos, ca. 350-330 B.C. (?)(Drawing by David Boggs 2006, after Love 1972, fig. 9)

Knidian tholos in Hadrian's Villa at Tivoli.[138]) Praxiteles' sculpture was meant to be viewed from all sides – the goddess was situated to be seen – and the tholos' circular form both facilitated and communicated this idea.

The theatrical viewing demanded by the Knidian Aphrodite was hardly unique in the early Hellenistic period. Indeed, a concern with fully three-dimensional sculpture and the need to view and appreciate these objects in the round is one of the most well known aesthetic concerns of fourth century B.C. sculpture.[139] More importantly, if the traditional date and function of the Knidian tholos are correct, then Leochares could have been directly inspired by the temple/theatre there. Leochares knew Praxiteles, he was active in Karia and the moldings on his statue base in the Philippeion can be directly traced through a Knidian prototype as was noted above.[140] The chain of influence is firm. That the Knidian tholos held the image of a goddess should not damage this hypothesis, especially if Philip and his family were shown in heroic or divinizing guise. By the early 330s B.C., there would have been nothing surprising about a tholos used as a gallery for the display of heroic, semi-divine or divine figures. That an architectural frame of this sort would have reinforced the overall heroic and/or divine sense of the images (whatever they looked like) seems obvious.

The Philippeion's famous descendant, the Lysikrates Monument (Fig. 26), provides another good example of a tholos being used as a *theatron*, albeit in somewhat different manner. The comparison is relevant since it is well

Fig. 26. The Lysikrates Monument in Athens, 335/34 B.C. (Drawing by David Boggs 2006, after Bauer 1977, pl. 9)

known that the little building was intimately connected to the Philippeion on stylistic and typological grounds.[141] In terms of function and significance (beyond advertising Lysikrates' victory in the boys' dithyramb in 335/4 B.C.) the small building's purpose was to facilitate the exhibition of Lysikrates' tripod and, more importantly, the statue of Dionysos that the monument contained. The small tholos was designed as a miniature *theatron*. Critical here, of course, is Heinrich Bauer's demonstration that the Lysikrates Monument was originally designed to encourage the view of the statue of Dionysos from all sides. The panels which now close the bays between the monument's columns were added only later as support for the entablature.[142] The building was designed to be walked around and the image within intended to be scrutinized from multiple vantage points. This is proved by the design of the frieze. While the primary view of the statue was from the east, Wolfgang Ehrhardt has now shown that the frieze's full narrative can only be understood *via* circumnavigation.[143] In other words, the monument itself promoted a very particular sort of behavior on the part of the ancient viewer: the tholos forced the audience to walk *around* the image that it contained.

Here again, it is the peculiar and defining *circularity* of the tholos form that lends itself to the framing of fully realized sculpture. More important, however, is the fact that the connection between the Lysikrates Monument and the Philippeion is secure and that there is no question that one purpose of the former was to serve as an architectural setting for the display of a free standing sculptural monument. Since Leochares' presence in Athens during the 330s B.C. and later is certain, the possibility that the two monuments could have been governed by similar aesthetic concerns hardly seems strange. Again, that the little tholos held an image of a god seems very much in line with the possible heroic or divine depictions of the Argead dynasts.

But what of the Philippeion's two most famous predecessors, the tholoi at Epidauros and Delphi?[144] Here as well, the notion of circular tholoi as spaces designed for divine spectacle – or maybe it should be said *epiphanies* – seems to manifest.

Pausanias (2.27.3) saw important paintings by the fourth century B.C. painter Pausias in the tholos at the Asklepieion at Epidauros.[145] At least in Roman times, the Epidaurian tholos was used for display or presentation, although Pausias' fourth century B.C. date suggests that this function could have been original. Also supporting an original, theatrical function for the Epidaurian tholos are the fourth century building inscriptions (e.g. *IG* IV² 103) that call the building the *thymelē*. From the end of the fifth century B.C. onward (Pratin. fr. 708.2 P.), *thymelē* had blatantly theatrical connotations – specifically with song and dance – and signified the orchestra or the altar to Dionysos set therein.[146] Later, in the Hellenistic and Roman periods (Phrynichos 142; Plut. *Vit. Alex.* 67; *Vit. Dem.* 12) the word specifically meant theatre or stage. The possibility that the tholos at Epidauros was called the *thymelē* in the accounts simply as a means to distinguish it from the theater proper deserves serious thought.

Of even greater interest in this specific context is the fact that some would see the *thymelē* as the locus for the performance for the renowned Epidaurian paeans.[147] This controversial hypothesis is far beyond the scope of the current paper but even so, there is no doubt that Epidaurian tholos' strange basement when combined with the hole in the center of its floor transformed the entire building into a mighty acoustical chamber perfectly suited for the performance of the well-known hymns to Asklepios.[148] Again, it is the *circularity* of the tholos – this time as an ideal acoustical zone – that made it the perfect space for divine spectacle.

The famous tholos in the sanctuary of Athena Pronaia at Delphi also seems to have been designed for display and, in Pausanias' day (10.8.4), held imperial portraits placed on the wide shelf that supported the tholos' interior colonnade. In 1988, Georges Roux argued convincingly that this shelf was originally designed to hold sculpture, possibly images of deities, and that the Delphic tholos was designed from the beginning as a sort of gallery or spectacle-space.[149] Again, like the tholos at Epidauros, the tholos at Delphi would have provided the perfect locus for the performance of the famous paeans to Apollon, even if it is missing the fully developed underground resonance chamber seen in its slightly later Peloponnesian cousin.[150] While these observations prove nothing regarding the theatrical function of the Philippeion, they do show that the two poorly understood tholoi at Epidauros and Delphi could be read in a similar manner. At the very least, Pausanias' testimony regarding these two fourth century B.C. buildings – the only literary evidence available regarding their function – does not stand against the hypothesis that the Philippeion was conceived primarily as a space designed for viewing and displaying divine or heroic images.

By the middle of the fourth century, it seems possible to understand monumental tholoi as the ideal architectural settings for the divine spectacles of the age. Indeed, if this reading of these buildings is correct, then the notion of tholos as sacred viewing place might even have been a bit dated by the time Leochares sculpted the Argead dynasts in ca. 338-336 B.C.; the sculptor may simply have been operating within a fashionable new architectural tradition.[151] In other words, for the Athenian master, the notion of tholos as locus for divine display may not have been revolutionary. It may have been expected.

Now it is freely admitted that this hypothesis raises a number of interpretive problems and possibilities that require sustained treatment. These will be dealt with in detail at a later date. Even so, it might be useful to speculate how the idea of tholos as viewing place (like the Knidian tholos or the Lysikrates Monument) or spectacle space (like the tholoi at Epidauros and Delphi) was generated by fourth century B.C. sculptors and architects within the sphere of the plastic arts.

Three interconnected developments seem relevant. First, it is well known that the sculptors of the fourth century B.C. grew increasingly interested in fully three-dimensional compositions as the century progressed. Indeed, an obsession with three-dimensional form, characterized most famously by the work of Lysippos, a point made earlier, is one of the hallmarks of middle fourth B.C. century sculpture.[152] Second, it is equally well known that fourth century sculptors often did double duty as architects. The examples of Skopas (Paus. 8.45-7), Pytheos of Priene (Vitr. *De arch.* 7.pr.12-3; Plin. *NH* 36.30-1), Satyros of Paros (Vitr. *De arch.* 7.pr.12-3; Plin. *NH* 36.30-31) and Polykleitos the Younger (Paus. 6.6.2, 2.27.5) are only the most obvious examples. The exchange of ideas between the two disciplines was thus fluid and dynamic. Sculptural concerns were translated directly into architecture (and vice versa) while theories of vision and reception were readily passed between two fields the distinctness of which is almost wholly a modern construct. Finally, it is now clear that the development of the circular orchestra of the Greek theatre should also be dated to the middle of fourth century B.C. This point has been finally demonstrated by Clifford Ashby, Floris van den Eijnde and now Rush Rehm.[153] In this period of increasingly sophisticated ideas, it seems possible to suggest that the sculptor-architects of the age saw a new potential in the tholos form, namely that the tholos perfectly facilitated the framing and view-ing of fully three-dimensional art. While this notion of tholos as spectacle space is separated here (for the purposes of analysis) from the broader aes-thetic concerns of early Greek cult, music and theatre, a holistic interpretation of the fourth century B.C. Greek tholos could not make such distinctions. Indeed, it seems possible that the development of the Greek tholos as divine *theatron* can be shown to spring precisely from the hyper-intellectualized at-mosphere of fourth century B.C. art and cult as an indivisible whole. In this sense, the tholos represents an ideal architectural response to the new and far reaching aesthetico-religious concerns of the early Hellenistic period.

It is difficult to exclude Leochares from this matrix of ideas. Indeed, the master's presence at Halikarnassos along with Praxiteles and Skopas (Plin. *NH* 36.30) makes it certain that the Athenian sculptor was up to date with current aesthetic thought. This seems to be demonstrated by the Philippeion itself. Cleverly playing with ancient expectations, viewers entering the Philip-peion's theatrical realm became both spectator and spectacle. On one hand, the semi-circular statue base and the portraits themselves, when set in their circular frame, were meant to be circumnavigated and inspected on all sides. The statue base in the Philippeion was separated from the tholos' rear wall by over one meter so that it could be walked around. The base was also carefully finished on both front and rear and was meant to be seen from all sides. In this sense, the building's design facilitated the dramatic and holis-tic display of Leochares' Argead dynasts. The traditional patterns of theatri-cal viewing – seen first in the tholos at Knidos and, later, the Lysikrates Monument in Athens – were retained. The tholos could be seen as a straight forward gallery, a *theatron* in which Leochares' Argead dynasts were observed as heroic or divine actors performing on the stage of the world.

At the same time, however, it seem equally clear that when standing in the center of the tholos, the spectators themselves were metaphorically ob-served by the Argead dynasts and that Philip and his family were transformed into a divine or heroic audience. In this sense, the arrangement of the Philippeion represents an interesting inversion of the usual patterns of theatrical viewing. In this *theatron*, spectators entered and observed but were then simultaneously subjected to symbolic scrutiny. The enclosed space of the Philippeion emphasized the size of the Makedonian dynasts and controlled a spectator's distance from the images. Unlike the tholos at Knidos or the Lysikrates Monument, but very much like the tholos at Delphi, the Philippeion's round architecture and semi-circular base enclosed and encircled the viewer, making them subject to the royal, divine gaze of Philip and his family. The blatantly political (and possibly religious) intent of the monument could not have been more perfectly communicated. With a stroke, Leochares' portrait group was transformed into the eternal audience and the heroic lords of all they could see and it was precisely the tension and suspension of the traditional categories of "divine" image and mortal viewer that promoted the overall effect.

Now, the appropriate response demanded from a fourth century B.C. Greek as he or she stood before the Argead dynasts – the potentially rich (but at present speculative) *performative* functions of the Philippeion and the manner in which this contributed to total religious, political and propagandistic effect of the monument – is still under investigation.[154] One final topographical point, however, can be made. One neglected facet of the Philippeion's design and placement in Olympia is the building's position in relation to what has traditionally been seen as the massive altar of Zeus.[155] Since most scholars now favor an eastern facing door for the Philippeion – a door that opened on a direct axis with Zeus's altar – this line should be allowed to effect the possible significance of the building. A Zeus-like Philip and his heroic family standing on axis with Zeus's altar would have left little to the imagination.

Acknowledgements:

I am grateful to the A.G. Leventis Foundation for supporting the initial research for this paper in the Fall of 2002, and to the State Scholarship Foundation of Greece (IKY) for facilitating the completion of research in the Fall of 2003 and the Spring of 2004. (Another version of this article – with less emphasis on the religious and iconographic ramifications of the speculative reconstruction introduced here and more detailed archaeological analysis – can be found in Schultz 2007a) It is also a pleasure to thank the following friends and colleagues who have discussed various aspects of this project with me: Richard Anderson, Brian Bosworth, Anne Marie Carstens, Antonio Corso, Dimitris Damaskos, Georgios Despinis, Sheila Dillon, Craig Hardiman, Ralf von den Hoff, Catherine Keesling, Lauren Kinnee, Michaelis Lefantzis, Barbara McCauley, Robin Osborne, John Pollini, Guy Sanders, Jan Sanders, David Scahill, Michael Scott, Edward Schmoll, Kris Seaman, Olin Storvick, Mary Sturgeon, Stephen Tracy, Bonna Wescoat and Cornelie Zanon.

Peter Schultz

I am particularly grateful to Klaus Herrmann (for generously sharing aspects
of his recent work on the Philippeion with me), to Bronwen Wickkiser (for
discussing with me the hymns of Asklepios and Apollon and for sharing
aspects of her forthcoming research on fourth century political paeans), and
to Spencer Pope (for examining and discussing the statue base and architecture of the Philippeion with me in Olympia during October of 2002). To
Chrys Kanellopoulos and David Boggs, whose drawings have increased the
value of this study beyond measure, I owe special debts. Talks with Chrys
in Olympia and in Athens during the years of 2001-2003 taught me a great
deal and provided the inspiration for many of the ideas explored below.
Discussions with David in Moorhead helped clarify numerous design issues,
particularly regarding the aesthetic relationship between Leochares' portraits
and the architecture of the Philippeion. I cannot thank these gentlemen
enough. Finally, I am happy to thank my students Maria Christodoulou,
Andrew Luxem and Takis Michaelidis who pointed out problems in the
manuscript and generated many useful (and provocative!) ideas.

In addition to the 2004 colloquium in Århus from which this article de-
rives, versions of this paper were presented in Athens in November of 2002
(at a colloquium organized by myself and Ralf von den Hoff entitled *Early
Hellenistic Sculpture: Image, Style, Context*), in Montréal in January of 2006 (at
the Archaeological Institute of America's Annual Meetings) and at Clemson
University in April of 2008 (at a colloquium entitled *Philip II and Alexander
III: Father, Son and Dunasteia. Fourth International Symposium on Alexander the
Great* organized by Elizabeth Carney) I am also grateful to Nancy Bookidis
for inviting me to present aspects of this paper in her seminar on the archaeology of Olympia at the American School of Classical Studies, Athens in
February 2004; comments from seminar participants Kirsten Day, Nigel Kennell, Stefanie Kennell, Phil Sapirstein and – especially – Laura Gawlinski
greatly improved the quality of the argument.

The research necessary for the completion of this paper could not have
been contemplated without the support of the Ephoria of Prehistoric and
Classical Antiquities at Olympia (Z'ΕΠΚΑ) and its director, Xeni Arapogi-
anni, who kindly gave me permission to photograph and draw the material
evidence. Finally, I am happy to extend my deepest thanks to Demosthenes
Giraud (Director of the Restoration of Ancient Monuments for the Greek
Ministry of Culture), Olga Palagia (Professor of Archaeology at the University of Athens), Andrew Stewart (Chancellor's Professor of Ancient Mediterranean Art and Archaeology at the University of California, Berkeley) and
Petros Themelis (Professor of Archaeology at the University of Krete, Re-
thymno) for their many solid observations on the argument offered below.
I owe them debts that I can never repay. All mistakes are mine. This article
is dedicated to Professor Olin Storvick: mentor, friend and inspiration.

Notes

1 The bibliography on the subject is vast. Smith (1988), Stewart (1993 and 2003), Svenson (1995) and Bergmann (1998) give solid overviews and bibliographies. The theory of Hellenistic kingship – particularly the significance of Hellenistic royal power – employed here is based on Smith (1988, 32-53), Stewart (1993) and Chaniotis (2003).

2 Stewart (1993, 121-209) gives the fundamental treatment of the image and its meaning.

3 *OGIS* 6, translated by Austin 1981, no. 32. For the decree and cultural context see Chaniotis 2003, 439.

4 Eponymous Heroes Monument, see Shear 1970.

5 Kroll 2007.

6 Tracy (1995, 7-23), Habicht (1997, 6-35), and Palagia & Tracy (2003) give current bibliographies and detailed treatments of the period.

7 The famous lacuna at 5.17.4 makes is impossible to claim certainty as to the specific identity of this "Eurydike." Kenneth D.S. Lapatin (2001, 117 n. 198 with comprehensive bibliography), however, has shown that Pausanias must refer to Philip's mother, not the wife of the mentally challenged Arrhidaios and certainly not Philip's last wife Kleopatra who changed her name to Eurydike after marriage. While Palagia (2008) has recently argued for this later identification, for the purposes of this paper, Lapatin's argument is assumed correct.

8 For the Philippeion generally: Bringmann & Steuben 1995, no. 329; Kotsidu 2000, no. 305 and Schmidt-Dounas 2000, 102-7. For Leochares: Stewart 1990, 282-4; Todisco 1993 103-7 and Muller-Dufeu 2002, 523-9. Interest in the monument has increased in recent years. Leochares' portraits have been discussed in a recent study of Hellenistic cult statues by Dimitris Damaskos (1999, 263-9), a survey of family portraits by Christoph Löhr (2000, 115-8), an important monograph treating chryselephantine sculpture by Lapatin (2001, 115-9) and a major new article treating the contexts and complexities of the Philippeion's architecture by Rhys Townsend (2003). Further study of the architecture for the purposes of *anastylōsis* was completed by Kostas Zambas and Gerasimos Thomas under the auspices of the Committee for the Restoration of Ancient Monuments and the Deutsches Archäologisches Institut in 2002 and a comprehensive investigation and re-study of all architectural elements is currently being completed by Klaus Herrmann and Hajo van de Löcht. (Reports prepared by Herrmann, van den Löcht, Zambas and Thomas – Στατική μελέτη για τμηματική αναστήλωση του Φιλιππείου στην Ολυμπία and Αίτηση για τμηματική αναστήλωση του Φιλιππείου στην Ολυμπία – are currently unpublished. They were generously made available to me by Demosthenes Giraud, Director of Restoration of Ancient Monuments for the Greek Ministry of Culture and by Klaus Herrmann, architect of the DAI.)

9 Schleif & Zschietzschmann's (1944, 51) original discussion of the base was cursory; Seiler's (1986, 98) was restricted to the base's relationship to the architecture.

10 For divided patronage of the Philippeion see, for example: Schleif & Zschietzschmann 1944, 2; Roux 1961, 404; Miller 1970, 179; Mallwitz 1972, 128; Borbein 1973, 66-7; Romano 1990, 71; Hintzen-Bohlen 1992, 29 with n. 119; Hu-

wendiek 1996, 156-7; Damaskos 1999, 266 n. 52; Löhr 2000, 116-7; Lapatin 2001, 116 and Jeppesen 2002, 170.

11 Momigliano 1987, 174-7.

12 Huwendiek 1996, 156-7.

13 Miller (1973, 191 n.11) and Seiler (1986, 101 n. 424) had previously shown that there is no architectural evidence for a break in construction.

14 Herrmann 2000, 386.

15 The presence of these bands indicates that the marble used in the base and in the floor is not Lynchnites, the finest quality Parian stone. This might be seen as another, indirect, indicator for hasty construction. Had the project been planned well in advance, stone of the highest quality could easily have been quarried and shipped to the site. I am grateful to Klaus Herrmann and Olga Palagia for discussing the Philippeion's Parian marble with me.

16 The Hephaisteion in Athens (Wyatt & Edmondson 1984; Barringer, forthcoming) and the temple of Apollon at Bassai (Palagia 2002a, 376-8), for example, both employ different marble types and both projects experienced significant breaks in construction. On the other hand, the Siphnian Treasury at Delphi (Daux & Hansen 1987, 26-32; Palagia & Herz 2002, 242) and the temple of Athena Nike on the Akropolis (Palagia 2000, 350) both use two different marble types (significantly, within their sculptural programs) and both seem to have been completed within short, single building phases. The employment of different marble types, therefore, can only suggest multiple phases for any given construction project; it cannot demonstrate the existence of such phases unconditionally (unless, of course, solid source data makes the contemporary or near contemporary harvest of the different marble types impossible). The question of marble source should therefore be seen as one piece of a larger data set.

17 Methodology: Bessac 1988, 49. Such a fine claw chisel work seems rare in architecture and is much more common in fourth century sculpture. The claw chisel on the grave stele of Aristonautes (Athens, NM 738), for example, had 5 teeth every 0.013 m, the claw chisel used on the Alkmaionid pediment at Delphi had 5 teeth every 0.015 m while the claw chisel used on the pediments at Tegea was very rough indeed with 3 teeth every 0.01 m. (Adam 1966, 18 and 20); all these chisels produced a coarser finish than that seen on the Philippeion's statue base and architectural details.

18 Adams 1966, 18-22, 115-8; Bessac 1988. Even today, the tools used by masons working for the Akropolis Restoration project are shaped by hand and produce a *very* unique finish. I am indebted to Richard Anderson, Demosthenes Giraud, Michaelis Lefantzis, Tassos Tanoulas and Stephen Tracy for discussing this point with me.

19 Early builders did not always employ a single style of clamp (much less a single *size* of a single style clamp) in their monuments. This fact makes the consistency of the pi-shaped clamps in the Philippeion (both in terms of style *and* size) all the more significant. "Early" Z-shaped clamps, for example, are mixed regularly with double-T clamps (as in the temple of Aphaia on Aegina, the Marathon base in front of the Treasury of the Athenians in Delphi, the lower Tarantine base at Delphi, the Argive niche of the Epigonoi at Delphi, the Hephaisteion, the temple of Apollon at Bassai, the hall of the Thessalians at Delphi

and the temple of Zeus Ammon in Kallithea, Chalkidiki), dove-tail clamps are mixed with pi-shaped clamps (as in the fourth century temple of Apollon at Delphi, the *temenos* of Zeus Soter at Megalopolis, the temple of the Athenians on Delos and the temple of Athena Nikephoros at Pergamon) and double-T clamps are used with almost all other clamps types (as in the Hephaisteion in Athens, the Temple of Apollon Patroos in Athens, the Stoa of the Asklepieion in Athens, the Telesterion in Eleusis, the Treasury of Kyrene at Delphi, the Doric propylon in the Sanctuary of the Great Gods on Samothrake and the tholos at Epidauros, among others). Martin (1965, 242-53; 256-8; 264-71; 274-7) gives complete lists and bibliographies. W.B. Dinsmoor Jr. (1980, 28) also gives many good examples of clamp mixing; I am indebted to David Scahill for this reference.

20 Bommelaer 1991, fig. 117 with corresponding references.

21 Damaskos (1999, 266 n. 52) gives a comprehensive treatment of the problem. Löhr (2000, 117) argues for the use of the proper dative based on the supposed problem of chronology (but see below). I am indebted to Brian Bosworth for sharing his thoughts on this question with me.

22 Schalles (1995, 667) and Löhr (2000, 117) have revived the old idea (Bötticher 1886, 343) that the tholos and portraits were sponsored by Alexander alone. While the archaeology (specifically, the fact that the building and base belong to one phase) is not precise enough to support or reject this hypothesis, there is one piece of physical evidence that strongly suggests exclusive Philippic patronage or, at the very least, an adherence to his original design.

23 Burford 1969, 55.

24 Palagia 2001, 167-75 and Fredricksmeyer 2003, 257 n. 18 with bibliographies.

25 Ellis 1976; Hammond & Griffith 1979, 500-1, 670; Hammond 1994, 40, 69, 114, 120, 158.

26 Burford 1969, 247 with bibliography.

27 Shoe 1936, 24.

28 See, for example, Hammond & Griffith 1979, 692, 694-5; Romano 1990; Lawton 2003, 122.

29 While consensus will never prove anything, architects Richard Anderson, Demosthenes Giraud, Chrys Kanellopoulos, Michaelis Lefantzis, David Scahill and Petros Themelis all support the arguments given above and believe that if the building was begun after Chaironeia then the Philippeion must have been completed prior to Philip's death in 336. Obviously, the fashioning of the portraits did not have to wait for the completion of the architecture. Work would have proceeded on them while the tholos was being constructed. If Hektoridas and his apprentices, for example, could complete a complex pedimental group of ca. twenty marble figures at the temple of Asklepios at Epidauros in less than eighteen months (*IG* 4² I, 102, BI 87-8, 109-10; Yalouris 1992; Schultz 2007a, 209-10 and 228 n. 19 and Schultz, forthcoming), Leochares and his crew could easily have completed a commission of five figures in two years.

30 Shoe 1936, 19.

31 Other stylistic connections between the Philippeion and the temple of Athena Alea at Tegea: the engaged half-columns of the interior of the Philippeion (similar with those in Athena Alea's cella; see Norman 1984, 176-9), the cyma reversa on the Philippeion's toichobate (similar to Athena Alea's external to-

ichobate; see Shoe 1936, 81) and the Korinthian capitals of the engaged colonnade (similar to those in the Athena Alea's cella; see Dinsmoor 1950, 236). I am indebted to Erik Østby for discussing these points with me.

32 Weickert 1913, 74-5; Schleif & Zschietzschmann 1944, 51. Compare the argument below with Miller 1970, 183-4 n. 379.

33 Norman 1984, 191-4; Voyatzis 1999, 155. Erik Østby kindly informs me that new stratigraphic evidence absolutely confirms a date for the temple in the second half of the fourth century.

34 The Idrieus relief: Waywell 1993; Gunter 1995 and Jeppesen 2002, 171 with bibliographies. Archaeological attested contact between Tegea and Karia: Stewart 1977, 95-103; Leventi 1993.

35 Waywell 1993.

36 Schleif & Zschietzschmann 1944, 51 n. 2. Knidian column base: Pontremoli & Haussoullier 1904, 160.

37 Schleif & Zschietzschmann 1944, 50-1; Miller 1970, 179 and 190-2; Miller 1973, 203-4 with n. 66; Townsend 2003, 94 n. 8.

38 Leochares' commissions at Halikarnassos: Plin. *NH* 36.30; Vitr. *De arch.* 7. pr.12-3, 2.8.11 (less certainly); Scheibler 1975; Waywell 1978, 79-84; Cook 1989; Waywell 1997; Rolley 1999, 307-8. Leochares' possible commission on Knidos: Ashmole 1951; Stewart 1990, 189, 191 and 284; Todisco 1993, 104, 106-7; Rolley 1999, 289-90. Ridgway (1997, 249, 332-3) rejects the connection.

39 Borbein 1973, 66-7; Seiler 1986, 91-2, 98; Hintzen-Bohlen 1990, 133; Kotsidu 2000, 431-2.

40 Semi-circular statue bases in the early Hellenistic period: Onians 1979, 157-60; Gruben 1982, 654 n. 60; Lauter 1986 149, 238-9; Thüngen 1994, 39-42; Schmidt 1995, 111-23; Steuben 1999. Portrait of Pandaites: Keesling 2003, 166, 176, 192 and 196. Portrait of Konon and Timotheos: Keesling 2007. Leochares' portrait of Pandaites and his family: Keesling 2007 with bibliography.

41 Achaian dedication: Ajootian 2003 with bibliography. Argive dedications: Jacquemin 1999, 314 with bibliography.

42 Borza 1982; Scaife 1989; Badian 1994; 1996, 11; Borza 1999, 5-8. The genealogy is also given in Euripides' *Archelaos* (Austin 1968, II.V.20.)

43 Palagia 1986; Bosworth 1988, 281-4; Stewart 1993, 57-8, 78-9, 158-61, 303-6; Stewart 2003, 40.

44 Leochares and Isokrates: [Plut.] *X orat.* 838d. Aristotle's Hymn to Excellence: Fredricksmeyer 2003, 255-6 and n. 7.

45 Hammond & Griffith 1979, 457-8, esp. 458 n. 1.

46 Hammond & Griffith 1979, 476-8, 616.

47 I am indebted to Brian Bosworth for discussing these points with me.

48 Miller 1970, 181; Price 1973; Lauter 1986, 137-8, 149, 238-9, fig. 45b. Schmidt-Colinet (1991, 43-6) also gives a useful discussion of the exedra in Pella; I am indebted to Craig Hardiman for this reference.

49 Wescoat 2003, 114-5.

50 Philip's presence in Delphi in 338 B.C.: Hammond & Griffith 1979, 615.

51 Ajootian 2003. Leochares' compostion in the Philippeion as *Schaubild*: Borbein 1973, 67; Seiler 1986, 92; Hintzen-Bohlen 1990, 133. Leochares' theatrical mentality, in so far as it can be known independently from the Philippeion: Todisco 1993, 105-6.

52 Ajootian 2003, 157-9. Borbein's (1973, 51-4) discussion of the encompassing, theatrical effects these semi-circular bases were meant to provoke within the context of the Thasian choregic monuments is fundamental. See also Onians 1979, 157-60; Gruben 1982, 664 n. 60; Lauter 1986 149, 238-9; Thüngen 1994, 39-42, 183 and Schmidt 1995, 111-23. Foucault's famous concept of the *hetero-topia*, a theatrical space artificially separated from the normal constraints of time (usually "storing time" like a museum or memorial) might also be relevant here (Foucault 1986).

53 Seiler 1986, 91: "Beim Philippeion konzentriert sich die materielle und künst-lerische Qualität auf die Ausstattung mit der chryselephantinen Statuengrup-pe des Leochares auf der reich verzierten Marmorbasis; das Bauwerk dient ihrer *Inszenierung* (my italics)." See also Borbein 1973, 67; Hintzen-Bohlen 1990, 133 and Kotsidu 2000, 431-2. Royal Makedonian interest, understanding and patronage of the theatrical arts in all their guises: Cohen 1997, 156-9.

54 See, for example, Schleif & Zschietzschmann 1944, 51-2; Hitzl 1995, 12; Lapatin 2001, 116.

55 Saatsoglou-Paliadeli 1993; 1996. Drougou and Saatsoglou-Paliadeli 2000, 28-31. For the sanctuary of Eukleia generally: Saatsoglou-Paliadeli 1987.

56 I am indebted to Andrew Luxem for providing these dimensions.

57 The presence of this pry cutting (along with the fact that no other evidence for reuse or adjustment can be observed on the base blocks) seems to demonstrate that the entire base was not disassembled when the portraits of Olympias and Eurydike were transferred to the Heraion. Only the statues themselves were moved. Lapatin's (2001, 116) good observation that **B1** and **C5** displayed slight-ly different patterns of weathering before they were cleaned is absolutely cor-rect but, in my opinion, does not translate into multiple phases for the base. The fact that no other traces of reuse or adjustment can be found on the crown or within the plinth cuttings also seems to rule out Hitzl's (1995, 11-2) otherwise interesting hypothesis that portraits of Nero and Messallina were placed in the Philippeion and substituted for the Argead women sometime in A.D. 66-67 during the emperor's athletic tour of Greece. Such modification of the upper surface of the crowns would have left easily discernable physical evidence; compare, for example, Shear 1970, 163-5, fig. 8 and Themelis 2000, 68-9, figs. 55-7.

58 So Lapatin 2001, 116. With regards to the composition, Lapatin (2001, 107-9) has persuasively proposed a similar placement of Leto and Artemis on the ends of the semi-circular statue base in the Athenian temple on Delos. There, he suggested that the two goddesses framed Apollon and, possibly, his four Io-nian sons. The existence of this divine "dynasty" on an architecturally framed semi-circular base would not have been lost on Leochares.

59 Because of the irregularity of the beddings, these dimensions must be seen as very close approximations. To calculate square areas within these fields, the beddings were broken down into six (or more) rigid geometrical sub-units. All calculations are based on measurements taken independently by Chrys Kanel-lopoulos, Spencer Pope and myself in October 2002 and then again in March 2003.

60 Alexander also seems to have been physically small (Diod. Sic. 17.37.5, 17.66.3; Curt. 3.12.16, 7.8.9). This personal trait may have been employed as a form of

somatic individualization by at least one fourth century Attic sculptor in connection with Alexander's public image. The Alexander Rondanini's compact,
stocky physique (to be distinguished, of course, from scale) certainly seems to
point in this direction. Alexander Rondanini: Palagia 1980, 46-7 (for somatic
individualizations); Ridgway 1990, 113-6 (with an introduction to the debate
over the identity of the portrait); Stewart 1993, 113-21, 429 (for the fourth century B.C. date, the traditional identification and bibliography) and von den
Hoff 1997 (for a spirited revival of Schwarzenberg's 1976 thesis that the Rondanini Alexander is not Alexander but rather Achilleus). Since Alexander had
styled himself since childhood as the new Achilleus (Stewart 1993, 78-86; Cohen
1995; 1997, 106-12; Palagia 2001, 192; Fredricksmeyer 2003, 256 n. 8 – the confusion over the portrait could thus be the result of successful propaganda), since
the pose is picked up by other early Hellenistic kings (Laubscher 1985, 336-7;
Smith 1988, 154, no. 10) and since the search for diminutive Achilleus has,
unsurprisingly, come up short, the traditional identification is here retained.

61 Kallithea Monument: Steinhauer 1998, 83-4.
62 Geominy 2007 with bibliography.
63 Much has been made regarding the presence of Olympias in Leochares' group.
Indeed, the queen's loss of favor in Pella at the end of 338 B.C. has been taken
by many (e.g. Hitzl 1995, 12; Huwendiek 1996, 156-7; Löhr 2000, 117) as proof
that Alexander was responsible for the completion of the monument. Why?
Because, it is reasoned, Philip could never have included his disenfranchised
wife amongst his honored family after she has been expelled from the capital
and had roused her brother, Alexander of Epeiros, to war against Makedon.
Fortunately, this line of argument has now been completely dismantled by
Elizabeth Carney (1992; 1994; 2000a, 212 with n. 45; 2000b, 24-5. See also Perez
1998a; 1998b; 2000 and Ogden 1999) who has shown how the notion sprang
from a Victorianesque misunderstanding of Makedonian royal marriage and
polygamy. (The hypothesis also fails to account for the archaeological data
discussed above which shows that the monument belongs to Philip not Alexander) Two further points are worth mentioning.

First, in terms of iconography, the presence of the Argead queens in the
Philippeion is obviously and directly based on Karian dynastic portrait groups
which always included images of women (the Maussolleion at Halikarnassos
is only the most obvious example, for which see Waywell 1978 and now Jeppesen 2002, 171-8). These prototypes were intimately familiar to both Philip and
Leochares. Any discussion of the Philippeion that ignores this obvious connection (and thus the blatant need for a consistent female presence in the dynastic
group) must be regarded with suspicion. From a purely art historical perspective, the presence of Olympias (and Eurydike) in the Philippeion is not surprising.

Second, *IG* II² 236, the famous copy of the alliance made between Philip and
the Greek city states in 338/7 B.C., specifies (ll. 11-2) that the cities swear to not
overthrow the kingdom of Philip or, importantly, his descendants. The durability of the treaty, in other words, was directly dependant upon the durability
(and the stability) of the Argead royal line. The Argead portraits at Olympia,
under construction while the treaty was being forged, testified to the strength,
longevity and stability of that dynasty and – by extension – the strength, lon-

gevity and stability of the treaty itself. In essence, both building and treaty reflect and reinforce identical Makedonian plans and their corresponding propaganda. The violent reactions to the news of Philip's death in 336 B.C. (Plut. *Vit. Phoc.* 16; *Vit. Dem.* 22; *Vit. Alex.* 11.1; *De Alex. fort.* 327c-d; Diod. Sic. 17.3.3-5; Justin *Apol.* 11.1.2-3), the false rumors of Alexander's demise in 335 B.C. (Arr. *Anab.* 1.7.1-3; Plut. *Vit. Alex.* 11.3; Diod. Sic. 17.8.2; Justin *Apol.* 11.2.7-8) and the tumult that followed Alexander's actual death in 323 B.C. show how quickly the pact could be set aside. That Philip would, for some reason, advertise possible weakness within of the Makedonian succession at the precise moment when its strength was most crucial to his agenda runs counter to everything we know of the Makedonian king. Not only was Olympias' presence in the group unsurprising iconographically it was necessary politically. Her appearance in the Philippeion provides no basis whatsoever for an argument for Alexandrian patronage. Alliance and common peace: Adams 1999 with comprehensive bibliography. I am indebted to Robin Osborne for sharing a preliminary draft of his commentary on *IG* II² 236 and to Brian Bosworth for discussing these points with me.

64 Saatsoglou-Paliadeli 1993; 1996. Drougou and Saatsoglou-Paliadeli 2000, 28-31.

65 There is little reason to doubt the fact that this image is a portrait (Carney 2000a, 270 n. 28). Eukleia is never shown as an elderly, individualized woman nor is this particular personification normally shown in heavy, matronly garb (*LIMC* IV, s.v. *Eukleia*). That the inscription does not specifically name the image as portrait finds parallel, for example, in the near contemporary dedication on the statue base of the portrait of Nikokleia from Knidos (Eule 2001, 76-8, and now Dillon 2007).

66 Saatsoglou-Paliadeli 1987, 737 with n. 20. Many scholars – Greenwalt (1989, 42), Borza (1990, 192-3, 308-9); Mortensen (1992, 165) and Palagia (2002b, 4-5) – have pointed out an apparent problem with Saatsoglou-Paliadeli's date for the sanctuary in the early 330s B.C. The primary objection is that Eurydike seems to drop from historical record in 368/7 B.C. and that Aischines (2.28) does not mention her in his speech to Philip of ca. 346 B.C., a speech that specifically refers to the events surrounding her husband's death in the 360s B.C. If she had been alive, the argument goes, this omission seems strange.

67 Retrospective style associated with gods and heroes: Stewart 1979, 35 with n. 6; Ridgway 1997, 260, 328, 366. Stylistic retrospection generally: Fullerton 1990; 1998a; 1998b; 2003.

68 Attic workmanship: Drougou & Saatsoglou-Paliadeli 2000, 30-1. However, both Palagia and Themelis suspect local workmanship following an Attic style (personal communication). Attic influence on fourth century B.C. Makedonian culture generally: Stewart 2003, 34-5. Similar Attic influence on fourth century B.C. Makedonian architecture: Wescoat 2003.

69 Eirene: Boardman 1995, fig. 24 and Agnoli 1998 with bibliography; I am indebted to Antonio Corso for this reference. Connection between Eirene and Eurydike: Ridgway 1997, 347.

70 See, for example, the "Hestia Giustiniani" (Boardman 1991, fig. 74), the Demeters of Eleusis and Sparta (Palagia 1980, figs. 51-3) and the Torlonia Leto (Palagia 1980, figs. 58-9). The notion that the peplos possibly served as a divine or heroic signifier is not new. Böttiger (1794, 62), Müller (1878, 473) and Winckel-

mann (1968, 9), among others, all considered the peplos as the appropriate garb for heroines and goddesses. This hypothesis is now reviewed and supported by Mireille Lee (2000; 2001; 2003). Retrospective peplophoroi in fourth century B.C. sculpture: Palagia 1980, 26-7, ns. 126-31. See Dillon 2007 for other traditional early Hellenistic portraits of women and a comprehensive bibliography on heroizing/divinizing female costume.

71 Boardman 1995, 52; Palagia 1980, 27-30 with connections to Attic sculptors.

72 See now Perez 1998a, 1998b; 2000; Carney 2000a; 2000b for the image and importance of Eurydike in Pella and abroad.

73 Dillon 2007 and Geominy 2007.

74 See now Le Bohec-Bouhet 2002. I am indebted to Cornelie Zanon for this reference.

75 Schumacher 1990. See also Damaskos 1999, 265 n. 49.

76 *Anastolē*: Stewart 1993, 170 with n. 48. It should also be noted that the *anastolē* seen on these coins might also simply reflect fourth century B.C. iconography that connects the *anastolē* with wisdom and age, see Bergemann 1997, 113. Philip II and Zeus: Caltabiano 1999 and Kroll 2007.

77 Schmidt-Dounas 1993-94.

78 Habicht 1970, 14-6 and Schmidt-Dounas 1993-94.

79 Habicht 1970, 14-6. See also Bosworth 1988, 281 and Badian 1996, 13. Brian Bosworth kindly informs me that it is still his opinion that the derivation of a cult epithet from a mortal man may suggest that Zeus was fused with Philip and that they may have shared a joint cult.

80 The inscription is now in the Philippi Museum.

81 Ducrey 1988. This position is supported by Giallombardo 1999.

82 Hatzopoulos 1989, no. 473.

83 Chaniotis 2003, 434. See also Habicht 1970, 16; Walbank 1984, 90 and Pilhofer 2000, 167-9.

84 Pape 1975, 19 with n. 152.

85 Damaskos 1999, 264-5. The identifications of Priam and Nestor given to statues of "youths" (Dio Chrys. 37.43) do not necessarily stand against this hypothesis since we have no idea what these statues looked like. More importantly, see Keesling's (2007) discussion of Dion Chrysostom's treatment of these early Hellenistic portraits and the relationship between their original appearance and the appearance of the men and women they were used to represent.

86 Both Badian (1996, 13) and now Damaskos (1999, 266-7) have pointed out that this historical evidence does translate into proof for Philip's formal deification. Here, I see the debate over the existence of early ruler cult as distinct from the question of the divinizing image. The notion that a heavily constructed, "divinizing" royal portrait must somehow reflect pre-existing religious institutions seems problematic, especially when so little is understood about the origins of early Hellenistic "ruler cult" in the first place. It seems possible to argue that Philip self-consciously constructed his own *image* as "divine" – and thus utterly distinct from and above those he ruled (Smith 1988, 38-9; Stewart 1993, 95; Bergmann 1998, 26-40; Chaniotis 2003, 433) – without arguing that he called himself a god. But even so, see Pollitt 1986, 271-4; the patterns of intent are blurry and much will be gained as recent finds further complicate the picture. With regards to Philip's likeness nothing certain can be said, although many

have tried. Smith (1988, 147), Ridgway (1990, 141 n. 20) and, most vividly, Oikonomides (1989) give treatments of what evidence there is.

87 Stewart 1993, 161 n. 14. See also Stewart 1995, 258-60.

88 Alexander Doryphoros as purely Lysippan: Moreno 1974, 137; 1987a, 93; 1988, 259. Response: Smith 1988, 62; Stewart 1993, 161.

89 Stewart 1993, 162-71; 2003, 36-7.

90 Stewart 1993, 165-6 and 408 with comprehensive bibliography and discussion.

91 Himmelmann 1989, 99, 148; 1998, 156-86.

92 Himmelmann 1989, 94; Ridgway 1990, 135; Stewart 1993, 165 n. 30

93 So Stewart 1993, 166.

94 Bringmann & Steuben 1995, 406 and Kotsidu 2000, 432 with bibliographies.

95 Ridgway 1990, 135; Himmelmann 1989, 94; Stewart 1993, 165.

96 Schwarzenberg 1967, 74 ns. 91-2, 86-8; 1976, 250 n. 1.

97 In spite of the archaeological and iconographic evidence noted above – in particular the Schwarzenberg head's short hair – skeptics might see this association as hopelessly speculative. This may be. But it is no more speculative than other ideas that have circulated around this important portrait. Stewart (1993, 166) for example, would tentatively associate the Schwarzenberg head with a prototype of 334 B.C., while John Polini (personal communication) kindly informs me that, in his opinion, the piece is an Augustan period creation that can best be understood within the historical and aesthetic contexts of the end of the first century B.C. Olga Palagia (personal communication), on the other hand, has suggested that the piece is a modern forgery. Clearly, there is room for a wide range of opinion.

98 Polykleitan Doryphoros: Stewart 1997, 86-97 and Wesenberg 1997. For a fundamental revision of the piece's identity and appearance see Themelis 2000, 74-87; Franciosi 2003 (with comprehensive bibliography) and Themelis 2003, 126-8. For Makedonian concern with Argive models expressed in architectural terms, see Wescoat 2003, 114-5.

99 Hölscher 1971.

100 Stewart 1993, 164 and 168; 2003, 41.

101 Moltesen et al. 1995, 138-41, cat. no. 73.

102 Herrmann 1972, fig. 95; Stewart 1990, fig. 262; Boardman 1991, fig. 18.

103 Intellectualized fourth century B.C. art: Pollitt 1986, 13-6, 164-84; Moreno 1987b, 101-28; Stewart 1990; 2007; Schultz 2007b. Philip at Olympia: Hammond & Griffith 1979, 230, 246, 254, 307, 664, 685-98; Romano 1990.

104 Eckstein 1987, 249 n. 55 and now Jacquemin (2001, 296-7) who reaches the same conclusion independently.

105 Hitzl 1995, 12 n. 43.

106 Lapatin (2001, 116 n. 184) also noted the strangeness of the cuttings and the possibility that Pausanias made a mistake. He suggested that the chryselephantine statues may have been fashioned in an otherwise unknown technique, but did not offer comparanda. Professor Giorgios Despinis kindly expressed the same opinion privately to me in 2002 and has now published his remarks (Despinis 2004, 254-8) but, again, no archaeological comparanda is given. While the idea of a hybrid ivory/marble image seems quite possible (as Despinis has made absolutely clear), the lack of archaeological parallels makes me hesitate when a reasonable and very well attested alternative exists. More to the point,

even if this idea of ivory/marble portraits is accepted, it still must be acknowledged that Pausanias' testimony is incomplete. Thus the issue is methodological and epistemological – it is about why and how we choose to fill the inevitable gaps in his account.

107 Examples of identical plinth beddings dating from Archaic to Roman times are beyond number. A sample of famous fourth century monuments which preserve plinth bedding and marble statue: the Eleusis Asklepios (Adam 1966, pls. 50-1); the choregic dedications in the Dionysion on Thasos (Grandjean & Salviat 2000, figs. 46 and 48); the Daochos Monument at Delphi (Stewart 1990, figs. 552-3); the Vergina Eurydike (Drougou & Saatsoglou-Paliadeli 2000, fig. 30), the Themis of Rhamnus (Stewart 1990, fig. 602), the Demeter and Kore from Kallipolis (Themelis 1998, fig. 5) ... the list is almost endless.

108 Lapatin 2001, 105-9 with comprehensive bibliography.

109 Lapatin 2001, 63-79, esp. 70-3.

110 Lapatin 2001, 116.

111 I am indebted to Andrew Stewart for sharing this hypothesis with me. See also Habicht 1998, 112. Pausanias' preference of sacred to profane monuments: Habicht 1998, 23 with n. 91.

112 Habicht (1998, 146) refers, of course, to the tale of the fifth century B.C. Elean warrior whose body was miraculously found intact on the roof of the Heraion after 700 years.

113 Pritchett 1999, 82-95; Jacquemin 2001.

114 Habicht 1998, 28-63, 148-9.

115 Eckstein 1987, 249 n. 55. Dinsmoor (1950, 236) offered a similar solution to explain Pausanias's mistake with regards to the walls; he suggested that they were stuccoed and painted to look like brick.

116 For the polishing and care of votive portraiture, see Krumeich 2007.

117 Pausanias' (2.23.6) thoughts on the guides of Argos are worth remembering here: "The Argive guides themselves are aware that not all the stories they tell are true; yet they stick to them, for it is not easy to persuade common men to change their opinions." For other problems with Pausanias' guides, see Habicht 1998, 144-6.

118 Painting and gilding of ancient statuary and marble: Reuterswürd 1960; Tiberios et al. 2002; Artal-Isbrand et al. 2002 with bibliography. At the beginning of the nineteenth century, E.D. Clarke was told by members of the team working for Giovanni Battista Lusieri (Elgin's agent) that the artists drawing the pedimental sculpture of the Parthenon had observed traces of gilding on the statues along with traces of paint (Palagia 1993, 12). Neoptolemos of Melite also offered to gild an altar of Apollon in the Athenian Agora ([Plut.] *X orat.* 834f-44a); I thank Carol Lawton for this reference. *IG* I³ 343, l. 10 records a gilted kore in the treasures of the Parthenon. The personification of Messene seen by Pausanias (4.31.11) during his tour of the city is specifically described by the traveler as being made of gilded Parian marble. Since the practice is well known, this solution seems preferable to the idea that the portraits were crafted of ivory and marble.

119 Praxiteles's Phryne: Corso 1997 with bibliography.

120 Krumeich 1997, 25-7 with bibliography.

121 Stewart 1993, 413 with bibliography.

122 For other gilded Alexanders see Krumeich 2007. As noted above, it is also possible that the gilding of the portraits in the Philippeion took place at some later date.

123 Smith 1988, 15 with n. 6; Stewart 1998, 89; Damaskos 1999, 308-9. See also Dillon 2007; Geominy 2007 and Krumeich 2007.

124 Rhys Townsend's (2003) recent discussion of the Philippeion's architecture as signifying and symbolic matrix is fundamental. In the argument that follows, I assume familiarity with the ideas presented in that paper. It is also essential to note that Herrmann and van de Löcht's study for the purposes of *anastylōsis* has already revolutionized our conception of the Philippeion's design. More exciting information will be forthcoming in van de Löcht's final published study. For now, it is sufficient to point out that the new discoveries incorporated into Figs. 4-6 – such as the absence of evidence for windows in the Philippeion's cella (personal communication, Klaus Herrmann) and the reduction of the height of the elevation and Ionic colonnade by one drum length (personal communication, Klaus Herrmann) – have already effected the manner in which the portraits would have been seen. The absence of windows, for example, would have focused both light and attention – at least from outside the building – almost exclusively on the central figure Philip, while the reduction of column height has the inevitable effect of causing the portraits to appear larger in the correspondingly shorter space of the Philippeion's interior. (The significance of this last discovery cannot be overstated since my preliminary restorations of slightly over-life sized portraits in Schlief's original interior elevation seemed hopelessly small in their setting; van de Löcht's reduction of the building's height solved this problem immediately.) Also: Treatment of Stella Miller's (1970; 1973) hypothesis that the Philippeion architect may have been a Makedonian rather than an Athenian as previously supposed (Schleif & Zschietzschmann 1944; Dinsmoor 1950, 236; Roux 1961, 355) is outside the scope of the present paper. Here, I simply follow Seiler (1986, 91-3; see also Borbein 1973, 66-7 and Hintzen-Bohlen 1990, 133) in assuming that Leochares and the Philippeion architect (whoever he was) did not consider their works as distinct projects. This idea is supported by the evidence reviewed in part one of this paper. Like the sculpture of the Parthenon or the Maussolleion at Halikarnassos, the sculpture of the Philippeion was an integral part of the finished ensemble. As such, the sculptor would have been consulted on all points that effected the final presentation of the images.

125 Hellenistic portraits galleries: Lembke 2000; Adams 2002, 39-40 and Jeppesen 2002, 170-82 with bibliographies. See also Geominy 2007.

126 See, for example, Roux 1984, 169; Lapatin 2001, 117; Townsend 2003, 93-4.

127 Treasury: Townsend 2003, n. 14 and Krumeich 2007. Pan-Hellenic headquarters: Dörpfeld cited by Schleif & Zschietzschmann 1944, 2 and Hammond & Griffith 1979, 694. The argument was dismantled by Miller (1973, 191-2).

128 Philippeion as heroön: Habicht 1970, 140-1; Borbein 1973, 66-7; Green 1991, 80-2; Caltabiano 1999, 201-2, all with bibliographies. See Krumeich 2007 on the lack of evidence for cult.

129 Townsend 2003.

130 Treasuries at Delphi: Bommelaer 1991, fig. 4 and plans 2-3 and Partida 2001 with comprehensive bibliography. Treasuries at Olympia: Kaltsas 1997, fig. 14 with references.

131 See, for example, the rectangular temple/heroön of Herakles at Dodone (Dakaris 1993, 19-20), the trapezoidal heroön of Pelops at Olympia (Kaltsas 1997, fig. 14; Whitely 2001, 155), the rectangular heroön of Helen and Menelaos at Therapne near Sparta (Antonaccio 1995, 155-66), the triangular heroön at the west gate of Eretria (Bérard 1970), the rectangular heroön of Phrontis(?) at Sunion (Antonaccio 1995, 166-9) and the pentagonal shrine of Archemoros at Nemea (Antonaccio 1995, 176-7). Even so, it cannot be denied that Bronze Age tholos tombs functioned as the locus for hero and/or ancestor cult from at least the eighth century (Morris 1988; Alcock 1991 and now Huguenot 2003 with comprehensive bibliography) or that this practice continued well into the Roman period. The possibility that a connection exists between fourth century B.C. tholoi and those of the Greek Bronze Age might repay systematic investigation.

132 Ajootian 2003, 157-9. See also Onians 1979, 157-60; Borbein 1973, 51-4; Gruben 1982, 654 n. 60; Lauter 1986 149; 238-9; Thüngen 1994, 39-42; 183; Schmidt 1995, 111-23.

133 The choregic monuments in the Dionysion at Thasos: Grandjean & Salviat 2000, 92-4 with bibliography. The "dynastic" Monument at Delphi: Jacquemin 1999, 367 with bibliography. Schmidt-Colinet 1991 and Turner 1994 give bibliographies.

134 Borbein 1973, 53-4.

135 Love 1972 with bibliography. The Knidian Aphrodite and its theatrical setting: Borbein 1973, 188-94; Corso 1988, 42-6; Ajootian 1996, 98-103, esp. 102-3 with bibliography. Seaman (2004) gives a holistic treatment of the image and its art historcial contexts.

136 Bankel (1997) argued that the Knidian tholos was a temple of Athena and has dated the tholos to later in the second century B.C., but he failed to mention the discovery of an important third century B.C. decree (Blümel 1992, 105) pertaining to the cult of Aphrodite found directly outside the tholos. Corso (2000) gives a good summary of the evidence with the arguments for the traditional identification; Seaman (2004, ns. 84-90) gives a comprehensive bibliography.

137 Osborne 1994, 81-5; Stewart 1997, 97-106.

138 Ortolani 1998.

139 Osborne (1994, 82-3) and Stewart (1997, 100-3) have both stressed the explicit sexual drives that seem to have motivated the circular architectural and theatrical contexts of the Knidian Aphrodite. These important observations, of course, must be read within the context of the broad aesthetic concerns of fourth century B.C. sculptors. Skopas' Maenad (Stewart 1990, fig. 547; in which three-dimensional viewing is encouraged by formal torsion), Lysippos' Herakles (Stewart 1990, fig. 566; in which three-dimensional viewing is encouraged by narrative action) and the Aphrodite Kallipygos (Boardman 1995, fig. 82; in which three-dimensional viewing is encouraged by a combination of formal torsion, narrative action and visual/sexual titilation) are only the most well known examples within which full, circular viewing was stressed and ex-

pected by fourth century B.C. sculptors. I am indebted to Robin Osborne and Andrew Stewart for discussing this point with me.

140 Antonio Corso's (2000, 230) comparison of the fourth century B.C. Korinthian capital found in the Knidian tholos and the Korinthian capitals of the temple of Athena Alea at Tegea also deserves careful consideration. The connection between the Philippeion and the Tegean temple is firm and the possibility of the fourth century predecessor has been suggested. See also Stewart 1997, 97.

141 McCredie 1984 and Townsend 2003, 94 n. 8 and 98-9.

142 Bauer 1977, 204.

143 Ehrhardt 1993, 47-52 and figs. 1-4.

144 Delphi: Seiler 1986, 56-72. Epidauros: Seiler 1986, 73-89.

145 That the paintings seemed to have communicated explicitly musical and/or Dionysiac themes seems significant. Lynn LiDonnici (1995, 12) provocatively suggests that the paintings denote an artistic or, more importantly, musical function of the building. I am indebted to Bronwen Wickkiser for this reference.

146 See LSJ s.v. θυμέλη. That the word might also mean "burning place" does not effect this hypothesis since the firing of braziers during paeans and processions has a history that continues well into modern Greek religion.

147 A fully developed version of this hypothesis, which seeks to holistically reframe the famous paeans of Asklepios and Apollon within the aesthetic, architectural and political contexts of fourth century B.C. Pan-Hellenic shrines, is currently being pursued as a collaborative study by Chrys Kanellopoulos, Bronwen Wickkiser and myself. Preliminary reports: Kannelopoulos 2006; Schultz 2006 and Wickkiser 2006. For Epidaurian paeans and paeans generally see Wilamowitz-Moellendorf 1886; Käppel 1992; Rutherford 2001, esp. 41.

148 At the very least it seems clear that Polykleitos the Younger, supposedly the architect of both theater and *thymelē*, was obsessed with complex acoustic effects.

149 Roux 1988, 294. See also Miller 1973, 214 and Seiler 1986, 63-4. Lerat's (1985) reading of the Delphic tholos as a display case for elaborate armor placed on the broad shelf also works well with this hypothesis.

150 Brommelaer 1991, 67. Paeans at Delphi: CA 141-8, 149-59 and 165-71. See also Stewart 1982; Bélis 1988; Käppel 1992, 207-90 and Rutherford 2001. I am indebted to Bronwen Wickkiser for these references.

151 For the late fourth century B.C. architectural avant-garde see: Townsend 2003.

152 For the transformation of this idea in the late fourth and early third centuries, see Geominy 2007. In this context, Charles Edwards' (1996, 153) beautiful description of Lysippos' contribution to the principles of motion in middle fourth century B.C. sculpture is worth quoting in full: "What we might call Lysippos' contribution, is his study of motion and how motion is perceived in sculpture. Shifts in weight, unsteady poses, arms that change direction, risings from bent postures, even rocking, are experiments in movement which had never been explored so thoroughly. In order that the viewer appreciate the movement, the composition of a Lysippan statue refuses to resolve itself into a single, primary viewpoint from which everything can be understood. We keep moving, looking for the front, when there is none. By forcing the viewer to be con-

stantly on the move, the illusion of movement in a statue is increased. Lysippos knew that. Maybe we would do best to translate the quote from from Lysippos in Pliny simply and literarily: older sculptors made men as they are, he made them as they are seen to be." The tholos as *theatron* seems perfectly suited to facilitate this sort of aesthetic concern.

153 Ashby 1999, 25-6; Van den Eijnde 2000, 11-2, 103-8; Rehm 2002, 37-41, esp. 39 n. 17 with bibliography.

154 The possibility that paeans were sung in the tholoi at Epidauros and Delphi raises the possibility that similar hymns were sung in the Philippeion, an idea, which would further substantiate the idea that the building was the locus for divinizing imagery. Unlike these two tholoi, however, there is no primary evidence that can be used to support this conclusion. Even so, it does seem significant that beginning in the fourth century B.C. paeans were sung to men, particularly generals and kings who had received heroic or divine honors (Cameron 1995, 291-5 and now Chaniotis 2003, 431-2). The earliest paean of this sort seems to have been sung for Lysander at the beginning of the fourth century B.C. (ca. 400 B.C., Plut. *Vit. Lys.* 18; Athen. 15.695e). This famous example is followed by paeans to Hermeias (ca. 344 B.C., Athen. 15.696a-7b), Antigonos the One-Eyed (ca. 306 B.C.; Athen. 15.697a), Demetrios Poliorketes (ca. 306 B.C. and again ca. 291 B.C., Athen. 6.252f-3d, 15.697a), and Ptolemy Soter (ca. 304 B.C., *FGH* 515 F 19). Considering what is now known of Philip's own status, does it seem likely that he would have allowed himself to be outdone by Lysander or, even worse, Hermeias? Clearly, more investigation is warranted. The picture will become much more vivid.

155 But see now Rambach 2002.

Bibliography

Adams, N. 2002. "Another Hellenistic Royal Portrait from the Temple of Apollo at Cyrene?" *LibSt* 33: 29-44.

Adam, S. 1966. *The Technique of Greek Sculpture in the Archaic and Classical Periods*. British School of Archaeology at Athens Suppl. 3. London: Thames and Hudson.

Adams, W.L. 1999. "Philip II, the League of Corinth and the Governance of Greece." In *Ancient Macedonia 6.1, Papers Read at the Sixth International Symposium held in Thessaloniki, October 15-19, 1996*, 15-22. Institute for Balkan Studies 272. Thessaloniki: Institute for Balkan Studies.

Agnoli, N. 1998. "L'Eirene di Kephisodotos nella replica da Palombara Sabina." *XeniaA* 7: 5-24.

Ajootian, A. 1996. "Praxiteles." In *Personal Styles in Greek Sculpture*, edited by O. Palagia & J.J. Pollitt, 91-129. Yale Classical Studies 30. Cambridge: Cambridge University Press.

Ajootian, A. 2003. "Homeric Time, Space, and the Viewer at Olympia." In *The Enduring Instant/Der bleibende Augenblick. Time and the Spectator in the Visual Arts/Betrachterzeit in den Bildkünsten*, edited by J. Nathan & A. Roesler-Friedenthal, 137-63. Berlin: Mann.

Alcock, S.E. 1991. "Tomb Cult and the Post-Classical Polis." *AJA* 95: 447-67.

Antonaccio, C.M. 1995. *An Archaeology of Ancestors: Tomb Cult and Hero Cult in Early Greece*. Lanham, MD: Rowman and Littlefield.

Artal-Isbrand, P., L., Becker & M.T. Wypyski. 2002. "Remains of Gilding and Ground Layers on a Roman Marble Statue of the Goddess Hygeia." In *ASMOSIA 5. Interdisciplinary Studies on Ancient Stone, Proceedings of the Fifth International Conference of the Association for the Study of Marble and other Stones in Antiquity, Museum of Fine Arts, Boston 1998*, edited by J.J. Herrmann, Jr., N. Herz & R. Newman, 196-200. London: Archetype.

Ashby, C. 1999. *Classical Greek Theater. New Views on an Old Subject*. Iowa City: University of Iowa Press.

Ashmole, B. 1951. "Demeter at Cnidus." *JHS* 71: 13-28.

Austin, C. 1968. *Nova Fragmenta Euripidea in Papyris Reperta*. Kleine Texte für Vorlesungen und Übungen 187. Berlin: Walter de Gruyter.

Austin, M.M. 1981. *The Hellenistic World from Alexander to the Roman Conquest: A Selection of Ancient Sources in Translation*. Cambridge: Cambridge University Press.

Badian, E. 1994. "Herodotus on Alexander I of Macedon: A Study in Some Subtle Silences." In *Greek Historiography*, edited by S. Hornblower, 107-30. Oxford: Clarendon Press.

Badian, E. 1996. "Alexander the Great between Two Thrones and Heaven: Variations on an Old Theme." In *Subject and Ruler: The Cult of Ruling Power in Classical Antiquity. Papers presented at a Conference held in the University of Alberta on April 13-15, 1994, to celebrate the 65th anniversary of Duncan Fishwick*, edited by. A. Small, 11-26. *JRA* Suppl. 17.

Bankel, H. 1997. "Knidos. Der hellenistische Rundtempel und sein Altar. Vorbericht." *AA* 112: 51-71.

Barringer, J. Forthcoming. "A New Approach to the Hephaisteion. Heroic Models in the Athenian Agora." In *Structure, Image, Ornament: Architectural Sculpture in Greek World*, edited by P. Schultz and R. von den Hoff. Oxford: Oxbow.

Bauer, H. 1977. "Lysikratesdenkmal, Baubestand und Rekonstruktion." *AM* 92: 197-227.

Bélis, A. 1988. "A proposito degli 'Inni delfici' ad Apollo." In *La musica in Grecia*, edited by B. Gentili & R. Pretagostini, 205-18. Bari: Laterza.

Bérard, C. 1970. *Eretria. Fouilles et recherches III: L'Hérôon à la Porte d'Ouest*. Bern: Éditions Francke Berne.

Bergemann, J. 1997. *Demos und Thanatos. Untersuchungen zum Wertsystem der Polis im Spiegel der attischen Grabreliefs des 4. Jahrhunderts v. Chr. und zur Funktion der gleichzeitlichen Grabbauten*. Munich: Biering & Brinkmann.

Bergmann, M. 1998. *Die Strahlen der Herrscher: Theomorphes Herrscherbild und politische Symbolik im Hellenismus und in der römischen Kaiserzeit*. Mainz am Rhein: Philipp von Zabern.

Bessac, J.-C. 1988. "Problems of Identification and Interpretation of Tool Marks on Ancient Marbles and Decorative Stone." In *Classical Marble: Geochemistry, Technology, Trade. Proceedings of the NATO Advanced Research Workshop on Marble in Ancient Greece and Rome: Geology, Quarries, Commerce, Artifacts, Il Ciocco, Lucca, Italy, May 9-13, 1988,* edited by N. Herz & M. Waelkens, 41-53. NATO ASI Series, Series E: Applied Sciences 153. Dordrecht, Boston & London: Kluwer Academic Publishers.

Blümel, W. 1992. *Die Inschriften von Knidos 1.* Inschriften griechischen Städte aus Kleinasien 41. Bonn: Rudolf Habelt.

Boardman, J. 1991. *Greek Sculpture. The Classical Period.* Reprint. London: Thames and Hudson. Original edition, London: Thames and Hudson.

Boardman, J. 1995. *Greek Sculpture. The Late Classical Period.* London: Thames and Hudson.

Bommelaer, J.-F. 1991. *Guide de Delphes. Le Site.* École Française D'Athènes. Sites et monuments 7. Paris: Boccard.

Borbein, A.H. 1973. "Die griechische Statue des 4. Jahrhundrets v. Chr. Formanalytische Untersuchungen zur Kunst der Nachklassik." *JdI* 88: 43-212.

Borza, E.N. 1982. "Athenians, Macedonians, and the Origins of the Macedonian Royal House." In *Studies in Attic Epigraphy, History and Topography Presented to Eugene Vanderpool. Hesperia Suppl.* 19: 7-13.

Borza, E.N. 1990. *In the Shadow of Olympus: The Emergence of Macedon.* Princeton: Princeton University Press.

Borza, E.N. 1999. *Before Alexander: Constructing Early Macedonia.* Publication of the Association of Ancient Historians 6. Claremont, CA: Regina Books.

Bosworth, A.B. 1988. *Conquest and Empire: The Reign of Alexander the Great.* Cambridge: Cambridge University Press.

Bötticher, A. 1886. *Olympia. Das Fest und seine Stätte.* Nach den Berichten der Alten und den Ergebnissen der Deutschen Ausgrabungen. Berlin: Julius Springer.

Böttiger, C.A. 1794. *Über den Raub der Cassandra auf einem alten Gefässe von gebrannter Erde.* Weimar: Verlag des Industrie-Comtoirs.

Bringmann, K. & H. von Steuben. (eds.). 1995. *Schenkungen hellenistischer Herrscher an griechische Städte und Heiligtümer. Teil I: Zeugnisse und Kommentare.* Berlin: Akademie Verlag.

Burford, A. 1969. *The Greek Temple Builders at Epidauros. A Social and Economic Study of Building in the Asklepian Sanctuary, during Fourth and early Third Centuries B.C.* Liverpool Monographs in Archaeology and Oriental Studies. Liverpool: Liverpool University Press.

CA = Powell, J. U. 1925/1970. *Collectanea Alexandrina: Reliquiae minores poetarum Graecorum aetatis Ptolemaicae, 323-146 A.C.* Epicorum, Elegiacorum, Lyricorum, Ethicorum. Oxford: Clarendon Press.

Caltabiano, M.C. 1999. "The Identity of the Two Horsemen on Philip II's Coinage." In *Ancient Macedonia* 6.1, *Papers Read at the Sixth International Symposium held in Thessaloniki, October 15-19, 1996*, 197-207. Institute for Balkan Studies 272. Thessaloniki: Institute for Balkan Studies.

Cameron, A. 1995. *Callimachus and His Critics*. Princeton: Princeton University Press.

Carney, E.D. 1992. "The Politics of Polygamy: Olympias, Alexander and the Murder of Philip." *Historia* 41: 169-89.

Carney, E.D. 1994. "Women and Basileia: Legitimacy and Female Political Action in Macedonia." *CJ* 90: 367-91.

Carney, E.D. 2000a. *Women and Monarchy in Macedonia*. Norman and London: University of Oklahoma Press.

Carney, E.D. 2000b. "Initiation of Cult for Royal Macedonian Women." *CPh* 95: 21-43.

Chaniotis, A. 2003. "The Divinity of Hellenistic Rulers." In *A Companion to the Hellenistic World*, edited by A. Erskine, 431-45. Oxford: Blackwell.

Cohen, A. 1995. "Alexander and Achilles – Macedonians and 'Mycenaeans.'" In *The Ages of Homer: A Tribute to Emily Townsend Vermeule*, edited by J.B. Carter & S.P. Morris, 483-505. Austin: University of Texas Press.

Cohen, A. 1997. *The Alexander Mosaic. Stories of Victory and Defeat*. Cambridge Studies in Classical Art and Iconography. Cambridge: Cambridge University Press.

Cook, B.F. 1989. "The Sculptors of the Mausoleum Friezes." In *Architecture and Society in Hecatomnid Caria. Proceedings of Uppsala Symposium 1987*, edited by T. Linders & P. Hellström, 31-42. Acta Universitatis Upsaliensis Boreas. Uppsala Studies in Ancient Mediterranean and Near Eastern Civilizations 17. Uppsala: Academia Upsaliensis, distribution Almqvist & Wiksell International.

Corso, A. 1988. *Prassitele. Fonti epigrafiche e letteraie: Vita e opere*. Vol. 1, Fonti epigrafiche; fonti letteraie dall'età dello sculptore al medio impero (IV sec. A.C. – circa 175 d.C). Xenia Quaderni 10. Rome: De Luca Edizioni d'Arte.

Corso, A. 1997. "The Monument of Phryne at Delphi." *NAC* 26: 123-50.

Corso, A. 2000. "Praxiteles and the Parian Marble." In *Paria Lithos. Parian Quarries, Marble and Workshops of Sculpture. Proceedings of the First International Conference on the Archaeology of Paros and the Cyclades, Paros, 2-5 October 1997*, edited by D.U. Schilardi & D. Katsonopoulou, 227-36. Athens: Hatzigiannis and SIA O.E.

Dakaris, S.I. 1993. *Archaeological Guide to Dodona*. Translated by E. Kirk-Defterou. Athens: Zaravinos.

Damaskos, D. 1999. *Untersuchungen zu hellenistischen Kultbildern*. Stuttgart: Franz Steiner.

Daux, G. & E. Hansen. 1987. *Fouilles de Delphes II. Topographie et architecture. Le Trésor de Siphnos.* Paris: Boccard.

Despinis, G.I. 2004. *Zu Akrolithstatuen griechischer und römischer Zeit.* Nachrichten der Akademie der Wissenschaften zu Göttingen. I. Philologisch-Historische Klasse. Jahrgang 2004, 8. Göttingen: Vandenhoeck & Ruprecht in Göttingen.

Dillon, S. 2007 "Portraits of women in the early Hellenistic period." In *Early Hellenistic Portraiture: Image, Style, Context,* edited by R. von den Hoff & P. Schultz, 63-83. Cambridge & New York: Cambridge University Press.

Dinsmoor, W.B. 1950. *The Architecture of Ancient Greece. An account of its Historic Development.* 3rd ed. Revised. London, Toronto, Sydney & New York: Batsford LtD.

Dinsmoor, W.B. Jr. 1980. *The Propylaia to the Athenian Akropolis. Vol. 1, The Predecessors.* Princeton: The American School of Classical Studies at Athens.

Drougou, S. & Ch. Saatsoglou-Paliadeli. 2000. *Vergina: Wandering through the Archaeological Site.* 2nd ed. Athens: Ministry of Culture. Archaeological Receipts Fund.

Ducrey, P. 1988. "Des dieux et des sanctuaires à Philippes de Macédoine." In *Comptes et inventaires dans la cité Grecque. Actes du colloque international d'epigraphic tenu à Neuchâtel du 23 au 26 septembre 1986 en l'honneur de Jacques Trehéux,* edited by D. Knoepfler, 207-13. Genevè: Droz.

Dugas, C. 1924. *Le sanctuaire d'Aléa Athéna à Tégée.* Paris: Paul Geuther.

Eckstein, F. 1987. *Pausanias. Reisen in Griechenland.* Vol. 2, *Bücher V-VII.* Darmstadt: Wissenschaftliche Buchgesellschaft.

Edwards, C.M. 1996. "Lysippos." In *Personal Styles in Greek Sculpture,* edited by O. Palagia & J.J. Pollitt, 130-53. Yale Classical Studies 30. Cambridge: Cambridge University Press.

Ehrhardt, W. 1993. "Der Fries des Lysikratesmonuments." *AntP* 22: 7-67.

Ellis, J.R. 1976. *Philip II and Macedonian Imperialism. Aspects of Greek and Roman Life.* London: Thames and Hudson.

Eule, J.C. 2001. *Hellenistische Bürgerinnen aus Kleinasien. Weibliche Gewandstatuen in ihrem antiken Kontext.* Task Vakfı Yayınları 2. Kazı ve Araştırma Raporları Serisi 1. Istanbul: Task Vakfı.

Foucault, M. 1986. "Of Other Spaces." *Diacritics* 16: 22-7.

Franciosi, V. 2003. *Il "Doriforo" di Policleto.* Naples: Jovene Editore.

Fredricksmeyer, E. 2003. "Alexander's Religion and Divinity." In *Brill's Companion to Alexander the Great,* edited by J. Roisman, 253-78. Leiden: E.J. Brill

Fullerton, M.D. 1990. *The Archaistic Style in Roman Statuary. Mnemosyne Suppl. 110.*

Fullerton, M.D. 1998a. "Description vs. Prescription: A Semantics of Sculptural Style." In *ΣΤΕΦΑΝΟΣ: Studies in Honor of Brunilde Sismondo Ridg-*

way, edited by K.J. Hartswick & M.C. Sturgeon, 69-77. University Museum Monographs 100. Philadelphia: The University Museum. University of Pennsylvania. Philadelphia.

Fullerton, M.D. 1998b. "Atticism, Classicism and the Origins of Neo-Attic Sculpture." In *Regional Schools in Hellenistic Sculpture. Proceedings of an International Conference held at the American School of Classical Studies at Athens, March 15-17, 1996*, edited by O. Palagia & W.D.E. Coulsen, 93-9. Oxbow Monograph 90. Oxford: Oxbow Books.

Fullerton, M.D. 2003. "'Der Stil der Nachahmer:' A Brief Historiography of Stylistic Retrospection." In *Ancient Art and Its Historiography*, edited by A.A. Donohue & M.D. Fullerton, 92-117. Cambridge: Cambridge University Press.

Geominy, W. 2007. "The Daochos Monument in Delphi: the Style and Setting of a Family Portrait in Historic Dress." In *Early Hellenistic Portraiture: Image, Style, Context*, edited by P. Schultz & R. von den Hoff, 84-98. Cambridge & New York: Cambridge University Press.

Giallombardo, A.M.P. 1999. "Τεμένη Φιλίππου a Philipi: ai prodromi del culto del sovrano?" In *Ancient Macedonia 6.2. Papers Read at the Ssixth International Symposium held in Thessaloniki, October 15-19, 1996, 921-43.* Institute for Balkan Studies 272. Thessaloniki: Institute for Balkan Studies.

Grandjean, Y. & F. Salviat. 2000. *Guide de Thasos.* 2nd ed. École Française d'Athènes. Sites et monuments 3. Paris: Boccard.

Green, P. 1991. *Alexander of Macedon, 356-323 B.C. Historical Biography.* Rev. ed. Berkeley, Los Angeles & Oxford: University of California Press.

Greenwalt, W. 1989. "Polygamy and Succession in Argead Macedonia," *Arethusa* 22: 19-45.

Gruben, G. 1982. "Naxos und Paros. Vierter vorläufiger Bericht über die Forschungskampagnen 1972-1980. II. Klassiche und Hellenistische Bauten aus Paros." *AA* 97: 621-89.

Gunter, A.C. 1995. *Labraunda: Swedish Excavations and Researches 2.5. Marble Sculpture.* Stockholm: Paul Åström.

Habicht, C. 1970. *Gottmenschentum und griechische Städte.* 2nd ed. Zetemata 14. Munich: Beck.

Habicht, C. 1997. *Athens from Alexander to Antony.* Translated by D.L. Schneider. Cambridge, Mass. & London: Harvard University Press.

Habicht, C. 1998. *Pausanias's Guide to Ancient Greece.* Rev. ed. Sather Classical Lecture 50. London, Los Angeles & Berkeley: University of California Press.

Hampe, R. 1971. *Katalog der Sammlung antiker Kleinkunst des archäologischen Instituts der Universität Heidelberg II. Neuerwebungen 1957-1970.* Mainz am Rhein: Philipp von Zabern.

Hammond, N.G.L. 1994. *Philip of Macedon*. London: Gerald Duckworth & Co.

Hammond, N.G.L. & G.T. Griffith. 1979. *A History of Macedonia. Vol. 2*, 550-336 B.C. Oxford: Clarendon Press.

Hansen, W. 2000. "The Winning of Hippodameia." *TAPA* 130: 19-40.

Hatzopoulos, M.B. 1989. "Macédoine." *REG* 102: 428-36.

Herrmann, K. 2000. "Zur Verwendung des parischen Marmors im Heiligtum von Olympia." In *Paria Lithos. Parian Quarries, Marble and Workshops of Sculpture. Proceedings of the First International Conference on the Archaeology of Paros and the Cyclades, Paros, 2-5 October 1997*, edited by D.U. Schilardi & D. Katsonopoulou, 379-87. Athens: Hatzigiannis and SIA O.E.

Herrmann, H.-V. 1972. *Olympia. Heiligtum und Wettkampfstätte*. Munich: Hirmer.

Himmelmann, N. 1989. *Herrscher und Athlet: die Bronzen vom Quirinal*. Milan: Olivetti.

Himmelmann, N. 1998. *Reading Greek Art*. Princeton: Princeton University Press.

Hintzen-Bohlen, B. 1990. "Die Familiengruppe – Ein Mittel zur Selbstdarstellung hellenistischer Herrscher." *JdI* 105: 129-154.

Hintzen-Bohlen, B. 1992. *Herrscherrepräsentation im Hellenismus. Untersuchungen zu Weihgeschenken, Stiftungen und Ehrenmonumenten in den mutterländischen Heiligtümern Delphi, Olympia, Delos und Dodona*. Cologne & Weimar: Böhlau.

Hitzl, K. 1995. "Drei Beiträge zu Olympia." *Boreas* 18: 5-12.

Hölscher, T. 1971. *Ideal und Wirklichkeit in den Bildnissen Alexanders des Großen*. Abhandlungen der Heidelberger Akademie der Wissenschaften. Philosophisch-historische Klasse. Jahrgang 1971. 2. Abhandlung. Heidelberg: Carl Winter Universitätsverlag.

Huguenot, C. 2003. "La réutilisation des édifices funéraires helladiques à l'époque hellénistique." *Numismaticae Classicae Antique* 32: 81-140.

Huwendiek, J. 1996. "Zur Interpretation des Philippeion in Olympia." *Boreas* 19: 155-9.

Jacquemin, A. 1999. *Offrandes monumentales à Delphes. BÉFAR 304*. Paris: Boccard.

Jacquemin, A. 2001. "Pausanias, le sanctuaire d'Olympie et les archéologues." In *Éditer, traduire, commenter Pausanias en l'an 2000. Actes du colloque de Neuchâtel et de Fribourg, 18-22 septembre 1998*, edited by D. Knoepfler & M. Piérart, 283-300. Genève: Droz.

Jeppesen, K. 2002. *The Maussolleion at Halikarnassos. Reports of the Danish Archaeological Expedition to Bodrum Vol. 5, The Superstructure: A Comparative Analysis of the Architectural, Sculptural, and Literary Evidence*. Jutland

Archaeological Society Publications 15:5. Højbjerg: Jutland Archaeological Society, distribution Aarhus University Press.

Käppel, L. 1992. *Paian: Studien zur Geschichte einer Gattung. Untersuchungen zur antiken Literatur und Geschichte* 37. Berlin & New York: Walter de Gruyter.

Kaltsas, N. 1997. *Olympia*. Athens: Ministry of Culture. Archaeological Receipts Fund.

Kanellopoulos, C. 2006. "The Tholos at Epidauros and Vitruvian Resonating Chambers." Paper read at the *107ᵗʰ Annual Meeting of the Archaeological Institute of America*, 6 January 2006. Abstract: *107ᵗʰ Annual Meeting of the Archaeological Institute of America Abstracts*, 101.

Keesling, C.M. 2003. *The Votive Statues of the Athenian Acropolis*. Cambridge: Cambridge University Press.

Keesling, C.M. 2007. "Early Hellenistic Portrait Statues on the Athenian Acropolis: Survival, Reuse, Transformation." In *Early Hellenistic Portraiture: Image, Style, Context*, edited by P. Schultz & R. von den Hoff, 141-60. Cambridge & New York: Cambridge University Press.

Kotsidu, H. 2000. *TIMH KAI ΔΟΞΑ. Ehrungen für hellenistische Herrscher im griechischen Mutterland und in Kleinasien unter besonderer Berücksichtigung der archäologischen Denkmäler*. Berlin: Akademie Verlag.

Kroll, J. 2007. "The Emergence of Ruler Portraiture on Early Hellenistic Coins: the Importance of being Divine." In *Early Hellenistic Portraiture: Image, Style, Context*, edited by P. Schultz & R. von den Hoff, 113-22. Cambridge & New York: Cambridge University Press.

Krumeich, R. 1997. *Bildnisse griechischer Herrscher und Staatsmänner im 5. Jahrhundert v. Chr.* München: Biering & Brinkmann.

Krumeich, R. 2007. "Human Achievement and Divine Favor: the Religious Context of Early Hellenistic Portraiture." In *Early Hellenistic Portraiture: Image, Style, Context*, edited by P. Schultz & R. von den Hoff, 161-80. Cambridge & New York: Cambridge University Press.

Lapatin, K.D.S. 2001. *Chryselephantine Statuary in the Ancient Mediterranean World*. Oxford: Oxford University Press.

Lattimore, S. 1997. "Art and Architecture." In *The Greek World in the Fourth Century. From the Fall of the Athenian Empire to the Successors of Alexander*, edited by L.A. Tritle, 249-82. London & New York: Routledge.

Laubscher, H.P. 1985. "Hellenistische Herrscher und Pan." *AM* 100: 333-53.

Lauter, H. 1986. *Die Architektur des Hellenismus*. Darmstadt: Wissenschaftliche Buchgesellschaft.

Lawton, C. 2003. "Athenian Anti-Macedonian Sentiment and Democratic Ideology in Attic Document Reliefs in the Second Half of the Fourth Century B.C." In *The Macedonians in Athens 323-229 B.C. Proceedings of an International Conference held at the University of Athens, May 24-26, 2001*, edited by O. Palagia & S.V. Tracy, 117-27. Oxford: Oxbow Books.

Le Bohec-Bouhet, S. 2002. "The Kings of Macedon and the Cult of Zeus in the Hellenistic Period." In *The Hellenistic World. New Perspectives*, edited by D. Ogden, 41-57. London: Classical Press of Wales & Duckworth.

Lee, M. 2000. "The Gendered Meaning of the Early Classical Peplos." *AJA* 104: 355-6.

Lee, M. 2001. "The Tragic Peplos: A Heroic Garment Transformed." Paper read at the *132nd Annual Meeting of the American Philological Association*, 6 January 2006. Abstract: *132nd Annual Meeting of the American Philological Association*, 203.

Lee, M. 2003. "The Peplos and the 'Dorian Question.'" In *Ancient Art and Its Historiography*, edited by A.A. Donohue & M.D. Fullerton, 118-47. Cambridge: Cambridge University Press.

Lembke, K. 2000. "Eine Ptolemäergalerie aus Thmuis/Tell Timai." *JdI* 115: 113-46.

Lerat, L. 1985. "Le énigmes de Marmaria." *BCH* 109: 255-64.

Leventi, I. 1993. "Τα αγάλματα του Ασκληπιού και της Υγείας στο ναό της Αθηνάς Αλέας στην Τεγέα." In *Sculpture from Arcadia and Laconia. Proceedings of an International Conference held at the American School of Classical Studies at Athens, April 10-14, 1992*, edited by O. Palagia & W.D.E. Coulson, 119-28. Oxbow Monographs 30. Oxford: Oxbow Books.

Lehmann, K. 1998. *Samothrace. A Guide to the Excavations and the Museum*. 6th ed. Rev. Thessaloniki: Institute of Fine Arts, New York University.

LiDonnici, L.R. 1995. *The Epidaurian Miracle Inscriptions: Text, Translation and Commentary*. Society of Biblical Literature. Texts and Translations 36. Graeco-Roman Religion Series 11. Atlanta: Scholars Press.

Löhr, C. 2000. *Griechische Familienweihungen. Untersuchungen einer Repräsentationsform von ihren Anfängen bis zum Ende des 4. Jhs. v. Chr.* Internationale Archäologie 54. Rahden: Marie Leidorf.

Love, I.C. 1972. "A Preliminary Report of the Excavations at Knidos, 1970 & 1971." *AJA* 76: 61-76, 393-405.

Mallwitz, A. 1972. *Olympia und seine Bauten*. Darmstadt: Wissenschaftliche Buchgesellschaft.

Martin, R. 1965. *Manuel d'Architecture Grecque I: Matériaux et Techniques*. Collection des manuels d'archéologie et d'histoire de l'art. Paris: A. & J. Picard.

McCredie, J. 1984. "The 'Lantern of Demosthenes' and Lysikrates, Son of Lysitheides, of Kikynna." In *Studies Presented to Sterling Dow on his Eightieth Birthday*, edited by K.J. Rigsby, 181-4. *GRBM* 10.

Miller, S.G. 1970. *Hellenistic Macedonian Architecture: Its Style and Painted Ornamentation*. Ph.D. diss., Bryn Mawr College.

Miller, S.G. 1973. "The Philippeion and Macedonian Hellenistic Architecture," *AM* 88: 189-218.

Moltesen, M. et. al. 1995. *Catalogue. Greece in the Classical Period. Ny Carlsberg Glyptotek.* Copenhagen: Ny Carlsberg Glyptotek.

Momigliano, A. 1987. Reprint. *Filippo di Macedone. Saggio sulla storia Greca del IV seccola a.C.*. Milano: Guerini Associalti. Original edition, Florence: Felice le monnier, 1934.

Moreno, P. 1974. *Lisippo. Vol. 1.* Storia e libri civiltà 11. Bari: Dedalo.

Moreno, P. 1987a. *Vita e arte di Lisippo.* Milan: Il Saggiatore.

Moreno, P. 1987b. *Pittura greca da Polignoto ad Apelle.* Milan: Arnaldo Mondadori.

Moreno, P. 1988. "Bronzi lisippei," in *Griechische und römische Statuetten und Großbronzen. Akten der 9. Internationalen Tagung über antike Bronzen, Wien, 21.-25. April 1986*, edited by K. Gschwantler & A. Bernhard-Walcher, 258-64. Vienna: Kunsthistorisches Museum, Wien.

Morris, I. 1988. "Tomb Cult and the 'Greek Renaissance': the Past in the Present in the 8th Century BC." *Antiquity* 62: 750-61.

Mortensen, K. 1992. "Eurydice: Demonic or Devoted Mother?" *Ancient History Bulletin* 6: 156-71.

Müller, K.O. 1878. *Handbuch der Archäologie der Kunst.* 3rd ed. Stuttgart: Albert Heitz.

Muller-Dufeu, M. 2002. *La sculpture grecque: sources littéraires et épigraphiques,* Paris: École nationale supérieure des beaux-arts.

Norman, N.J. 1984. "The Temple of Athena Alea at Tegea." *AJA* 88: 169-94.

Ogden, D. 1999. *Polygamy, Prostitutes and Death. The Hellenistic Dynasties.* London: Classical Press of Wales & Duckworth.

Oikonomides, A. N. 1989. "The Portrait of King Philip II of Macedonia." *AncW* 20: 5-16.

Onians, J. 1979. *Art and Thought in the Hellenistic Age. The Greek World View 350-50 B.C.* London: Thames and Hudson.

Ortolani, G. 1998. *Il Padiglione di Afrodite Cnidia a Villa Adriana: progetto e significato.* Rome: Dedalo.

Osborne, R. 1994. "Looking on – Greek style. Does the Sculpted Girl speak to Women too?" In *Classical Greece: Ancient Histories and Modern Archaeologies*, edited by I. Morris, 81-96. Cambridge: Cambridge University Press.

OGIS = Orientis Graeci inscriptiones selectae, edited by W. Dittenberger. Leipzig: Hirzel 1903-1905.

Palagia, O. 1980. *Euphranor.* Monumenta Graeca et Romana 3. Leiden: E.J. Brill.

Palagia, O. 1986. "Imitation of Herakles in Ruler Portraiture: A Survey from Alexander to Maximinus Daze." *Boreas* 9: 137-51.

Palagia, O. 1993. *The Pediments of the Parthenon.* Monumenta Graeca et Romana 7. Leiden: E.J. Brill.

Palagia, O. 2000. "Parian Marble and the Athenians." In *Paria Lithos. Parian Quarries, Marble and Workshops of Sculpture. Proceedings of the First International Conference on the Archaeology of Paros and the Cyclades, Paros, 2-5 October 1997*, edited by D.U. Schilardi & D. Katsonopoulou, 347-54. Athens: Hatzigiannis and SIA O.E.

Palagia, O. 2001. "Hephaestion's Pyre and the Royal Hunt of Alexander." In *Alexander the Great in Fact and Fiction*, edited by A.B. Bosworth & E.J. Baynham, 167-206. New York & Oxford: Oxford University Press.

Palagia, O. 2002a. "A New Metope from Bassai," in *ASMOSIA 6. Interdisciplinary Studies on Ancient Stone. Proceedings of the Sixth International Conference of the Association for the Study of Marble and other Stones in Antiquity, Venice, June 15-18, 2000*, edited by L. Lazzarini, 375-82. Padova: Bottega d'Erasmo.

Palagia, O. 2002b. "News: The 'Tomb of Eurydice,' Vergina, Plundered." *Minerva* 13.1: 4.

Palagia, O. 2008. "Philip's Eurydice in the Philippeion at Olympia." Paper read at *Philip II and Alexander III: Father, Son and Dunasteia. Fourth International Symposium on Alexander the Great*, 3 April 2008. Abstract: http://people.clemson.edu/~elizab/Alexander %20conference.html#Abstracts

Palagia, O. & N. Herz. 2002. "Investigations of Marbles at Delphi." In *ASMOSIA 5. Interdisciplinary Studies on Ancient Stone. Proceedings of the Fifth J66International Conference of the Association for the Study of Marble and other Stones in Antiquity, Museum of Fine Arts, Boston, 1998*, edited by J.J. Herrmann, Jr., N. Herz & R. Newman, 240-9. London: Archetype.

Palagia, O. & S. Tracy (eds.). 2003. *The Macedonians in Athens 322-229 B.C. Proceedings of an International Conference held at the University of Athens, May 24-26, 2001*. Oxford: Oxbow Books.

Pape, M. 1975. *Griechische Kunstwerke aus Kriegsbeute und ihre öffentliche Aufstellung in Rom. Von der Eroberung von Syrakus bis in augusteische Zeit*. Ph.D. diss., University of Hamburg.

Partida, E. 2001. *The Treasuries at Delphi: An Architectural Study*. Jonsered: Åströms.

Perez, M.D. 1998a. "Olimpia, Euridice y el origen del culto dinastico en la Grecia helenistica." *FlorIl.* 9: 215-35.

Perez, M.D. 1998b. "Como convertirse en diosa: Mujeres y Divinidad en la Antigüedad Clasica." *Arenal* 5.1 (enero-junio): 23-46.

Perez, M.D. 2000. "Transmitters and Representatives of Power: Royal Women in Ancient Macedonia." *AncSoc* 30: 35-52.

Pilhofer, P. 2000. *Philippi. Vol. 2, Katalog der Inschriften von Philippi*. Wissenschaftliche Untersuchungen zum Neues Testament 119. Tübingen: J.C.B. Mohr Siebeck.

Pollitt, J.J. 1986. *Art in the Hellenistic Age*. Cambridge: Cambridge University Press.

Pontremoli, E. & B. Haussoullier. 1904. *Didymes. Fouilles de 1895 et 1896*. Paris: Ernest Leroux.

Price, T.H. 1973. "An Enigma in Pella: The Tholos and Herakles Phylakos." *AJA* 77: 66-71.

Pritchett, W.K. 1999. *Pausanias Periegetes II*. APXAIA EΛΛAΣ: Ancient Greek History and Archaeology 7. Amsterdam: J.C. Gieben.

Rambach, J. 2002. "Dörpfelds Bau VII in der Altis von Olympia. Ein früh-eisenzeitliches Apsidenhaus und 'Haus des Oinomaos.'" *AA* 117: 119-34.

Rehm, R. 2002. *The Play of Space: Spatial Transformation in Greek Tragedy*. Oxford & Princeton: Princeton University Press.

Reuterswürd, P. 1960. *Studien zur Polychromie der Plastik. Griechenland und Rome. Untersuchungen über die Farbewirkung der Marmor und Bronzeskulpturen*. Stockholm: Skandinavian University Books.

Ridgway, B.S. 1990. *Hellenistic Sculpture I: The Styles of ca. 331-200 B.C.* Madison: University of Wisconsin Press.

Ridgway, B.S. 1997. *Fourth-Century Styles in Greek Sculpture*. Madison: University of Wisconsin Press.

Rolley, C. 1999. *La sculpture grecque. 2: La période classique*. Paris: A. & J. Picard.

Romano, D.G. 1990. "Philip of Macedon, Alexander the Great and the Ancient Olympic Games." In *The World of Philip and Alexander. A Symposium on Greek Life and Times*, edited by E.C. Daniel, 63-79. University Museum Public Forum Series 1. Philadelphia: University Museum of Archaeology and Anthropology, University of Pennsylvania.

Roux, G. 1961. *L'Architecture de l'Argolide aux IVᵉ et IIIᵉ Siècles avant J.-C. BÉFAR* 199. Paris: Boccard.

Roux, G. (ed.). 1984. *Temples et sanctuaires*. Séminaire de recherché 1981-1983 sous la direction de G. Roux. Travaux de la Maison de l'Orient 7. Lyon: GIS – Maison de l'Orient & Boccard.

Roux, G. 1988. "La tholos d'Athéna Pronaia dans son sanctuaire de Delphes." *CRAI*: 290-309.

Rutherford, I. 2001. *Pindar's Paeans: A Reading of the Fragments with a Survey of the Genre*. New York & Oxford: Oxford University Press.

Salvait, F. 1979. "Vedettes de la scène en province: Signification et date des monuments chorégiques du Thasos." In *Thasiaca*, 155-67. BCH Suppl. 5.

Saatsoglou-Paliadeli, C. 1987. "Εὐρυδίκα Σίρρα Εὐκλαίαι." In: AMHTOΣ, *Τιμητικός τόμος για τον καθηγητή Μανόλη Ανδρόνικο*, 733-44. Thessaloniki: The Aristotle University.

Saatsoglou-Paliadeli, C. 1990 [1993]. "Βεργίνα 1990. Ανασκαφή στο Ιερό της Εύκλειας." *AEMΘ* 4: 21-34.

Saatsoglou-Paliadeli, C. 1996. [1997]. "Το Ιερό της Εύκλειας στη Βεργίνα." *AEMΘ* 10 A: 55-68.

Scaife, R. 1989. "Alexander I in the Histories of Herodotos." *Hermes* 117: 129-37.

Schalles, H.-J. 1995. Review of *Herrscherrepräsentation im Hellenismus. Untersuchungen zu Weihgeschenken, Stiftungen und Ehrenmonumenten in den mutterländischen Heiligtümern Delphi, Olympia, Delos und Dodona*, by B. Hinzten-Bohlen. *BJb* 195: 666-71.

Schleif, H. & W. Zschietzschmann. 1944. "Das Philippeion." *OlForsch* 1: 1-52.

Schmidt, I. 1995. *Hellenistische Statuenbasen*. Archäologische Studien 9. Berlin, Bern, Frankfurt am Main & New York: Peter Lang.

Schmidt-Dounas, B. 1993-94. "Statuen hellenistischer Könige als Synnaoi Theoi." *Egnatia* 4: 71-141.

Schmidt-Dounas, B. 2000. *Schenkungen hellenistischer Herrscher an griechische Städte und Heiligtümer. Vol 2, pt. 2.2, Geschenke erhalten die Freundschaft. Politik und Selbstdarstellung im Spiegel der Monumente. Archäologische Auswertung*. Berlin: Akademie Verlag.

Scheibler, I. 1975. "Leochares in Halikarnassos. Zur Methode der Meisterforschung." In *Wandlungen. Studien zur Antiken und neueren Kunst*, edited by I. Scheibler & H. Wrede, 152-62. Munich: Stifland Verlag Waldsussen, Bayern.

Schmidt-Colinet, A. 1991. "Exedra duplex. Überlegungen zum Augustusforum." *Hefte des Archäologischen Seminars der Universität Bern* 14: 43-60.

Schultz, P. 2006. "Propaganda and Performance in the Philippeion at Olympia." Paper read at the 107th *Annual Meeting of the Archaeological Institute of America*, 6 January 2006. Abstract: 107th *Annual Meeting of the Archaeological Institute of America Abstracts*, 101.

Schultz, P. 2007a. "Leochares' Argead Portraits in the Philippeion." In *Early Hellenistic Portraiture: Image, Style, Context*, edited by P. Schultz & R. von den Hoff, 205-36. Cambridge & London: Cambridge University Press.

Schultz, P. 2007b. "Style and Agency in an Age of Transition." In *Debating the Athenian Cultural Revolution. Art, Literature, Philosophy and Politics 430-380 B.C.*, edited by R. Osborne, 144-87. Cambridge & London: Cambridge University Press.

Schultz, P. Forthcoming. "Accounting for agency at Epidauros: *IG* IV^2 102 AI-BI and the economies of style." In *Structure, Image, Ornament: Architectural Sculpture in the Greek World*, edited by. P. Schultz & R. von den Hoff. Oxford: Oxbow.

Schumacher, L. 1990. "Zum Herrschaftsverständnis Phillipps II. von Makedonien." *Historia* 39: 426-44.

Schwarzenberg, E. von 1967. "Der lysippische Alexander." *BJb* 167: 58-118.

Schwarzenberg, E. von 1975. "The Portraiture of Alexander." In *Alexandre le Grand: Image et réalité, Vandœuvres, Genève, 25-30 août 1975*, edited by E. Badian, 223-78. Entretiens sur l'Antiquité classique 22. Genève: Foundation Hardt.

Seaman, K. 2004. "Retrieving the Original Aphrodite of Knidos." *RendLinc* 15: 531-94.

Seiler, F. 1986. *Die griechische Tholos. Untersuchungen zur Entwicklung, Typologie und Funktion kunstmäßiger Rundbauten.* Mainz am Rhein: Philipp von Zabern.

Shear, T.L. Jr. 1970. "The Monument of the Eponymous Heroes in the Athenian Agora." *Hesperia* 39: 145-222.

Shoe, L.T. 1936. *Profiles of Greek Mouldings.* Cambridge, Mass.: Harvard University Press.

Smith, R.R.R. 1988. *Hellenistic Royal Portraits.* Oxford Monographs on Classical Archaeology. Oxford: Clarendon Press.

Steinhauer, G. 1998. *Τα Μνημεία και το Αρχαιολογικό Μουσείο του Πειραιά.* Athens: Michalis Toumbis.

Steuben, H. von 1999. "Statuengruppen auf gekrümmten Basen." In *Hellenistische Gruppen, Gedenkschrift für Andreas Linfert*, 29-52. Schriften der Liebieghauses. Museum alter Plastik, Frankfurt am Main. Mainz am Rhein: Philipp von Zabern.

Stewart, A. 1977. *Skopas of Paros.* Park Ridge, NJ: Noyes Press.

Stewart, A. 1979. *Attica: Studies in Athenian Sculpture of the Hellenistic Age. JHS Suppl. Paper* 14.

Stewart, A. 1982. "Dionysos at Delphi: The Pediments of the Sixth Temple of Apollo and Religious Reform in the Age of Alexander." In *Macedonia and Greece in Late Classical and Early Hellenistic Times*, edited by B. Barr-Sharrar & E.N. Borza, 205-27. Studies in the History of Art 10. Washington, DC: National Gallery of Art.

Stewart, A. 1990. *Greek Sculpture: An Exploration.* New Haven: Yale University Press.

Stewart, A. 1993. *Face of Power. Alexander's Image and Hellenistic Politics.* Berkeley, Los Angeles & Oxford: University of California Press.

Stewart, A. 1995. "Notes on the Reception of the Polykleitan Style: Diomedes to Alexander." In *Polykleitos, the Doryphoros, and Tradition*, edited by W.G. Moon, 246-61. Wisconsin Studies in Classics. Madison: University of Wisconsin Press.

Stewart, A. 1997. *Art, Desire, and the Body in Ancient Greece.* Cambridge: Cambridge University Press.

Stewart, A. 1998. "Goddess or Queen? A Colossal Marble Head in the Athenian Agora." In *Regional Schools in Hellenistic Sculpture. Proceedings of an International Conference held at the American School of Classical Studies at Athens, March 15-17, 1996*, edited by O. Palagia & W.D.E. Coulsen, 83-91. Oxbow Monographs 90. Oxford: Oxbow Books.

Stewart, A. 2003. "Alexander the Great in Greek and Roman Art." In *Brill's Companion to Alexander the Great*, edited by J. Roisman, 31-66. Leiden: E.J. Brill.

Stewart, A. 2007. "Alexander, Philitas and the skeletos: Poseidippos and Truth in Early Hellenistic Portraiture." In *Early Hellenistic Portraiture: Image,*

Style, Context, edited by P. Schultz & R. von den Hoff, 123-40. Cambridge & New York: Cambridge University Press.

Svenson, D. 1995. *Darstellungen hellenistischer Könige mit Götteratttributen*. Archäologische Studien 10. Frankfurt am Main, Berlin, New York, Paris & Vienna: Peter Lang.

Themelis, P.G. 1998. "Attic Sculpture at Kallipolis (Aitolia). A Cult Group of Demeter and Kore." In *Regional Schools in Hellenistic Sculpture. Proceedings of an International Conference held at the American School of Classical Studies at Athens, March 15-17, 1996,* edited by O. Palagia & W.D.E. Coulsen, 47-59. Oxbow Monograph 90. Oxford: Oxbow Books.

Themelis, P.G. 2000. Ἥρωες καὶ Ἥρῶα στην Μεσσήνη. The Archaeological Society at Athens Library 210. Athens: Archaeological Society of Athens.

Themelis, P.G. (ed.). 2003. *Ancient Messene*. Site and Monuments. Edition of the Region of Peloponnese 1998. Athens: D. & G. Kalofolias Publication Inc.

Tiverios, M.A. & D.S. Tsiafakis (eds.). 2002. *Color in Ancient Greece. The Role of Color in Ancient Greek Art and Architecture 700-31 B.C. Proceedings of the Conference held in Thessaloniki, 12th-16th April, 2000 organized by the J. Paul Getty Museum and Aristotle University of Thessaloniki.* Thessaloniki: Aristotle University of Thessaloniki.

Thüngen, S.F. von 1994. *Die frei stehende griechische Exedra*. Mainz am Rhein: Philipp von Zabern.

Todisco, L. 1993. *Scultura greca del IV secolo, Maestri e scuole di statuaria tra classicità ed ellenismo*. Milan: Longanesi & Co.

Tracy, S.V. 1995. *Athenian Democracy in Transition. Attic Letter-Cutters of 340 to 290 B.C.* Berkeley, Los Angeles and London: University of California Press.

Trianti, I. 2002. "Neue technische Beobachtungen an den Skulpturen des Zeustempels von Olympia." In Olympia 1875-2000: 125 Jahre Deutsche Ausgrabungen. Internationales Symposion, Berlin 9.-11. November 2000, edited by H. Kyrieleis, 281-300. Mainz am Rhein: Philipp von Zabern.

Turner, L. 1994. "The History, Monuments and Topography of Ancient Lebadeia in Boeotia, Greece." PhD diss., University of Pennsylvania.

Townshead, R.F. 2003. "The Philippeion and Fourth Century Athenian Architecture." In *The Macedonians in Athens 323-229 B.C. Proceedings of an International Conference held at the University of Athens, May 24-26, 2001,* edited by O. Palagia & S.V. Tracy, 93-101. Oxford: Oxbow Books.

Van den Eijnde, F. 2000. *The Theatre Cavea in Early Greece. A Study on the History and Form of the Greek Cavea, 2000-330 B.C.* Ph.D. diss., University of Amsterdam.

Von den Hoff, R. 1997. "Der 'Alexander Rondanini.' Mythischer Heros oder heroischer Herrscher?" *MJB* 48: 7-28.

Voyatzis, M.E. 1999. "The Role of Temple Building in Consolidating Arkadian Communities." In *Defining Ancient Arcadia. Symposium, April, 1-4 1998. Acts of the Copenhagen Polis Center 6*, edited by T.H. Nielsen & J. Roy, 130-68. Historisk-filosofiske Meddelelser 78. Copenhagen: The Royal Danish Academy of Science and Letters.

Wallbank, F.W. 1984. "Monarchies and Monarchic Ideas." In *Cambridge Ancient History* 7.1. 2nd ed., edited by F.W. Wallbank, A.E. Astin, M.W. Frederiksen & R.M. Ogilvie, 62-100. Cambridge, London, New York, New Rochelle, Melbourne & Sydney: Cambridge University Press.

Waywell, G.B. 1978. *The Free-Standing Sculptures of the Mausoleum at Halicarnassus in the British Museum. A Catalogue*. London: British Museum Publications.

Waywell, G.B. 1993. "The Ada, Zeus and Idrieus Relief from Tegea in the British Museum." In *Sculpture from Arcadia and Laconia*, edited by O. Palagia & W.D.E. Coulson, 79-86. Oxbow Monographs 30. Oxford: Oxbow Books.

Waywell, G.B. "The sculptors of the Mausoleum at Halicarnassus." In *Sculptors and Sculpture of Caria and the Dodecanese*, edited by I. Jenkins and G.B. Waywell, 60-7. London: The British Museum Press.

Weickert, C. 1913. *Das lesbische Kymation. Ein Beitrag zur Geschicte der antiken Ornamentik*. Leipzig: Verlag von Wilhelm Schunke.

Wescoat, B.D. 2003. "Athens and Macedonian Royalty on Samothrace: The Pentelic Connection." In *The Macedonians in Athens 323-229 B.C. Proceedings of an International Conference held at the University of Athens, May 24-26, 2001*, edited by O. Palagia & S.V. Tracy, 102-16. Oxford: Oxbow Books.

Wesenberg, B. 1997. "Für eine situative Deutung des polykleitischen Doryphoros." *JdI* 112: 59-75.

Wickkiser, B. 2006. "Paean Performance in the Fourth-Century Tholoi at Delphi and Epidauros." Paper read at the 107th Annual Meeting of the *Archaeological Institute of America*, 6 January 2006. Abstract: 107th *Annual Meeting of the Archaeological Institute of America Abstracts*, 101-02.

Wilamowitz-Moellendorff, U. von 1886. *Isyllos von Epidauros*. Philologische Untersuchungen 9. Berlin: Weidmann.

Winckelmann, J.J. 1968. *History of Ancient Art*. Vol. 2. Translated by G.H. Lodge. New York: Frederick Ungar Publishing Co.

Whitley, J. 2001. *The Archaeology of Ancient Greece*. Cambridge World Archaeology. Cambridge: Cambridge University Press.

Wyatt, W.F. Jr. & C.N. Edmondson. 1984. "The Ceiling of the Hephaisteion." *AJA* 88: 135-167.

Yalouris, N. 1992. *Die Skulpturen des Asklepiostempels in Epidauros. AntP* 21.

Music and Cult in Ancient Greece: Ethnomusicological Perspectives

Tore Tvarnø Lind

What did music in ancient Greece sound like? Or, rather, how do we imagine the sound of ancient Greece to be? The answer is inevitably bound to the limitations of our historical and musical imagination. The conference "Aspects of Ancient Greek Cult" was a call for an interdisciplinary, collaborative approach to the study of cult and cult practice including music. Ethnomusicologists devote an increasing amount of their attention to both anthropological and historical considerations, which suggests that ethnomusicology, or musical anthropology, is itself interdisciplinary: the more one attempts to distinguish between the anthropological and the historical disciplines, the more they seem to overlap.[1] In this article, I will present some thoughts on how ethnomusicology might be of valuable assistance to the study of the music in ancient Greek culture and cult. In so doing, I will touch upon theoretical, socio-cultural and historical issues, all of which are concerns for the modern ethnomusicologist. In addition, my essay will draw attention to the specific musical reconstruction work by Atrium Musicae de Madrid and address our position as scholars in relation to Greek antiquity in terms of cultural and historical distance.[2]

My field of research is the Byzantine musical tradition of the Greek Orthodox Church in its medieval, Post-Byzantine, and, especially, contemporary expressions and settings. My methodology in this essay is to apply my experience with religious music from other periods of Greek history to the study of music and cult of the pre-Christian era. My essay thus aims at suggesting a set of issues that, from an ethnomusicological perspective, are both important and necessary to consider when approaching the field of ancient Greek music. For example, issues such as historicity, the creation of Self and Other, and cultural identity are important to consider not least because our cultural understanding is still influenced by prevailing evolutionist and colonialist views in the humanities. This call for an anthropological approach to the musical culture of the ancient Greeks and has been presented by Donatelli Restani, relating directly to the reflection and debate offered by the ICTM study group on Anthropology of Music in Mediterranean Cultures.[3] A change in perspective with regard to the musical culture in ancient Greece might, in Restani's words, "[open] the way toward a complete overhaul of our approach to the music of the Greeks."[4]

Silence and historical distance

When studying a music in the remote past of Greek antiquity—a historical field often characterized as *the* beginning of (Western) music history—ethnomusicologists are faced with two immediate and obvious problems: (1) the lack of sound, and (2) the impossibility of doing fieldwork in the conventional sense of the term.

Ever since H.G. Wells's famous novel *The Time Machine* (1895), the sheer fascination of time-traveling has been part of how we imagine human deed and thought in time and space. Journeys into remote areas, as if a *terra incognita* still existed as a white spot on the map, are often described as a traveling back through history, a thought that has prevailed in the colonialist view of "Island Culture," in which groups are seen as self-contained and internally organized with no contact to the surrounding world, and thus outside history.[5] Meanwhile, archaeologists continue digging while ethnomusicologists and anthropologists are forced to employ other modes of operation, besides day dreaming, of observing and recording the ceremonies at Delphi, attending a performance of the Delphic hymn to Apollon in the ceremonial context of 135 B.C., and experiencing the behavior, actions, thoughts, and emotions of those present in the Apollon temple.

We cannot dig out sound from the dirt. The types of musical evidence handed down to us are all physical: literature, such as treatises on music, etc., archaeological remains, including small pieces of instruments, graphic and plastic art, and very few fragments of musical compositions in musical notation of which most are of a post-Christian date.[6] These are the material sources on which musicology and music archaeology—or archaeomusicology—base its understanding of how music may have functioned and sounded in the context of Greek cult ceremonies and other facets of ancient Greek daily life.[7] Music archaeology seeks to place unearthed objects into social and cultural contexts, which has inspired the label "prehistoric anthropology of music."[8] However, the term "prehistoric" is an ambiguous term. On the one hand it refers to musical cultures before modern history, but herein lies also the implication that these cultures are outside history, which connects the term to evolutionary worldviews.

It is hardly satisfying to any musical study not to be able to listen to music. The famous Italian composer Giuseppe Verdi once argued with reference to the "paean" to Apollon: "Research into the art of Greek music is pointless!"[9] Verdi was arguably addressing the lack of sound, and in this he may have had a point. Verdi's notion of the pointlessness of studying Greek music, however, is the viewpoint of a composer, not an historian. But as historians, too, we ought to ask ourselves the same sort of question: exactly why is Greek music worth researching? And what precisely can we expect to find out considering the scarcity of evidence available? Sound is non-existent.

Reconstructions of instruments, tunings, playing techniques, and compositions are hypothetical. Any notions of distant echoes of the past are senti-
mental constructs. Indeed, the most palpable phenomenon in the musical
study of the ancient Greek world seems to be its limitations.

Experience as cultural knowledge

The sound of music is not the only thing we cannot dig out of the dirt and
experience ourselves. Although there is a vast body of music theory and
philosophy, we simply do not know what the individual worshipper thought
of the music he or she listened to, what attitudes he or she had towards it,
and what music *meant* in everyday life to individuals and groups. The aspect
of how the audience—such as worshippers—acted and perceived the music
is too easily overlooked. How did the audience express their feelings, and
what were their reactions to music heard at ceremonies? What were the
norms of music performance and musical behavior, and how were these
norms met in everyday life? What was perceived as musically significant by
different groups in ancient Greek society and what was not? What role did
music play in the formation of social and cultural identity?

These are just a few of the questions that the study of archaeological
objects alone cannot satisfactorily answer. Ethnomusicological fieldwork—
given the possibility of conversations, or semi-structured interviews—would
involve not only teachers, theoreticians and philosophers (characters whose
thoughts we encounter in writing) but anybody whose opinion would be
considered central to a thorough investigation of a music in a given society:
musicians, music students, instrument builders, priests, book keepers, audiences, worshippers and many others.

Musical norms in a structured society are often defined by influential
actors, such as philosophers and theoreticians who, in their writing, present
philosophical and metaphysical aspects of music and highly dense music
theory. Examples can be found in the works of Aristoxenos and Plato in the
fourth century B.C., Ptolemy in the second century A.D., and later Quintil-
ian—works that are mainly based on Pythagoras' music theory—whose work
has also formed a considerable part of basic concepts of Western music
theory and terminology. The anonymous audiences, musicians, and others,
by contrast, often provide a variety of views, practices, and musical experiences that challenge the ideal and idealized musical behavior and thought
presented by the texts, and bring to the fore insights that historical documents seldom provide. As the ethnomusicologist Martin Stokes advocates:
"We might perhaps first look at what musics often *do* rather than what they
are held to *represent* (the two not always being the same thing)."[10]

As has recently been shown in studies of Byzantine music, treatises on
music theory often express the ideal of a music culture that served as role

models for teaching, more than they represent the actuality of music training or experience. Ancient works of music theory were copied in the Byzantine era, but theory seems to have had its own life alongside musical practices, both oral and written. So it seems that theory often does not correspond to the aural and practical reality. This, however, does not mean that theory is falsely applied or inaccurate; it merely points to the fact that music is subject to conceptualizations and usages in various ways and on different levels.[11] This might strengthen the warnings against reducing ancient Greek musical life to theory, metaphysics, and mathematics.[12]

Ethnomusicology and Antiquity

Many studies have dealt with the issues and aspects of ancient Greek musical life that I treat in this essay.[13] These studies are primarily based on the interpretation of various evidence; Gullög Nordquist's iconographically oriented studies of musicians and music instruments in Greek cult are of special relevance in this context.[14] Restani's work also emphasizes the value of Greek music imagery, and she paves the way for a new perspective with regard to the relationship between music and myth in ancient Greece.[15]

The interdisciplinary — or anthropological — strategy is meant to complement other strategies employed in the latest monographic works on ancient Greek music, such as the explicit musicological work by Mathiesen (1999), and the classicist works by Comotti (1979/1989), West (1992), Anderson (1994), and others. The study of the roles music has played in Greek cult would find much inspiration by looking at studies of other musical traditions of religious or spiritual practices. One fine example of such a study is *Enchanting Powers. Music in the World's Religions* by Lawrence Sullivan, in which the reader finds a plethora of studies of different religious and musical settings, such as Tantrism at Java, Dagbamba of Ghana, music in Islam, Jewish Mysticism, and others.[16] By invoking so-called "ethnographic parallels," analogies between existing and ancient musical cultures, I by no means wish to return to earlier stages in musicology where scholars were concerned with the "origins" of music, but rather to support ethnomusicologist Martin Clayton's notion that comparison between cultures is an important and even necessary implication in any cultural study of music.[17]

This is the principle that has guided my own study of Byzantine music: the study of contemporary settings, forms, and conceptualizations of the music amongst today's performers and audiences is indeed valuable for a better understanding of the music genres as they were performed and listened to in ancient times. Of course, there might be differences in the perceptions of music from one age to another, in that music exerts in each age a different kind of power.[18] Take for example the shift in the perception of the term "Byzantine," which was quite unwanted in the years following the

Greek War of Independence (the late 1820s) with its associations to what was perceived to be Eastern or Oriental,[19] and later the increasing popularity of the term in both historiography and everyday speech because of its obvious notion of coherence with the past tradition of Byzantium, and, ultimately with ancient Greek musical traditions.[20]

While it is difficult to compare musical practices of the past in the ancient temples at Delphi, Athens, or Mount Athos with contemporary cultures—on account of the many possible differences in perceptions of music from one age to another—the historian Lionell Trilling optimistically turns things upside-down when he argues: "To suppose that we can think like men of another time is as much of an illusion as to suppose that we can think in a wholly different way."[21] This calls attention to the need for an ethnomusicological approach to studies of past musical cultures to complement palaeo-organology, palaeography, Classical philology, and others.

In this context, it seems important to emphasize that the ancient world should not be treated as a monolithic era, but as a culture with varied urban and regional traditions spread in the vast area of the Mediterranean that developed and changed throughout many centuries. Likewise, we should not assume a homogenous culture of musical practices. Even within very small areas today, musical practices occasionally vary greatly. Thus, music of the ancient Greek world might as well be understood as a plurality of performing practices, a multiplicity of styles, genres, and usages that were subject to changes in terms of form, aesthetics, and meanings. Therefore, the plural forms of "pasts" and "musics" are sound indeed.

When we study Greek antiquity, we look through a complex set of "coloured" lenses, which is why we should consider our relative position towards it. First, we look through Roman lenses.[22] For example, the terms cult (*cultus*) and religion (*religio*) are themselves of Roman (Latin) origin, not Greek. Second, we generally look through both a Christian and a modern secularized filter, as well as many others. Third, and perhaps most important, we understand ancient Greek culture through the "Greek Renaissance" of the late eighth century B.C.[23] A variety of Greek texts were copied extensively throughout the Byzantine era, a sign of a "revival of interest in the heroic past" and a "general trend to panhellenism."[24]

Widely believed to be seminal to the Early formation of Europe is the synthesis of three central elements: The Roman administrative apparatus, the Hellenistic cultural heritage, and Christian religion.[25] What lacks in this picture is perhaps a consideration of the Oriental influence. Archaeologist Warwick Ball refers to this formative period in European history as the "Oriental Revolution";[26] however, I should like to widen this perspective in arguing that Western ideas of the Oriental Other, the dual myth of the Oriental—the "bad Turk" and the "sensual Orient"—probably have had as great an influence on European history as the Oriental influence itself, the two not always being as easy to distinguish from one another as we would like to believe.[27]

To the notion of Christian religion replacing earlier pantheist cult practices, it is worth mentioning the case of the monastic society at Mount Athos. It was formally established in the year A.D. 963 as the "Garden of the All Holy Mother of God," that is, as Christian land, but it had with certainty been a refuge for Christian spiritual worship already since the eighth century, perhaps even earlier.[28] Before that, however, as the archaeological evidence reveals, Mount Athos housed several Greek temples, such as a temple of Apollon placed near the northeastern sea shore where the monastery of Iveron was erected. The columns from this temple were used centrally in the Katholikon (i.e., the main church building) after the Christian monks from Iveron had applied a Cross to each of them.

Reconstructing the other

Reconstructions of instruments, playing techniques, and performances are of great importance to the understanding of ancient Greek musical culture. Perhaps better than anything else, reconstructions of ancient musical performances remind us how distant we are positioned in relation to early music both in time and culture. There is no stronger reminder of this distance, I suggest, than the sound of the musical reconstruction.

Imagine if we could hear what ancient music really did sound like? It would arguably cause a massive culture shock. And what if we came to realize that the sound of ancient music was much farther away from what we had imagined: what disappointment! We would stand face to face with the (relative) uselessness of our work, as suggested by Verdi. However, the real question does not concern what the music *really* did sound like. As I see it, the real question concerns how we like to imagine the sound of ancient Greek music to be, and the possible reasons why we like to imagine it in a specific way. It is related to the question I asked above: why is Greek music worth researching? Exactly what makes ancient Greek music an important field of study?

Any possible answer to this question is intertwined both with the history of archaeology as a discipline and with Western cultural and historical identity. The culture might be "Greek," but archaeology is profoundly concerned with European culture and the Western cultural Self. As Chris Gosden notes, methods created in the early, colonial days of anthropology and archaeology, "were all to do with Us studying Them, where the Us in question were white, middle-class people in developed nations and They were small groups of far-away people ..."[29] As such the early stages of humanistic studies were bound to Romantic ideas, colonialist power, and evolutionistic views of man and nature. The idea that it is possible to trace Western history back

to a time of purity and philosophical brilliance, back to the era widely believed to be the "cradle of humanity" is *per se* a Romantic search for the
Urquelle of European-ness before—and this is an inescapable implication—
it got mixed up with the tanned and uncivilized Oriental neighbors. What
literally lies between the ancient and the modern is "the intellectual history
of imagining the Mediterranean as a border between the West and what lies
beyond," as Philip Bohlman argues, and this idea still marks the limit with
regard to the expansion of the European Union today—to such a degree that
it almost seems "natural." [30]

In archaeology and other disciplines, the evolutionist point of view has
been challenged by more nuanced arguments, and not entirely without irony:
the white columns, buildings, sculpture and votive reliefs that for long nur-
tured the idea of the superior ancient Greek culture as essentially being a
"white" culture, were in fact not white but colored.[31] In the early days of
archaeology—when Lord Elgin took with him what he felt belonged to
him—so the history of the discipline has shown, archaeologists cleansed a
great many columns and sculptures from the remaining colour pigments,
believing, as they did, that the paint was of so-called "barbaric" origin and
of a much later date. This is a striking example of how wanted pasts are
created to match current worldviews.

This discussion of chromaticism relates directly to widely held ideas of
the sound of music in Early Europe. Within the field of Byzantine music, for
example, scholars have disputed for many years whether or not chromatic
modes existed in the music of the historical period of Byzantium (i.e., until
1453). The discussion is blurred by the assumption that chromatic modes
are essentially of Oriental origin (leaving aside the fact that the Turkish and
Arabic *makam*-systems, or "modes," are based on the same ancient Greek
music theory as the Byzantine modes). Following this logic, however, the
music of the post-Byzantine era was chromatisized, as it were, during the
Ottoman rule.

Edward Said's critical arguments on "orientalism" are still highly relevant
to many musicological studies as well as to archaeology, judging from Warwick Ball's recently published and highly praised work, *Rome in the East*.[32]
Although Ball sympathetically calls for an Eastern viewpoint, he nevertheless draws an exotic picture of the East. In discussing the "baroque" style of
Classical buildings, he juxtaposes East and West:

> "The forms of Classical architecture were rigidly dominated by
> strict rules and order […] In the East […] the natural Near East-
> ern love of flamboyance and elaboration had free reign […] it
> lent the monuments spontaneity and humour that is often lack-
> ing in the purer but colder Classical monuments further west.

In the East, it becomes warmer, more living, more experimen-
tal."[33]

Ball's so-called Eastern viewpoint never rises above the level of postulation
and self-delusion. Instead of overcoming the eurocentrism and orientalism
he himself criticizes, he simply wraps the same prejudices in a new—perhaps
more "friendly"—way.[34] Ball juxtaposes East and West in stereotyped, binary oppositions, which seems to be a return to cultural essentialism: West
is cold, rigid, and pure, East is warm, spontaneous, and colourful. If this
marks the end of orientalism, it simultaneously heralds the arrival of neo-
orientalism.[35] Although mentioning that Roman architecture may seem an
excursus in the context of Greek music and cult, I use the quotation from
Ball's book to show how important it is to both recognize one's own relative
cultural position as a researcher, and to realize the implications of pretend-
ing the viewpoint of the Other. Ball does not address the obvious question:
precisely for which Oriental peoples' viewpoint does he speak? Those of the
present? The past? The one group or the other? In the Near Orient, too, we
must assume that people were as different in the past as they are today.

To gain insight into the worldview of the Other, one needs to be willing
to risk one's own worldview and identity, at least partially and temporarily.
This is one of the most important experiences for anthropological fieldwork.
A brilliant study dealing with issues related to the colonialist roots of archaeology and anthropology is Gosden's work on the changing relationship
between the two disciplines. His dual consideration is indeed important and
necessary, as each of the disciplines has continuously influenced each other.[36]
Ethnomusicology, as another humanistic discipline, might as well be added
to the list.

The *kiste*-effect

Historical ethnomusicology emphasizes the specificity and historicity of
events and meanings that are thought of as musically significant by different
human beings who are positioned in different cultures at different times.
This principle guides not only the study of music, but also relates to all other
aspects of ancient culture. We might dig relics out of the dirt, but not cultural systems of relationships. Poststructural anthropology emphasizes that
since cultural relations are not material, they cannot even be observed. Cultural relations can only be experienced through participation.[37]

The study of music in a Greek cultic context must, of course, relate to
"historical facts." Then, historiography is basically the act of filling the gaps
between the historical facts much in the same manner as a musical reconstruction. We can do nothing but turn to our historical imagination and interpretative skills, which are already fostered by our biases, preunderstand-

ings, and predefinitions. There is, after all, an inherent element of intellectual, or creative, interaction in history writing. This does not mean that historiography should not be carried out with minute care, thoroughness and much precaution; on the contrary. It rather emphasizes the need to be aware of what we really do when we write history.

The archaeological discussion of the contents of the *kiste* in votive reliefs serves as an illustrative example.[38] What were the contents of the container (the *kiste*), and what was it made of? A point worth mentioning—which was clearly emphasized during the conference discussion on this matter—is that no agreement exists among scholars that the 'cube-like-container-with-the-somewhat-slightly-rounded-corners' really is a *kiste*! It could be something else. So, even a discipline as material and systematic as archaeology, which occasionally still makes claims to positivistic objectivity, does speculate. In other words, when evidence is scarce, archaeologists can only try to imagine the contents of (what is believed to be) the *kiste*. I refer to this as the *kiste-*effect, which designates the situation where curiosity, persistency, and sheer eagerness of wanting to know turns into a highly creative discussion of different hypotheses. The *kiste*-effect is a good metaphor for the principle that is at work, for example, in the reconstruction of the sound of the *kithara* by looking at the sound box and number of strings on a black-figure vase-painting of a *kithara*. Numerous studies reveal an abundance of information, but what can we possibly say about the sound of the *kithara* by looking at a black figure vase-painting? The *kiste*-effect inevitably takes over when evidence is exhausted.

Music as context

Turning to music in the context of ancient cult, it could broadly be defined as sacred music functioning in the context of a religious practice or *cultus*, the Antique cult being defined as a system of religious devotion, and a service or act of worship. However, the music cannot satisfactorily be seen as background for other parts of a ceremony in relation to which it is understood as less significant. Music is not mere accompaniment, not only a means to fill the various gaps during ritual and ceremonial act. Any given set of sacred music cannot be separated from the ritual or ceremonial practice it inhabits, as shown by numerous studies of religious music.[39] It is therefore problematic to speak about cult music as "music" in any conventional sense. A brief look at how the concept of music was applied in ancient Greek society does not make things easier. The term "music" derives from "the art of the muses" (μουσικὴ τέχνη) and was used to designate a simultaneity of musical sound production, dance, and poetry as late as the fifth century B.C.[40] As Cowan maintains, this performative and philosophical unity was expressed both in secular song and ritual drama.[41]

The practices of a cult cannot fully be understood as providing the contextual setting for the music. Music itself creates context, or co-creates context. Thereby music produces locality, hereness, and a sense of belonging for those who are present.[42] This enables us to speak simultaneously about music in culture and society, and society and culture in music.[43] As phrased by the ethnomusicologist Martin Stokes:

> "Musics are invariably communal activities, that bring people together in specific alignments, whether as musicians, dancers or listening audiences. The 'tuning in' (Schutz 1977) through music of these social alignments can provide a powerful affective experience in which social identity is literally 'embodied'."[44]

Music as spiritual medium

An important aspect of the production of "hereness" in many contexts of religious music is that the connection between the earthly and the heavenly, or spiritual, spheres is manifested. The presence of a deity is made factual in the form of a concrete encounter between worshipper(s) and god(s) with music as the mediator. This event, or "sound event," strengthens a religious tradition in binding the present performance to the tradition's past, while simultaneously making the promise that the future will be tied to the same shared past. This is a means of ensuring the continuation of the religious and musical tradition.

One of the unique abilities of music is "to represent the ideal in sensuous, immaterial, audible form. It liberates by negating the restrictions of matter. And because music is able to express the inner life of the soul, it can represent man's entire emotional universe."[45] The notion of the "entire emotional universe," as Rowell puts it, I take to embrace also the spiritual aspect of human experiences, a thought that is common to many cultures and not far from the ancient Greek scheme of musicking and musical thinking. After all, ancient Greece is not the only culture to make a connection between the universe and musical sound, nor between music and transforming emotional and spiritual states. The enchanting powers of ancient Greek music should not be neglected merely as "legendary powers of Greek music," as Mathiesen characterizes it.[46] Rather, it seems as if the power of music was culturally recognized in ancient Greece, a power that was thought of as both musically and philosophically significant, and possibly even fundamental to Greek society.

Ritual and authority

We already know that music performance in ancient Greece was highly institutionalized, and that music played a central role in the civic and the religious life. Music is an important agent in the establishment of authoritarianism, power, and religious hierarchy, two traits common to all kinds of cult.[47] This is also true for the establishment and perseverance of a tradition's values and longevity, both of which legitimate cult. In his book on *Church and Cult*, Wookey mentions traits such as manipulation and mind-control as some of the issues that relate to cults (in modern times), a notion supported by the classicist Walter Burkert, who mentions the possible veiled interests of religious groups and phenomena.[48] Authority could be proliferated by a strong and conscious performance practice with articulate aesthetic ideas and expressions in the music performed at cult ceremonies. Likewise, elitist traits ("We, and only we, are right!") also would be mirrored in the attitude towards performing practices and ideals of, for example, timbre, gesture, and vocal use ("We, and only we, know how this music should be performed"). Such attitudes are always legitimated by implied notions of longevity and reliance on oral tradition and musical reminiscence. In the case of Byzantine music, it is interesting to see how the oral tradition within a single monastic setting has more weight than written sources hundreds of years old. Without oral knowledge, so the Vatopedian monks argue, the performer will neither get the full meaning of the notation, nor be able to make a "correct" performance.

Specific examples of a strong and conservative musical performance practice could be found, perhaps, in vase-paintings. What I find striking in the imagery of "auletes" (*aulos*-players), as in Nordquist's study, is the simultaneity of the stereotyped and the idiosyncratic.[49] There is, of course, a stylistic explanation to this, but being part of a well-defined and tightly controlled series of ceremonial acts as musicians in cult settings presumably were, their performance style, so the vase-paintings suggest, seems to have been highly stereotyped, but at the same time there seems to be an indication of local variation. The typical is also a prominent trait in temple buildings, to name but another example.[50] That the musicians "look" typical, or stereotyped, is what can be expected when it comes to liturgical or ceremonial music. Most elements in a given ritual act are formulaic, prescribed. That is the whole meaning of a ritual. The verbal, the bodily, the theatre-like acts and gesticulations are all meant to be repeatable, meant to be performed in the same way at every ceremony, although great variation even within a single region or locality might be observed.[51]

The historicity of reconstruction

When musicians try to reconstruct the sound of ancient Greek music and fill the *lacunae* in the musical fragments, they must rely on their historical knowledge, their musical training, and their personal and shared musicalities (the music they usually perform and listen to). The gaps can be filled either by playing or singing something that most plausibly could have been played or sung, or by letting silence take over. In either case, the final result will always be an interpretation influenced by the current trends and conventions within performance practices of so-called "ethnic," "folk," or "historical" musics, genres that would be found under the all-encompassing rubric of "World Music" in today's record store. Labels such as these must—from a scholarly viewpoint—be considered pejorative and analytically dubious. All music is in a sense ethnic music and folk music, since music is an action entirely human. The musician Big Bill Broonzy, when asked whether the tunes he played were folk tunes, once replied: "I never heard a horse sing 'em!"[52] What we recognize is that these labels are entirely meaningless when not applied from a specific viewpoint.

Atrium Musicae de Madrid's reconstruction of ancient Greek music bears associations to a wide range of different musics, such as Gregorian chant (track 7), Indian citar sound with South American pan flutes (track 4), and folk music and modern, atonal composition (track 1). The whole enterprise of reconstruction is inevitably bound to the time the recording was made (in 1979), and thus echoes a variety of musics from the musical soundscape of the late 1970s. That some instruments resemble what can be heard as "exotic" instruments is, to be sure, not a coincidence. They picture the distance to the realm of the alleged 'origins' of music. The implications of evolutionist and Romantic worldviews are hard to miss. It is as if the reprint of the recording—it was reprinted twice, in 1986 and 1999—itself adds a further aspect of historical distance: for a 2004-ear, the recording is no longer merely a reconstruction of approximately 2500-year old Greek music, it also presents the somewhat distant sound of 1979! It is not a coincidence, I believe, that this first attempt to reconstruct ancient Greek music took place in the period of the Early Music movement: the so-called "historical" recordings of the late 1970s and 1980s. Various musical works were subject to recording projects that made claim to original performance practices on "historical" instruments. All instruments on the Atrium Musicae de Madrid's recording (they mention more than 65 instruments) are reconstructions or replicas, built and played by the musicians themselves.

"Tuning in": music examples

The reconstructions of ancient Greek music carried out by Atrium Musicae de Madrid are based on written fragments from the two known ancient notational forms, the instrumental and the vocal. The result presents a highly creative approach to the music as well as a sincere attempt to recapture a "totally unknown" music, as the musicians themselves phrase it in the booklet. The musicians explicitly try to "tune in" the audience to ensure a certain listening-attitude towards the music. In encouraging the reader of this article to get hold of the CD and listen while reading, let me to quote the statement of the ensemble from the booklet of the recording:

> "We commence the record with a sonorous explosion which, in the manner of the 'Anakrousis' [i.e., prelude] recreates the silence necessary to enter into contact with a music as remote as and unknown as this."[53]

The audible sound of music is—and was—perhaps a means of knowledge because of its ability to reveal the inaudible, a thought taken from Indian music.[54] However, these thoughts are not without paradox. Performed music is never remote but sounds utterly present.

On a record, it is virtually impossible to start with silence, since the two most plausible (and understandable) reactions would be either to think that the record has not started yet, or that the volume is turned to zero. Therefore Atrium Musicae de Madrid opens the first track with an explosion of sound. All reconstructed ancient instruments play a *tutti fortissimo*. Thus, the following silence has the effect of sharpening the ear towards the next sound to come. In other words, the musicians play with the listeners' expectations.

The "tuning in" through music of a historically remote cultural space is a powerful experience that literally embodies it in the present. We might ask ourselves, then, what would we expect to hear? What did, or, better, what should, this "totally unknown" music actually sound like? I have already suggested an answer above. Our expectations would always be limited by our own time, our own culture, our own present. And these limitations also apply to the musicians, which is why the music in a sense sounds quite known, and sounds very much like the late 1970s, which is not so mystically "unknown." We are not able to listen beyond the music that has shaped our musical education and our cultural ear. A future comparative study of different "takes" on ancient Greek music, that is different reconstructions, would eventually show that changing national and political agendas, current trends and musical fashions, are as much a part of musical reconstruction work as the practical reconstruction itself.[55]

Historical narrative

The television broadcasting of the latest Olympic Games at Athens in 2004 showed clearly how the history of the ancient games is interwoven with modern Greek national identity markers. Trailers and historical programmes on television, and breaks during many of the indoor disciplines of the event, played Greek bouzouki-music from the 1960s and later, accompanying the return of the Olympic Games to their original historical framework, "to the city where it all began."[56] The opening ceremony of the Olympic Games staged "ancient Greek" elements in the shape of reconstructed clothing and dances. Also "ancient Greek" music was played: parts of the Atrium Musicae de Madrid's reconstructions echoed in the arena. Assumably, their recording is still an authority. Thus music plays a fundamental role in the highly self-conscious performance of Greekness. Displaying music in this manner is a strong means of fusing historical depth into the narrative of the modern Greek nation-state, which strengthens its international position among other great nations. Musical reconstruction has no relevance, and does not touch us, unless the music relates to our own time. Both the study and reconstruction of ancient Greek music is an engagement with the past that takes place in a present. Thus working with ancient Greek music remains inevitably an issue of Self and historical identity that has recourse in narrating a distant Other.

On the relation between identity and history, ethnomusicologist Philip Bohlman argues: "The otherness of the past as an experience in which one did not participate is often inseparable from the selfness of the past as an experience to which one draws closer through its narration."[57] In other words, the selfness of past is a constructed, or imaginary, experience. But the point is not to discover the "truth" of one's past, rather it is an issue of identity.

The return to history: concluding remarks

I strongly advocate a wide range of scholarly and creative approaches to an interdisciplinary study of ancient Greek music. We should allow ourselves to let our historical knowledge of "an irretrievably lost and unknown music" be enriched and widened by multiple (musical) experiences from contemporary cultures. This will enable us to ask questions in new ways and this, in turn, will nurture our historical imagination as well as increase the awareness about the historicity of musical research and reconstruction. Only by reflecting on musicology's and ethnomusicology's embeddedness in the humanistic scholarly tradition will we ensure that our own interests are made explicit. Both theoretical and self-critical reflection will enable us to ask new questions. Only with theoretical ambition will the historical as well as anthropological study of music ever reach a level beyond a mere museum enterprise and thereby add something new and valuable to the world of history and music.[58] One characteristic for which music reconstructors must be admired is that they dare to sound the silence in creative ways.

Atrium Musicae de Madrid's record displays the second Delphic hymn to Apollon (128 B.C.).[59] The sound of the reconstructed instrument *hydraulos* is dominated by the bubbles of water—hydraulic air compression is required for the instrument to produce sound—and its organ-pipe-like tones resemble a ferryboat leaving the harbour heading for the open sea. This could be seen as a strong symbol of a sacred journey into the unknown, unexplored past. Travelling into cultures of the Other is often used as a metaphor for travelling back in history, and vice versa, and as such the boundaries between cultural and historical Other, between anthropology and history, become blurred and give shape to a theoretical terrain shared by anthropological and historical perspectives.[60] Following one of the main arguments in David Lowenthal's work, *The Past is a Foreign Country*, the main concern for any historical study is to recognize the impact of the present on the past.[61] Our historical imagination is inevitably embodied in the present. This does not mark the end of history, but rather the return to history, as also Lowenthal has it: "If today's insights can be seen as integral to the meaning of the past, rather than subversive of its truth, we might breathe new life into it."[62]

Acknowledgements:

This article is an altered and revised version of the paper presented at the conference "Aspects of Ancient Greek Cult," 9-10 January, 2004, Centre for the Study of Antiquity and the Department of Classical Archaeology, University of Aarhus. My thanks to archaeologists Jesper Tae Jensen and Mette Korsholm for drawing my attention to a number of important references.

Notes

1 Bohlman 1997b.
2 See Discography.
3 Restani 1997. The ICTM (International Council for Traditional Music) study group on "Anthropology of Music in Mediterranean Cultures" held three meetings, Venice 1992, 1995, and Bari-Molfetta 1996. See the e-journal *Ethnomusicology OnLine* 3 (1997); see also Restani 1997; Bohlman 1997b, see also http://www.ethnomusic.ucla.edu/ICTM.
4 Restani 1997.
5 See for example Gosden 1999, 180.
6 Cf. Mathiesen 1999, 7; see catalogue and transcriptions of musical fragments in West 1992.
7 Note that Schneider lists seven types of sources; however, these categories do not contradict the four types I have listed. See Schneider 1999, 36. For music archaeology generally, see Schneider 1999.
8 Or the German *'Vorgeschichtsmusikanthropologie'*; Lund 1980, reference in Schneider 1999, 34.
9 Mathiesen 1999, 5.
10 Stokes 1994, 12. Parenthesis and italics original.
11 See Lind 2003.
12 See Restani 1997.
13 See for example the selective but quite extensive reference list in Mathiesen 2002.
14 Nordquist 1992; 1994.

15 Restani 1997.
16 See Sullivan 1997 for references.
17 Clayton 2003, 57.
18 Cf. Bohlman 1997a; 1997b.
19 Romanou 1990, 93.
20 See Lind 2003, 83, 153-68.
21 Trilling 1942, 192.
22 Cf. the discussion at the conference that followed L.B. Christensen's paper on the concept of cult, see Christensen, this volume.
23 See Antonaccio 1995, 5; reference to Hägg 1983.
24 Antonaccio 1995, 5, 8 respectively.
25 See for example Ostrogorsky 1957, 25.
26 Ball 2000, 7.
27 See also the arguments of Said 1978.
28 See Morris 1996, 37-46.
29 Gosden 1999, 180.
30 Bohlman 1997b.
31 See for example Østergaard et al. 2004; cf. the recent exhibition "ClassiColor" on ancient polychromatic sculpture, Ny Carlsberg Glyptotek, Copenhagen, 12 March – 30 May 2004.
32 Said 1978; Ball 2000.
33 Ball 2000, 382.
34 Ball 2000, 2.
35 Cf. Hastrup 1999.
36 Gosden 1999.
37 See for example Hastrup 1990.
38 See Hamilton in this volume.
39 See for example Blacking 1973; 1995; Qureshi 1991; Bohlman 1997a; Bergeron 1998; Lind 2003. See also Sullivan 1997.
40 Comotti 1979/1989, 3.
41 Cowan 1999, 1022.
42 Lind 2003.
43 Cf. Blacking 1973.
44 Stokes 1994, 12, with reference to Schutz 1977.
45 Rowell 1983, 125, comment to a part of Hegel's "The Philosophy of Fine Art."
46 Mathiesen 1999, 4.
47 Wookey 1996, 14.
48 Wookey 1996, 2; Burkert 1996, 22.
49 Nordquist 1992.
50 Burkert 1996, 26.
51 See Lind 2003.
52 Broonzy quoted in Nettl 1983, 303.
53 Atrium Musicae de Madrid 1979, from the CD booklet [1999].
54 Rowell 1992, 38.
55 For examples on different reconstructions, see, e.g., the recordings listed in the Discography.
56 For example "Historien bag historien" [transl., "The History Behind the Story"] on the Danish television program TV2's daily coverage of the Olympic Games

at Athens 2004. TV2's homepage, tv.tv2.dk/tv, August 24, 2004 (translation mine).

57 Bohlman 1997a, 149, reference to Ricoeur 1992, 140-68.

58 I paraphrase Kirsten Hastrup's beautiful Danish expression, "hagiografisk kustodevirksomhed;" see Hastrup 1999, 5.

59 Listen to track 21 on the CD, play from [02:45] to hear the reconstructed *hydraulos*.

60 See Bohlman 1997b; Lind 2003.

61 Lowenthal 1985.

62 Lowenthal 1985, 410.

Bibliography

Anderson, W.D. 1994. *Music and Musicians in Ancient Greece*. Ithaca & New York: Cornell University Press.

Antonaccio, C.M. 1995. *An Archaeology of Ancestors. Tomb Cult and Hero Cult in Early Greece*. Greek Studies in Interdisciplinary Approaches. Lanham, MD: Rowman & Littlefield.

Ball, W. 2000. *Rome in the East. The Transformation of an Empire*. London & New York: Routledge.

Bergeron, K. 1998. *Decadent Enchantments. The Revival of Gregorian Chant at Solesmes*. Los Angeles & New York: University of California Press.

Blacking, J. 1973. *How Musical Is Man?* Seattle & London: University of Washington Press.

Blacking, J. 1995. *Music, Culture & Experience. Selected Papers of John Blacking*. Edited by R. Byron. Chicago: University of Chicago Press.

Bohlman, P.V. 1997a. "Fieldwork in the Ethnomusicological Past." In *Shadows in the Field. New Perspectives for Fieldwork in Ethnomusicology*, edited by Gregory F. Barz & Timothy J. Cooley, 139-62. London & Oxford: Oxford University Press.

Bohlman, P.V. 1997b. "Music, Myth, and History in the Mediterranean: Diaspora and the Return to Modernity." *Ethnomusicology OnLine* (EOL). http://research.umbc.edu/efhm/3/bohlman/index.html.

Bryant, W. 1999. "Ancient Greek Music." In *The Garland Encyclopedia of World Music, Europe*. Vol. 8, edited by T. Rice, J. Porter & C. Goertzen, 46-8. New York: Garland Publishers.

Burkert, W. 1996. "Greek Temple-builders: Who, Where and Why?" In *The Role of Religion in the Early Greek Polis: Proceedings of the Third International Seminar in Ancient Greek Cult, organized by the Swedish Institute at Athens, 16-18 October 1992*, edited by R. Hägg, 21-9. Stockholm: Svenska Institutet i Athen, distribution Paul Åström.

Clayton, M. 2003. "Comparing Music, Comparing Musicology." In *The Cultural Study of Music. A Critical Introduction*, edited by M. Clayton, T. Herbert & R. Middleton, 57-68. New York: Routledge.

Comotti, G. 1979/1989. *Music in Greek and Roman Culture*. Translated by R.V. Munson. Baltimore & London: Johns Hopkins University Press.

Cowan, J.K. 1999. "Greece." In *The Garland Encyclopedia of World Music, Europe*. Vol. 8, edited by T. Rice, J. Porter & C. Goertzen, 1007-28. New York: Garland Publishers.

Gosden, C. 1999. *Anthropology and Archaeology. A Changing Relationship*. London & New York: Routledge.

Hastrup, K. 1990. "The Ethnographic Present: A Reinvention." *Cultural Anthropology* 5.1: 45-61.

Hastrup, K. 1999. *Viljen til viden. En humanistisk grundbog*. Copenhagen: Gyldendal.

Hägg, R. 1983. *The Greek Renaissance of the Eight Century B.C.: Tradition and Innovation, Proceedings of the Second International Symposium at the Swedish Institute in Athens, 1-5 June, 1981*. SkrAth 4°, 30. Stockholm: Svenska Institutet i Athen, distribution Paul Åström.

Lind, T.T. 2003. "The Past Is Always Present. An Etnomusicological Investigation of the *Byzantine Musical Tradition at Athos*." Ph.D. diss., University of Copenhagen.

Lowenthal, D. 1985. *The Past is a Foreign Country*. Cambridge & New York: Cambridge University Press.

Lund, C. 1980. "Methoden und Probleme der nordischen Musikarchäologie." *Acta Musicologica* 52: 1-13.

Mathiesen, T.J. 1999. *Apollo's Lyre. Greek Music and Music Theory in Antiquity and the Middle Ages*. Publications of the Center for the History of Music Theory and Literature 2. Lincoln & London: University of Nebraska Press.

Mathiesen, T.J. 2002. "Ancient Greece." In *The New Grove Dictionary of Music and Musicians*, Vol. V. 2nd ed., edited by S. Sadie, 327-48. London & New York: Macmillan.

Morris, R. 1996. "The origins of Athos." In *Mount Athos and Byzantine Monasticism*, edited by A. Bryer & M. Cunningham, 37-46. Society for the Promotion of Byzantine Studies 4. Hampshire: Ashgate Publishing, Variorum.

Nettl, B. 1983. *The Study of Ethnomusicology: Twenty-Nine Issues and Concepts*. Chicago: University of Illinois Press.

Nordquist, G.C. 1992. "Instrumental Music in Representations of Greek Cult." In *The Iconography of Greek Cult in the Archaic and Classical Periods. Proceedings of the first International Seminar on Ancient Greek Cult, organized by the Swedish Institute at Athens and the European Cultural Centre of Delphi, Delphi, 16-18 November, 1990*, edited by R. Hägg, 143-68. Athens and Liège: Centre d'Étude de la Religion Grecque Antique.

Nordquist, G.C. 1994. "Some Notes on Musicians in Greek Cult." In *Ancient Greek Cult Practice from the Epigraphical Evidence, Proceedings of the Second*

International Seminar on Ancient Greek Cult, Athens, 1991, edited by R. Hägg, 81-93. SkrAth 8°, 13. Stockholm: Svenska Institutet i Athen, distribution Paul Åströms Förlag.

Ostrogorsky, G. 1957. *History of the Byzantine State*. Translated by J. Hussey. New York: Rutgers University Press.

Qureshi, R.B. 1991. "Sufi Music and the Historicity of Oral Tradition." In *Ethnomusicology and Modern Music History*, edited by S. Bluhm, P.V. Bohlman, and D.M. Neuman, 103-20. Chicago: University of Illinois Press.

Restani, D. 1997. "Music and Myth in Ancient Greece." http//www.muspe. unibo.it/period/MA/index/number2/restani/dona0.html.

Ricoeur, P. 1992. *Oneself As Another*. Chicago: University of Chicago Press.

Romanou, K. 1990. "A New Approach to the Work of Chrysanthos of Madytos. The New Method of Musical Notation in the Greek Church and [the Great Theory of Music]." *Studies in Eastern Chant* 5: 89-100.

Rowell, L. 1983. *Thinking About Music. An Introduction to the Philosophy of Music*. Boston: The University of Massachusetts Press.

Rowell, L. 1992. *Music and Musical Thought in Early India*. Chicago: University of Chicago Press.

Said, E.W. 1978. *Orientalism*. New York: Vintage Books.

Schneider, A. 1999. "Archaeology of Music in Europe." In *The Garland Encyclopedia of World Music, Europa*. Vol. 8, edited by T. Rice, J. Porter & C. Goertzen, 34-45. New York: Garland Publishers.

Stokes, M. (ed.). 1994. *Ethnicity, Identity and Music. The Musical Construction of Place*. Oxford & Providence: Berg.

Schutz, A. 1977. "Making Music Together: A Study in Social Relationship." In *Symbolic Anthropology*, edited by J. Dolgin, D. Kemnitzer & D. Schneider, 106-119. New York: Columbia University Press.

Sullivan, L.E. (ed.). 1997. *Enchanting Powers. Music in the World's Religions*. Cambridge, MA: Harvard University Press.

Trilling, L. 1942. "The Sense of the Past." In *The Liberal Imagination. Essays on Literature and Society*, 356-77. London and New York: Penguin Books.

West, M.L. 1992. *Ancient Greek Music*. Oxford: Clarendon Press.

Wookey, S. 1996. *When a Church Becomes a Cult. The Marks of a New Religious Movement*. London: Hodder & Stoughton.

Østergaard, J.S. et al. 2004. *ClassiColor. Om farver i antik skulptur*. Copenhagen: Ny Carlsberg Glyptotek.

Discography

Musique de la Grèce Antique. Atrium Musicae de Madrid, dir. Gregorio Paniagua. Harmonia Mundi. France, HMA 1901015, CD. 1979 [reprint 1986, 1999].

Music of Ancient Greece. dir. C.Hilaris. Orata ORANGM 2013. 1992.

Music of the Ancient Greeks. De organographia. Pandourion 1001, CD. 1995.

Musiques de l'antiquité grecque. Ensemble Kérylos, dir. A. Bélis, K617069, CD. 1996.

Von Hammurabi tot Karel de Grote. Dreiduizend jaar muziek van 2000 v. Chr tot 800 n. Chr. Ensemble Aeide Mousa. Amsterdam, EAM01, CD. 1999.

Cultic Persona and the Transmission of the Partheneions

George Hinge

The chorus was one of the most important expressions of Greek cult. In words and movements, the chorus embodied the myth of the cult and gave life to its rituals. In addition, the young boys and girls of the chorus were integrated into the civic body by imitating the history of the *polis*. In Sparta, a corpus of these choruses was published in Hellenistic times in six books under the name of the seventh-century poet Alkman.[1] Unfortunately, this collection disappeared before or during the Middle Ages. Only about 3% has survived, either as quotations in other authors or in papyrus fragments from Egypt.[2] Many of these fragments belong to so-called partheneions, i.e. choral songs performed by young girls, *parthenoi*.[3]

The most famous of Alkman's partheneions, which is known primarily thanks to the Louvre Papyrus, lists the names of eleven girls.[4] Two girls are in the front – two protagonists, so to speak – whose names occur more times in the extant lines: Hagesichora (vv. 54, 57, 79, 90) and Agido (vv. 40, 42, 58, 80). The chorus compares their attractiveness (vv. 39-59):[5]

> ... ἐγὼν δ᾽ ἀείδω
> Ἀγιδῶς τὸ φῶς· ὁρῶ
> .᾽ ὥτ᾽ ἄλιον, ὅνπερ ἄμιν
> Ἀγιδὼ μαρτύρεται
> φαίνεν· ἐμὲ δ᾽ οὔτ᾽ ἐπαινὲν
> οὔτε μωμέσθαι νιν ἁ κλεννὰ χοραγὸς
> οὐδ᾽ ἁμῶς ἐῇ· δοκεῖ γὰρ ἤμεν αὐτα
> ἐκπρεπὴς τὼς ὥπερ αἴτις
> ἐν βοτοῖς στάσειεν ἵππον
> παγὸν ἀεθλοφόρον καναχάποδα
> τῶν ὑποπετριδίων ὀνείρων·
> ἦ οὐχ ὁρῆς; ὁ μὲν κέλης
> Ἐνετικός· ἁ δὲ χαίτα
> τᾶς ἐμᾶς ἀνεψιᾶς
> Ἁγησιχόρας ἐπανθεῖ
> χρυσὸς [ὡ]ς ἀκήρατος·
> τό τ᾽ ἀργύριον πρόσωπον

διαφάδαν τί τοι λέγω;
Ἁγησιχόρα μὲν αὕτα·
ἁ δὲ δευτέρα πεδ᾽ Ἀγιδὼ τὸ εἶδος
ἵππος Ἰβηνῶι Κολαξαῖος δραμεῖται

I sing of the light of Agido. I see her (?) like the sun, of whose
light Agido is a witness. Our illustrious chorus-leader will not
in any way allow me to praise her or blame her. For she seems
to be herself excellent as if one would put on grass a horse,
strong, prize-winning, thunder-footed, belonging to the dreams
from beneath the rocks (?). Don't you see it? The first is a fast
Enetian, but the mane of my cousin Hagesichora is blossoming
like pure gold. Her silvery face – why spell it out? That is Hagesichora. Agido runs after her the second in beauty, like a Ko-
laxaian horse against an Ibenian.[6]

Then nine other girls are introduced (vv. 64-77):

οὔτε γάρ τι πορφύρας
τόσσος κόρος ὥστ᾽ ἀμύναι,
οὔτε ποικίλος δράκων
παγχρύσιος, οὐδὲ μίτρα
Λυδία, νεανίδων
ἰανογ[λ]εφάρων ἄγαλμα,
οὐδὲ ταὶ Ναννῶς κόμαι,
ἀλλ᾽ οὐ[δ᾽] Ἀρέτα σιειδής,
οὐδὲ Σύλακίς τε καὶ Κλεησισήρα,
οὐδ᾽ ἐς Αἰνησιμβρ[ό]τας ἐνθοῖσα φασεῖς·
Ἀσταφίς [τ]έ μοι γένοιτο
καὶ ποτιγλέποι Φίλυλλα
Δαμαρ[έ]τα τ᾽ ἐρατά τε Ἰανθεμίς·
ἀλλ᾽ Ἁγησιχόρα με τείρει.

For there will not be enough purple to defend oneself, nor a
colourful snake of solid gold nor a Lydian diadem, the pride of
the violet-eyed young girls, nor the hair of Nanno, nor godlike
Areta nor Sylakis and Kleesisera; and you will not go home to
Ainesimbrota and say: May Astaphis be mine, may Philylla look
my way, or Damareta or lovely Ianthemis. No, it is Hagesichora
that torments me.

These girls are normally identified as the rest of the chorus. There are some
badly preserved verses later in the poem saying something about being ten

instead of eleven.[7] These seem to correspond with the total number of names mentioned in the poem (ten with Ainesimbrota, eleven without her). In this group, Hagesichora and Agido occupy a central place in the collective consciousness of the chorus.

The name Hagesichora means literally "she who leads the chorus," and it has therefore generally been assumed that she was also the chorus-leader or *chorēgos* mentioned often in the poem. Agido, on the other hand, means "a girl belonging to the family of the Agiads." The Agiads were one of the two Spartan royal houses. Gregory Nagy draws an important conclusion from the fact that the names of the two protagonists have a straightforward meaning, namely that they do not designate historical persons, but generic *roles* employed by different persons in different performances of the choral song in question.[8] It was not *Gelegenheitsdichtung* composed for a single occasion or for a very specific group of girls. The chorus represented the *polis* as such, and the poem was, so to speak, timeless. I agree with Nagy's analysis, since it converges with the conclusions about the performance of choral lyrics that I would like to draw from the linguistic form of the transmitted poems.

In general, one must be cautious not to draw too far-reaching conclusions from the meaning of a personal name. Nagy may be right that names of poets like Homer, Hesiod and Stesichoros may in fact originally designate generic figures rather than historical persons, since their names fit so perfectly to their status. Homer is the "collector," i.e. the proto-rhapsode (ὁμο- + ἀραρίσκω), Hesiod is "he who releases the song" (ἵημι + ϝοδός), and Stesichoros is "he who puts up the choruses" (ἵστημι + χορός).[9] They are both, after all, shrouded in mythology. On the other hand, the danger of the method becomes clear when one considers a name like Aristotle; it means in fact "the best end," and since *telos*, "end, purpose," is a cornerstone in Aristotelic terminology, we would have called Aristotle a generic name, the prototype of the Peripatetic philosopher, if we didn't know better. So, parents may in fact just be lucky (or provident[10]) when they give names to a newborn child. It could thus simply be a happy coincidence that a girl named Hagesichora happened to be the chorus-leader in the year when Alkman composed his famous partheneion.

The eleven names in the Partheneion are uncommon. That is, three of them are frequent girls' names in inscriptions throughout the Classical age, *Areta* "virtue," *Philylla* "sweetheart" and *Damareta* "virtue of the people." The other names, however, are rather extraordinary. In fact, six of them are not attested in other sources, namely *Hagēsichora, Agidō, Ainēsimbrota, Astaphis, Ianthemis,* and *Sylakis,* and one is attested only in literary texts, namely *Kleēsisēra; Nannō* occurs a couple of times. There are, of course, many names that are attested only once, and female names in particular, which are much rarer in the sources, tend to be singular. In the *Lexicon of Greek Personal Names,*

2,630 female names altogether are enumerated for the Peloponnese and Magna Graecia.[11] 1,739 of these names or 66.1% occur only once and 501 or 19% twice or three times. So it must not be discriminating *per se* that six or 54.5% of the names in Alkman's partheneion occur only there. What makes them suspicious is not so much their infrequency, but rather the fact that some of them fit their role so remarkably well.

Mario Puelma argues that Hagesichora cannot be the chorus-leader, since the word *ho choragos* is introduced in verse 44 before the first mention of the name Hagesichora in verse 53; it must refer to the only person who is called by her name earlier in the poem, namely Agido, who is mentioned in the previous sentence.[12] According to this analysis, it is mere coincidence that Hagesichora has a name that means "chorus-leader."[13] It is, however, perfectly possible that the chorus referred to their leader with the title and no name the first time, since they themselves would of course have known who was who. At any rate, if we accept that the persons are in fact generic roles, it is no problem at all. The words *choragos* and *Hagēsichora* would then be equivalent both semantically and functionally and therefore mutually interchangeable.

I will claim that all names of the partheneion are role-names.[14] When Alkman composed his partheneion, he did not have in mind concrete girls with names like Philylla, Nanno or Sylakis. The choral song is a drama with certain roles, which would be cast with the girls who happened to be available for the year of the performance. Of course the casting was not random. The part of the beloved was not given to the ugliest or less sympathetic girl of the group. Beauty and attractiveness could hardly be considered objective criteria anyway, but were measured by the position of the girl's family. Thus, the part of Agido would always be played by a girl from the family of the Agiads.

The roles of the other names in Alkman's first partheneion are less evident. As we have seen, the names are rare, but we know too little about early Lakonian female onomastics to exclude the possibility that they were in fact commonplace names, as were Areta, Philylla and Damareta in later times. The triviality of these names is in fact no less suspicious than the rarity of the other names. One could say that they simply designate the common role of the dancing and admiring girl. The name Nanno, which is probably some kind of *Lallwort*, is in classical literature only known as the name of a flute-playing hetaera in Mimnermos.[15] If we are allowed to transfer this connotation to Sparta (Mimnermos is contemporaneous with Alkman), it would not be a very appropriate name for a Spartan girl of noble rank. The name Sylakis is not particularly innocent either: *thylakos* means "leather sack," and the feminine *thylakē* is used, at least later, for the scrotum.[16] We know nothing about the bodily movements of the dance, but it is not impossible that it involved obscene roles, too.

Let us turn to some of the other extant partheneions to see if the names included in them can also be analysed as generic. The most problematic in this respect would be Alkman fr. 5 P, which is quoted in a papyrus commentary only, since it seems to have mentioned the Spartan king Leotychidas:

"νῦν δ᾽ ἴομες τῶ δαίμονος" ἔω(ς) τοῦ "παι[δῶν] ἀρίσταν"·
Λεωτυχίδας Λ]ακεδαι[μονί]ων βασιλεύς. ἄδηλον δὲ [... θ]
υγάτηρ ἡ Τιμασιμβρότα ... τινος. "φυὰν δ᾽ ἔοικεν [π]αιδὶ
ξανθῷ Πολυδώ[ρ]ω[]" Λεωτυχίδα υἱός ἐστι τοῦ Λακεδαιμονίων]
βασιλέ[ω]ς· [το]ῦ δ᾽ Εὐρυκ[ρ]άτους υἱὸς Πολύδ]ωρος καὶ
Τιμ[ασιμ]βρότα θυγά[τηρ.

"But now let us go to the god's" until "the best of his children". Leotychidas, the king of the Lakedaimonians. It is unclear [...] daughter was Timasimbrota ... "Is similar in build to the blond child (of?) Polydoros" He is the son of the king of the Spartans. Polydoros was Eurykrates' son and Timasimbrota his daughter.

This information has been taken as a decisive verification of the traditional date of Alkman.[17] It is in this context more interesting that the presence of a historical king in a partheneion may be considered an inconvenient impediment to the hypothesis about the generic character of these poems. However, the king can be seen as a generic figure as well, even if his name is historical; he is the representative of a power, which embodies the city as such and is repeated generation after generation for centuries. At any rate, it is uncertain if the name of Leotychidas did in fact stand in the poem. If the poem told that Timasimbrota was the best of Leotychidas' children, there would have been nothing to comment upon, but the commentator states that it is unclear and ends up with another conclusion, it seems. Furthermore, *Leōtychidas, -ēs* is the Attic-Ionic form of the name; it is rather unlikely that the commentator would choose that form if he had just read the Doric *La(o) tychidas* in the poem.[18] Another possibility, therefore, is that it was said that Timasimbrota was the best of the king's children, and that the commentator has himself calculated that Leotychidas was king at the time of Alkman. Timasimbrota in the next lemma is compared with a youth called Polydoros. Since Leotychidas' son had another name, the commentator concludes that they were the children of the other king, Eurykrates, instead.

Pindar's second partheneion (= fr. 94(b) SM) is written for the daphnephoric procession in the honour of Apollon. In the middle of the song, the chorus calls on the son of Damaina to lead it, and adds that the daughter will follow as the first one (vv. 66-72):

Δαμαίνας πα[ῖ, ἐ]να[ισίμ]ῳ νῦν μοι ποδὶ
στείχων ἀγέο· [τ]ὶν γὰρ ε[ὔ]φρων ἕψεται
πρῶτα θυγάτηρ [ό]δοῦ
δάφνας εὐπετάλου σχεδ[ό]ν
βαίνοισα πεδίλοις,
Ἀνδαισιστρότα ἂν ἐπά-
σκησε μήδεσ[ι.....]ρο[ ]

... of Damaina, stepping forth now with a ... foot, lead the way
for me, since the first to follow you on the way will be your kind
daughter, who beside the branch of leafy bay walks on sandals,
whom Andaisistrota has trained in skills ...
(Transl. W.H. Race)

It is normally assumed that Damaina's son is Pagondas mentioned in the
beginning of the poem (v. 10), and it is his daughter that follows after him;
Agasikles, mentioned in v. 38, is considered his son. Thus the poem is associated with a particular historical family and therefore not particularly
generic. This, however, is not the only interpretation: Damaina's son could
be Agasikles, and "the daughter" not the daughter of Damaina's son, but
the daughter of Damaina herself. Another supplement of verse 66 reads *patēr*,
"father," so that Damaina is the name of the daughter.

At any rate, it is striking how the different names resemble the names of
Alkman's partheneions semantically. The leading boy has a name derived
from *hēgeomai*, the very same verb that is used in the exhortation (v. 67 ἀγέο).
Agasikles' role was presumably similar to that of Hagesichora. The children's
mother has a name, which can be interpreted as "the praise of the people"
(δῆμος + αἶνος). The closest parallel to that is Alkman fr. 10(b) P, where the
leader of the chorus is called Hagesidamos, son of Damotimidas. The structure of the two partheneions is similar: after a narrative excursus, the chorus
invokes its leader and comments upon the dance.

The chorus-leader is acting with one particular girl, who is in both cases
defined genealogically: *Ag-idō* (Alkman): *thygatēr* (Pindar). At the beginning
of Pindar's partheneion, the chorus states that it will sing about the "dwell-
ing of Aioladas and his son Pagondas" (vv. 8-11 πάν|δοξον Αἰολάδα
σταθμόν | υἱοῦ τε Παγώνδα | ὑμνήσω). I suppose that this is meant only
as a general reference. The cult was in the hands of a *genos* that claimed
Pagondas as a prominent member, just like the cult of Alkman's first partheneion is associated with the *genos* of the Agiads by virtue of the girl's name
Agido (and fr. 5 P perhaps with the Eurypontids due to the name Polydoros).
The references to the excellencies of the parents in the middle of the poem
are also general. Even if the mention of these influential families in Pindar
and Alkman may be the poet's indication of the patronage of the song, a sort

of *sphragis*, we know from Pausanias that the children leading the daphnephoric procession had to come from a noble family (9.10.4):

τόδε γε καὶ ἐς ἐμὲ ἔτι γινόμενον οἶδα ἐν Θήβαις· τῷ Ἀπόλλωνι
τῷ Ἰσμηνίῳ παῖδα οἴκου τε δοκίμου καὶ αὐτὸν εὖ μὲν εἴδους,
εὖ δὲ ἔχοντα καὶ ῥώμης, ἱερέα ἐνιαύσιον ποιοῦσιν· ἐπίκλησις
δέ ἐστίν οἱ δαφναφόρος, στεφάνους γὰρ φύλλων δάφνης
φοροῦσιν οἱ παῖδες.

The following custom is, to my knowledge, still carried out in
Thebes. A boy of noble family, who is himself both handsome
and strong, is chosen priest of Ismenian Apollon for a year. He
is called Laurel-bearer, for the boys wear wreaths of laurel leaves.
(Transl. Jones/Ormerod)

It is clear from this description that the boy was acting a generic role characterised by two qualities, beauty and breeding. Hagesichora and Agido
were probably cast for their roles on account of the same two qualifica-
tions.

In Alkman's partheneion, Ainesimbrota has a special role. The chorus
says that it doesn't bother about Nanno, Areta, Sylakis, Astaphis, Philylla,
Damareta, or Ianthemis; it is Hagesichora it loves. It says literally: "*You will
not go home to Ainesimbrota and ask, may Astaphis be mine, or may Philylla look
my way.*" It has been claimed that choral poems like the famous partheneion
were performed in a competition between two choruses, or two halves of
the chorus, and that Ainesimbrota was the leader of the other team.[19] Martin
West has proposed that Ainesimbrota was some kind of witch who would
give love mixtures to convince the unwilling heart of a girl, just like the
pharmakeutria, "mixer of love potions," in Theokritos' Second Idyll.[20] It is,
however, better to compare her role with Pindar's Andaisistrota, as Claude
Calame does, being like her the third person besides the chorus-leader and
the favourite girl.[21] The chorus of Pindar's partheneion explicitly describes
Andaisistrota as the trainer (v. 71 ἂν ἐπάσκησε).

An-daisi-strota literally means "she who divides the people" (ἀνα-δαίω +
στρατός).[22] It is therefore very likely that it is yet another role name that was
employed by different women in different performances. *Ainēsi-mbrota* means
"she who praises people" (αἰνέω + βροτός), and *Timasi-mbrota* in fr. 5 P and
Klēsi-mbrota in fr. 4 P have pretty much the same meaning (τιμάω and κλέω).
We have seen that the mother of the children (or the daughter) in Pindar's
second partheneion and the father of the chorus-leader in Alkman fr. 10(b)
P also have names, which mean something like "praise of the people," *Damaina* and *Damo-tim-idas* respectively. In Alkman's second largest partheneion,
fr. 3 P, a person called *Asty-meloisa*, or "she who cares for the city" (ἄστυ +

μέλω), plays a central role in the ritual, and her role is emphasised further with the prepositional phrase κατὰ στρατόν "throughout the people" (v. 74).[23]

It is significant that we have repeatedly more or less the same semantic describing either the trainer of the chorus or the parent of the chorus-leader. Since the chorus embodies the people as such, the person casting it and training it may consequently be called "the one who distributes the honours to the people." There can be no doubt that Alkman was in fact conscious about the etymological value of the names in question. In fact, in fr. 3 P, he even has the chorus glossing Astymeloisa *melēma damōi* "a delight for the people" (v. 74).

Since the unison voice of the chorus calls Hagesichora its cousin (v. 53 τᾶς ἐμᾶς ἀνεψιᾶς), it is likely that the members were somehow related.[24] Another fragment of a partheneion, fr. 10(b) P, has a chorus that consists of *Dymainai*, i.e. female members of the Doric *phylē* of the Dymanes. Like many other Doric cities, Sparta was divided into three so-called *phylai*, a kind of clan that claimed a common origin. If the chorus of the large partheneion was recruited in the same way, it could easily claim to be related – "cousins" so to speak.[25]

A papyrus commentary to a partheneion of Alkman, fr. 11 P, speaks about *Dymainai* and *Pitanides*. Unfortunately, it is very fragmentary, so it is impossible to see if the commentator is speaking about one and the same group of girls or two different groups. *Pitanides* means girls from Pitane, one of the old Spartan villages (*kōmai*); unlike most other Greek cities, the *polis* of Classical Sparta consisted of five independent villages instead of a synoecized city, and a town wall was not built until Hellenistic times. Since the "constitution" of Sparta, the famous *rhētra* quoted in Plutarch, *Vit. Lyc.* 6, prescribes that the people shall be divided into *phylai* and *ōbai*, it is generally assumed that *phylē* was a tribal division and *ōbē* a geographical division, identical to the villages of Sparta.[26]

In other words, the *Dymainai* and the *Pitanides* belonged to two different orders of organisation.[27] One could of course claim that either Alkman or his commentator has got it all wrong. On the other hand, the two levels are compatible if the *ōbai* and the *phylai* overlapped, so that each *ōbē* was divided into three parts according to the three *phylai*.[28] Such a division is a commonplace in the Greek world; these kinship subdivisions are called either *ph(r)atria* or *patra* according to the dialect of the text.[29] In fr. 5 P, the commentator does in fact speak about a *patra*, if the supplement is correct: φυλ[ικὸς χ]ορός (ἐστι) Δυμα[... πά]τρα Δυμά[νων "it is a *phylē* chorus; Dyma[... a *pa*]*tra* of the Dyma[nes."

A probable scenario is that the single pieces of choral lyric were re-performed by a certain *patra* in connection with a certain festival. Each year group of a *patra* probably formed a club, a *thiasos*.[30] These *thiasoi* rehearsed and performed the traditional songs generation after generation until Hellenistic times. Taking the broad range of possible re-occurring festivals and the number of *patrai* (15? 27?) into consideration, it is not surprising that the Hellenistic philologists were able to collect at least two papyrus rolls with maiden songs ascribed to Alkman (in all ca. 20-25 songs). It is not, however, self-evident that each *patra* had equal access to all festivals. Some festivals were perhaps reserved for a certain lineage. It is remarkable that all known references to a *phylē* in Alkman mention the Dymanes. There are also other indications that this *phylē* was traditionally associated with cult practice.[31]

The *Dymainai* chorus of fr. 10(b) P was led by a male chorus-leader with the name Hagesidamos. The similarity with the name Hagesichora is probably not a coincidence. Names with *Hagēsi-* were known in the Agiad house in the Archaic age, so Alkman may have constructed role names with this verb in order to mark them as belonging to this family. Aristotle says that Alkman was originally a slave of Agesidas, but was set free because of his talents (*Politeia Lakōnōn*, fr. 611.9 Rose); Agesidas is possibly a corruption of the name Hagesidamos occurring in fr. 10(b) P.[32] This tradition may point to a dependence of Alkman on the Agiad dynasty, and it may be derived from a misunderstanding or over-interpretation of some parts of Alkman's poetry, where a chorus expresses its affection for its leader.[33]

However, the Agiads belonged to the *phylē* of the Hylleis, since they claimed to be descendants of Herakles' adoptive son Hyllos. In other words, if Hagesidamos is Agiad, we have a man from the Hylleis *phylē* leading a chorus of girls from the Dymanes *phylē*. In fr. 1 P, on the other hand, the chorus and their female leader belong to the same *phylē*. Since the relation between chorus and leader must be different in the two cases anyway because of the different sex, the difference in *phylē* is not so surprising after all. The *phylē* of the Hylleis seems to have been associated with the ruling class.[34] The combination of dancing Dymainai and a leading Hylles corresponds to this division of the roles.

According to Pausanias, the royal tombs of the Agiads were situated in the *kōmē* of Pitane (3.14.2), whereas the tombs of the Eurypontids were located in the *kōmē* of Kynosura (3.12.8). It would perhaps not be too audacious, then, to assume a link between the Agiad house and the *ōbē* of Pitane. Alkman's own grave monument was situated in the same part of the city as well (3.15.3), near the Dromos, where, still according to Pausanias, young men competed, and near Platanistas, where the race of the young girls in Theokritos' Idyll 18 seems to be situated. Claude Calame thinks that the same ritual was the occasion of Alkman's first partheneion as well.[35] In other words, fr. 1 P was meant to be performed by girls belonging to the Hylleis *patra* of the Pitane *ōbē*. The poem was re-performed year after year by new girls, who played fixed roles in the group and in the ritual. One of the girls was appointed the leader of the chorus and carried the name "Hagesichora." Another girl obtained the role of the beautiful number two, and she was called "Agido." There was also a third girl, "Ainesimbrota," possibly one from an older year group, who assumed the role of the trainer and divided the parts between the girls.

The only external testimony to the transmission of Alkman's poetry is found in the *Deipnosophistai* of Athenaios. It is a quotation of the Lakonian historian Sosibios (15, 678[b-c] = *FGrH* 595 F 5):

θυρεατικοί· οὕτω καλοῦνταί τινες στέφανοι παρὰ Λακεδαιμονίοις, ὥς φησι Σωσίβιος ἐν τοῖς Περὶ θυσιῶν, ψιλίνους αὐτοὺς φάσκων νῦν ὀνομάζεσθαι, ὄντας ἐκ φοινίκων· φέρειν δ᾽ αὐτοὺς ὑπόμνημα τῆς ἐν Θυρέα γενομένης νίκης τοὺς προστάτας τῶν ἀγομένων χορῶν ἐν τῇ ἑορτῇ ταύτῃ, ὅτε καὶ τὰς Γυμνοπαιδιὰς ἐπιτελοῦσιν. χοροὶ δ᾽ εἰσὶν γ᾽· ὁ μὲν πρόσω παίδων, <ὁ δ᾽ ἐκ δεξιοῦ γερόντων,> ὁ δ᾽ ἐξ ἀριστ<ερ>οῦ ἀνδρῶν, γυμνῶν ὀρχουμένων καὶ ἀδόντων Θαλητᾶ καὶ Ἀλκμᾶνος ᾄσματα καὶ τοὺς Διονυσοδότου τοῦ Λάκωνος παιᾶνας.

Thyreatikoi. This is the name of some wreaths among the Spartans, as it is told in Sosibios, *On cult.* He says that they are now called *psilinoi*, because they are made of palm leaves. In commemoration of the victory at Thyrea, they are carried by the leaders of the choruses that are held in the festival, when they are also celebrating the Gymnopaidiai. There are three choruses: in the front one of boys, <to the right one of old men,> and to the left one of men, who are dancing naked and singing the lyrics of Thaletas and Alkman and the paeans of Dionysodotos the Lakonian.

Starting from this fragment of Sosibios, the establishment of the choruses is dated to the year of the victory at Thyrea in 546 B.C. Since this date is later than all conventional estimations of Alkman's lifetime, he could not possibly have written the poems specifically for the festival in question. It would have to be a poem written for some other occasion, but revived at a later time.[36] It is, however, not the Gymnopaidiai as such that were instituted after the victory at Thyrea, but only a minor festival, if one reads Athenaios' summary of Sosibios closely. The name of this festival was probably Parparonia.[37] The Gymnopaidiai were most likely celebrated in commemoration of another battle between Sparta and Argos over the same piece of land, namely the battle at Hysiai in 669 B.C.[38] In other words, there is nothing that speaks against the conclusion that Alkman composed songs for choruses participating in the Gymnopaidiai, a central festival in the initiation cycle of the boys.

I assume that Alkman's poetry was transmitted inside the cultic context for centuries, until it was collected in the third or second century B.C. and published in a scholarly edition in Alexandria. It is normally believed that the poems of Alkman were written down by the poet himself or at least in his own lifetime, and that this hypothetical proto-edition circulated in the Greek world in the Archaic and Classical ages, until the poems were reedited in an orthographically and typographically up-to-date version in the Hellenistic age. There are virtually no sources supporting this hypothesis. The main arguments are the sophistication of the texts and the incorrupt transmission. Thus, John Herington writes in his *Poetry into Drama*:[39]

> "The archaic Greek song culture differed most radically from the song cultures of Appalachia, or of most others known to history, in this: although its *performances* were universally oral, it rested on a firm substructure of carefully meditated written texts. Only the existence of texts can account for its astounding sophistication, refinement, and variety and also for the transmission and preservation of its songs in reasonably uncorrupt form."

However, sophistication and literacy are not co-dependent. Both the Iranian *Avesta* and the Indian *Rigveda* have been composed and transmitted for more than thousand years without a written text. This picture is simply anachronistic and ethnocentric. As to the uncorrupt transmission, we have really no proof that the extant fragments of Alkman have come to us in an unaltered form. On the contrary, the linguistic peculiarities of the text of the Egyptian papyri and of many quotations occurring in later Greek authors, suggest that the Hellenistic text reflects a fourth-century pronunciation rather than a seventh-century orthography.

As a matter of fact, the poetry of Alkman was almost unknown outside of Sparta until the Hellenistic age. It is striking that Plato does not mention Alkman at all, even though he speaks about Lakonian poetry in great length in the second book of the *Laws*. He only refers to Tyrtaios, the elegiac poet, who composed exhortative songs during the Messenian wars; Plato says that because of its militaristic constitution Sparta has not been able to produce any beautiful songs.[40] This unfair judgement is only possible if Plato was totally unaware of the sweet muse of Alkman. There is nothing militaristic about *his* partheneions.

There are, nevertheless, some poems that seem to have been known outside of Sparta already in the Classical period. They are characterised by another linguistic surface than the one seen in Egyptian papyri and in most quotations. To my mind, this is an evident indication of a different transmission. This small group of poems has no local dialect features at all. It has for instance θ and ου, where the main transmission shows Lakonian σ and ω. Both traditions have the Doric ᾱ, but this feature is the rule not only in Pindar, but also in the choral lyric of Attic drama.[41] One such poem is a fragment consisting of four hexameter verses (fr. 26 P):

> οὔ μ᾽ ἔτι, παρθενικαὶ μελιγάρυες ἱερόφωνοι,
> γυῖα φέρειν δύναται· βάλε δὴ βάλε κηρύλος εἴην,
> ὅς τ᾽ ἐπὶ κύματος ἄνθος ἅμ᾽ ἀλκυόνεσσι ποτῆται
> νηλεὲς ἦτορ ἔχων, ἁλιπόρφυρος εἴαρος ὄρνις.

> Honey-singing holy-voiced girls, no longer can my limbs carry me. If only I were a *kērylos*, that flies over the top of the waves together with the halcyons, with a strong heart, a sea-blue bird of the spring.[42]

It is alluded to in Aristophanes' *Birds*, without the name of the author, but the similarity between the verses makes the allusion certain (*Av.* 298-300). Among the fragments of Alkman that were quoted in later authors, there are other dactylic hexameters (fr. 28, 77, 80, 107 P), whereas hexameters are totally absent in the fragments transmitted in the Egyptian papyri. This discrepancy suggests that the papyri do not represent the Alkman corpus equally. They contain primarily ordinary choral lyric poems, which are characterised by varying metres as part of larger stanzas. It cannot be excluded, of course, that the four hexameters of fr. 26 P were combined with lines of another type in the original poem, but it would be atypical, to say the least. Thus, the metre points to another type of poetry than the one represented by the partheneions.

Another fragment, which is transmitted in a non-Lakonian form, is fr. 98 P:

> θοίναις δὲ καὶ ἐν θιάσοισιν
> ἀνδρείων παρὰ δαιτυμόνεσσι πρέπει παιᾶνα κατάρχειν

> At the meals and at the banquets of the mess, among the guests, it is time to begin the paean.

This is found in the *Geography* of Strabon in a context where he quotes the historian Ephoros (10.4.18 = *FGrH* 70 F 149). Ephoros writes in the middle of the fourth century B.C., so the fragment is older than the Hellenistic edition of Alkman. According to my analysis, it therefore belongs to the limited group of poems exported already in Classical times. Like fr. 26 P, it has θ and ει instead of the Lakonian σ and η.

In a description of the Lakonian sacrificial meals, Herodotos uses the exact same word for the participants as does the Alkman fragment, namely *daitymōn*.[43] It is common in the *Odyssey*, too, where it is used, among other things, of the dinner guests of Menelaos in Sparta (4.621), and it is not rare in prose either. It is, however, remarkable that Herodotos has put it in the exact same epic form as Alkman, *daitymonessi*. It may be a reminiscence of this verse.[44] The scene of Alkman fr. 98 P is some kind of cultic meal in a ritual society, described with words *thoinē* and *thiasos*; it says that it is time to begin a paean, but it is probably not a paean itself.

A work of choral lyric is not just a text and a melody, but also a complex dramatic dance, and so it is not so easily exported. A poem like the famous Partheneion of Alkman could, of course, be performed by one person, but the implicit references are almost unintelligible without the dance and the ritual context to make the roles clear. It is therefore, I think, no coincidence that the partheneions did not reach a larger public in the Classical period and were not submitted to writing until the Hellenistic age when they were studied by an esoteric group of learned philologists. The poems that were in fact "exported" to other areas in Classical times, were different. They were more accessible; the text was not full of arcane references to a specific cult. They were composed for a different performance and a different forum.

The hexameter is normally meant for solo performances, typically accompanied by the lyre, what is also called *kitharōidia*. One particular type of poem performed by a *kitharōidos* is the *prooimion*, "prelude."[45] The so-called Homeric hymns were called *prooimia* in Classical times (Thuc. 3.104.4-5 of the *Apollon Hymn*), and they were probably meant as an introduction to a choral performance. According to the interpretation of fr. 26 P in Antigonos of Karystos, the poet expresses his concern that he cannot follow the movements of the chorus actively anymore.[46] It was probably an independent kitharodic introduction to a partheneion, in which the poet spoke in his own voice and introduced the chorus.[47]

In the same way, fr. 98 P presents itself as a *prooimion* of a paean that was performed during a sacrificial meal. One important forum for the distribution of poetry in antiquity was without doubt the symposium. It was common that a virtuoso, accompanied by the kithara, sang a piece of music either from his own production or one of the more famous poems. Sparta had the institution of the *syssition*, during which the men ate together. We know from Philochoros that at their meals the Spartans used to present pieces of Tyrtaios by turns (Athen. 14, 630e-f = *FGrH* 328 F 216):

Φιλόχορος δέ φησιν κρατήσαντας Λακεδαιμονίους Μεσσηνίων διὰ τὴν Τυρταίου στρατηγίαν ἐν ταῖς στρατείαις ἔθος ποιήσασθαι, ἂν δειπνοποιήσωνται καὶ παιωνίσωσιν, ᾄδειν καθ᾽ ἕνα <τὰ> Τυρταίου· κρίνειν δὲ τὸν πολέμαρχον καὶ ἆθλον διδόναι τῷ νικῶντι κρέας.

> Philochoros says that after having conquered the Messenians under the command of Tyrtaios, the Spartans introduced the habit that whenever they had dinner and sang paeans they would sing Tyrtaios' pieces in turn. The polemarch would be the judge and give meat as a prize to the winner.

The fame of Tyrtaios' poetry outside of Sparta already in the Classical age is without doubt due to the fact that elegy was easily transferred from *syssition* to symposium. If certain pieces of Alkman were performed at the *syssitia*, they were possibly picked up by other Greeks as well. These fragments were performed in a neutral Greek and eventually written down in this form (just like the fragments of Tyrtaios, which are in Ionic).

Most of Alkman's poems consisted of choral lyric which was bound to its cultic context until it was eventually "discovered" by the Hellenistic philologists and published according to the contemporary living performance. The choral hymns were inaccessible because of the many implicit references to the cultic situation and therefore less suitable for a performance outside of this context. The fragmentary nature of the extant texts has of course not made comprehension of the poems any easier. Even the largest fragment of them all, fr. 1 P, poses more questions than it answers, and in spite of more than 150 years of scholarship, what is going on and who is who is still a matter of debate. The rich commentaries in the margin of the papyrus itself and in the independent papyrus commentary *P.Oxy.* 2389 show that the task was no less complicated for the Hellenistic scholars, even if they were able to read the whole text. As a matter of fact, the text of this poetry would only appeal to antiquarians and philologists with a keen interest in Lakonian history or language, and it was never part of the common syllabus.

Several of the extant fragments are quoted in the *Deipnosophistai* of Athenaios (ca. A.D. 200). He has probably not collected the verses himself, but relies on quotations found in older handbooks. Sometimes he is explicit about his sources, as at 3, 114f (= fr. 94 P):

αἱ δὲ παρ' Ἀλκμᾶνι θριδακίσκαι λεγόμεναι αἱ αὐταί εἰσι ταῖς
Ἀττικαῖς θριδακίναις. λέγει δὲ οὕτως ὁ Ἀλκμάν ʽθριδακίσκας
τε καὶ κριβανωτώς'. Σωσίβιος δ' ἐν γ' περὶ Ἀλκμᾶνος κριβάνας
φησι λέγεσθαι πλακοῦντάς τινας τῷ σχήματι μαστοειδεῖς.

The (cakes) called *thrikadiskai* by Alkman are the same as the Attic *thridakinai*. Alkman says '*thridakiskai* and *kribanōtoi*'. Sosibios says in *On Alkman*, Book 3, that *kribanai* are a kind of breast-shaped cake.

He returns to the same matter later (14, 646a):

> κριβάνας πλακοῦντάς τινας ὀνομαστικῶς Ἀπολλόδωρος παρ᾽
> Ἀλκμᾶνι. ὁμοίως καὶ Σωσίβιος ἐν γ᾽ περὶ Ἀλκμᾶνος, τῷ
> σχήματι μαστοειδεῖς εἶναι φάσκων αὐτούς, χρῆσθαι δ᾽ αὐτοῖς
> Λάκωνας πρὸς τὰς τῶν γυναικῶν ἑστιάσεις, περιφέρειν τ᾽
> αὐτούς, ὅταν μέλλωσιν ᾄδειν τὸ παρεσκευασμένον ἐγκώμιον
> τῆς παρθένου αἱ ἐν τῷ χορῷ ἀκόλουθοι.

> *Kribanai* is the name of some sort of cake in Alkman according
> to Apollodoros. Similarly Sosibios in *On Alkman*, Book 3, saying
> that they are breast-shaped, and that the Lakonians use them at
> the festivals of the women, carrying them around, when the
> attendants in the chorus are going to sing the hymn they have
> prepared for the girl.[48]

Sosibios is mentioned as an authority in connection with two other quotations of Alkman, at 3, 81f (= fr. 100 P), about the quince, and at 14, 648b (= fr. 96 P), about a ritual muesli. There is a handful of other fragments concerning ritual meals, which may very well have come from the same source, even though Sosibios is not mentioned in the context, e.g. 3, 100f (= fr. 19 P):

> μακωνιᾶν δ᾽ ἄρτων μνημονεύει Ἀλκμὰν ἐν τῷ ε᾽ οὕτως·
> ᾽κλῖναι μὲν ἑπτὰ καὶ τόσαι τράπεσδαι μακωνιᾶν ἄρτων
> ἐπιστέφοισαι λίνω τε σασάμω τε κὴν πελίχναις πέδεστι
> χρυσοκόλλα<ς>᾽ ἐστὶ <δὲ> βρωμάτιον διὰ μέλιτος καὶ λίνου.

> Poppy-seed breads are mentioned by Alkman in Book 5: 'Seven
> couches and seven tables groaned with poppy-seed breads, lin-
> seed and sesame, and there is gold-solder in the bowls.' It is a
> dish made of honey and linseed.

We have the same metre as in fr. 96 P (catalectic iambic trimeter), and the two fragments may very well have come from one and the same hymn.[49]

Sosibios is probably to be dated around 200 B.C.[50] Apparently, he wrote a treatise on Alkman in at least three books (and probably many more, if it was a running commentary). The excerpts explain implicit references to rituals in Alkman's poetry. In other words, the Lakonian scholar refers to the "esoteric" choral hymns of Alkman, which were unknown outside of Sparta in the Classical age and virtually incomprehensible without a commentary. It is therefore extremely interesting that the linguistic surface of these quotations is perfectly Lakonian. It happens to be apparent only in fr. 94 P (κριβανωτώς[51]) and 19 P (ἐπιστεφοίσαι = -ουσαι, τραπέσδαι = -ζ-, λίνω and σασάμω = -ου, πέδεστι = μετ-). What is more, fr. 19 P is quoted with reference to the book in which it appears, which is a clear proof that a proper edition with a fixed order of the poems existed at the time of the quotation.

Athenaios' excerpts from Sosibios' *Peri Alkmanos* are probably the earliest indirect testimony to the Hellenistic edition of Alkman. As we have seen, the few older quotations originate from an independent transmission of a minor group of easily accessible poems. In the third century, someone took on the task of editing something like the "Complete Works of Alkman" in six volumes, including approximately 60 cult hymns that had previously been unknown to the reading public.[52] One may only guess what the impetus for this edition was. Under the reign of Agis IV (ca. 244-241 B.C.) and Kleomenes III (ca. 235-222 B.C.), Sparta experienced some kind of renaissance during which old institutions were revitalised. The edition of the choral lyrics may very well have been part of this programme, an attempt to erect an eternal monument in memory of the golden age of Sparta and, at the same time, to codify the ritual choruses, which were considered indispensable for the famous Spartan *agōgē* and, by consequence, for the establishment of civic identity.

The choral lyric of Alkman was not ephemeral literature that happened to be preserved because of its beauty. It was tied to its cultic context and remained in it throughout the Classical period. Except for a limited number of poems known outside of Sparta in the Classical age that were primarily poems that could be performed by *kitharōidoi* in the context of the symposium, the poems were not written down until the Hellenistic age but were transmitted in uninterrupted re-performance by the Spartan youth.

Alkman's poetry was not meant for one occasion. The personal names occurring in the partheneions are not historical persons, but roles, which new girls took upon them generation after generation. The same holds true, it seems, for the partheneions of Pindar. The partheneions were performed by groups of girls coming from specific tribes and families. The political division in *phylai* and *ōbai* played a central role in the formation of these groups since the choruses marked the integration of the youth into the civic structure. The partheneions remained the property of the kinship groups until they were eventually collected and submitted to writing in the third century B.C.

Acknowledgments:

Even though this article may be described as an abridged elaboration of some of the points made in Hinge 2006, 282-314, I am grateful for having the opportunity to present my thoughts to a different audience and in a more accessible form. At the same time, since the work with this article happened to coincide with the last revision of my book, it contributed to strengthening many of the arguments put forward there. For this reason – and for many others – I am in great debt to Jesper Tae Jensen.

Notes:

1 *Suda*, s.v. (= TB1 Davies): ἔγραψε βιβλία ἐξ, μέλη καὶ Κολυμβώσας "He wrote six books of melic poetry and (including?) the *Kolymbōsai*."

2 The fragments count ca. 3,745 syllables. The total of six books would have been ca. 7,800 verses or ca. 117,000 syllables. In the papyri we have ca. 602 verses (7.7%), but, due to the bad preservation of the lines, only ca. 1,985 syllables (1.7%); the quotations include ca. 181 total or partial verses (2.3%) and ca. 1,898 syllables (1.6%). Only ca. 116 syllables are preserved in both quotations and papyri. Cf. Hinge 2006, 314-6.

3 The most thorough study of the partheneions is Calame 1977, to which I am of course indebted.

4 *P.Louvr.* E 3320, first century B.C. = fr. 1 P. The papyrus preserves three columns or 101 verses. Of the fourth column, only a coronis is visible, which indicates that the poem ended after another four verses. If the poem was indeed the first poem of the collection (or at least of the papyrus), it probably had 10 stanzas of 14 verses each; this, however, is anything but certain (cf. the editions of Davies (1991) and Calame (1983)).

5 Throughout the present article, the text of Alcman is printed according to the orthography found in the manuscripts, not in the reconstructed versions found in the standard editions of Page (1962), Davies (1991) and Calame (1983), which tend to exaggerate the dialect features of the text. The fragments are identified with the numbers found in Page 1962 (followed by Campbell 1988 and Davies 1991).

6 Linguistically, it is more straightforward to take πεδ᾽ Ἀγιδώ as a preposi- tional phrase, i.e. "she runs after Agido" (as is done by most scholars: Page 1951, 48; West 1965, 196-7; Puelma 1977, 29-32; Campbell 1988, 365; Pavese 1992, 65-6). In the context of the poem, however, it is not comfortable if Hagesichora takes the second place. It is therefore more attractive to interpret Ἀγιδώ as the subject (together with ἁ δὲ δευτέρα) and to take πεδ᾽ with the verb in tmesis (cf. Calame 1977, vol. 2, 71 n. 50; 1983, 330). Since the nominative and accusa- tive of the ō-stems were kept apart in Dorian vase inscriptions (-OI: -O = -ῶι: -ῶ < IE *-ōy: *-oym; cf. Wachter 2001, 254), there would probably have been no danger of misunderstanding the phrase in spite of the unusual word order (the papyrus has in fact ἀγιδῶι, but the iota has been struck out). Cf. Hinge 2006, 161-2.

7 Vv. 98-99 ἀντ[ὶ δ᾽ ἕνδεκα] παίδων δεκ[ὰς ἅδ᾽ ἀείδ]ει "instead of eleven girls this group of ten is singing"; supplemented by Wilamowitz and Blass in ac- cordance with the scholion: ἀλλὰ διὰ τὸ τὸν χορὸν ὅτε μὲν ἐξ ια᾽ παρθένων ὅτε δὲ ἐκ ι᾽· φη(σὶν) οὖν τὴν χορηγὸν ἐπαινῶν ἀντὶ ια᾽ ἄιδειν ι᾽ "but because the chorus (consists) sometimes of 11, sometimes of 10 girls. So he says, prais- ing the chorus-leader, that 10 are singing instead of 11."

8 Nagy 1990a, 345-70.

9 Nagy 1979, 296-7; 1990a, 47. Since the noun *ϝοδός (< IE *(h₂)wodós, related to αὐδή < *h₂(e)udeh₂) is otherwise unknown, it is probably more safe to analyse Ἡσί-οδος as "he who wants a journey" (ἵημι / ἀνδάνω + ὁδός), referring to Hesiod's one and only journey to Euboia to challenge Homer, cf. also *Etym. Magn.* s.v.: ὁ τὴν αἰσίαν ὁδὸν πορευόμενος "he who makes the auspicious journey" (apparently taking Ἡσι- as αἴσιος, cf. the "Aeolic" variant Αἰσίοδος in Herodian, *Peri pathōn* 2.362).

10 Cf. Sch. *Il.* 2.494 ἐπίθεσαν οἱ πλεῖστοι τῶν παλαιῶν προληπτικῶς τὰς ὀνομασίας τοῖς παισίν, ἀφ᾽ ὧν ἔμελλον οἱ παῖδες ἐπιτηδεύειν πραγμάτων "Most ancient people gave names to their children in anticipation of what the children would later pursue." It is, on the other hand, a matter of faith if one prefers to ascribe the etymology of the name of Jesus to luck, *vaticinium ex eventu* or divine providence (Hebr. *Jᵉhōšuᵃ'* = "JHWH saves": Matt. 1.21 with Philon, *Peri tōn metonomazomenōn* 121: Ἰησοῦς δὲ σωτηρία κυρίου "Jesus means 'the salvation of the Lord'"; cf. also *Ps.* 20.7; 118.25).

11 Fraser & Matthews 1997.

12 Puelma 1977, 25.

13 Cf. also Pavese 1992, 51-2 (who thinks that the *choragos* is neither Hagesichora nor Agido): "che la ragazza lodata si chiamasse Hagesichora è casuale e nulla ha a fare con la sua presente attività corale."

14 Calame 2000, 246-52, is aware of the expressivity of the names of the eleven girls, but he argues that the poet just explores the etymological potential of the actual names given to the girls in early childhood.

15 Cf. Hermesianax fr. 7 Powell, v. 37. Classical writers quote several elegiacs from Mimnermos' collection *Nanno*, even if none of the extant verses include the name Nanno (= fr. 4, 5, 8, 9, 10, 12, 24 West).

16 *Hippiatrica Berolinensia* 50.1, 50.2, 73.1.

17 Harvey 1967; Schneider 1985. *Suda* s.v. (TA12 Davies): ἦν δὲ ἐπὶ τῆς κζʹ Ὀλυμπιάδος, βασιλεύοντος Λυδῶν Ἄρδυος, τοῦ Ἀλυάττου πατρός "He lived in the 27th Olympiad [i.e. 672-668 B.C.], when Ardys, the father of Alyattes, was king of the Lydians"; Euseb. *Chron.* s. Ol. 42.4 (TA13 Davies): *Alcman, ut quibusdam videtur, agnoscitur* "(in the fourth year of the 42th Olympiad [i.e. 609/8]), Alkman is recognised according to some."

18 Cf. *La-bōtas, La-charēs, La-kratēs*.

19 Kukula 1907, 212.

20 West 1965, 199-200; Puelma 1977, 40-1.

21 Calame 1977, vol. 2, 95-7.

22 In Pindar, *stratos* normally has the meaning "people" (also Alkman fr. 3 P, v. 73).

23 Calame 1977, vol. 2, 105-6. For the meaning of the name and the role of Astymeloisa, see Peponi 2007, 356.

24 Page 1951, 67-8.

25 Calame 1977, vol. 2, 84-5.

26 Accordingly, in *IG* 5(1).26 (2nd/1st cent. B.C.), *Amyklai*, according to Pausanias a *kōmē*, "village" (3.19.6), is called an *ōbē*. Later, in the victory dedications of the Imperial age, *phylē* and *ōbē* are used indiscriminately.

27 Calame 1977, vol. 1, 382-3.

28 Forrest 1968, 42-6.

29 Att. *ph(r)atria*, Ion. *phrētria* is derived from the IE word for "brother," whereas Doric *patra* is of course derived from *patēr* "father." In a context where he speaks about the conditions in Sparta, Aristotle makes this general remark (*Pol.* 2, 1264a.6-8): οὐ γὰρ δυνήσεται μὴ μερίζων αὐτὰ καὶ χωρίζων ποιῆσαι τὴν πόλιν, τὰ μὲν εἰς συσσίτια τὰ δὲ εἰς φατρίας καὶ φυλάς "It would be impossible to construct the state (of Plato) without dividing things partly into *syssitia* and partly into *phratriai* and *phylai*".

30 The word is here taken in its modern, general sense. It is not implied that these year group clubs were in fact called *thiasoi* in seventh-century Sparta. Alkman uses the word once (fr. 98 P) of the clubs of the *syssitia*; see below.

31 Nagy 1990b, 276-93: the Dymanes, Hylleis and Pamphyloi correspond to Dumézil's three functions of the sovereign, the warrior and the peasant, most explicitly in a fourth-century *lex sacra* from Kos (*ICos* 140): θύονται κατὰ φυλάς, ὁ μὲν τῶν Ὑλλέων παρὰ τὸ Ἡράκλειον, ὁ δὲ τῶν Δυμάνων παρὰ τὰ Ἀναξίλεα, ὁ δὲ τῶν Παμφυλέων ἐν Εἰτέᾳ παρὰ τὸ Δαμάτριον "They practise their cult according to *phylai*, the Hylleis in the Heakleion, the Dymanes in the Anaxilea and the Pamphyloi in the Demetrion of Eitea." A similar fictitious kinship division is attested for the Scythians, cf. Hinge 2003.

32 Huxley 1974.

33 Cf. also the tradition, allegedly going back to Archytas (in Athenaios 13.600f), that Alkman was excessively in love with Megalostrata, which is most probably based on an inadequate reading of a choral song in which the chorus expressed its affection for its leader (cf. Calame 1977, vol. 1, 434-5, vol. 2, 93-4). Archytas has certainly not read the whole chorus song, whether fr. 59(b) P was the first lines of it or, better, an independent *prooimion* introducing the chorus and its leader (see below); otherwise, he would have understood that the poet referred to the sentiments of the chorus. The verses were probably quoted outside of their original context as a refrain in the symposium, which is supported by the fact that the linguistic form is neutral Doric (Μουσᾶν, παρθένων), not Lakonian (Μωσᾶν, παρσένων).

34 Nagy 1990b, 283-4.

35 Calame 1977.

36 It must be what Herington (1985, 25-6) has in mind when he claims that the re-performance mentioned in Athenaios was done "in memory of the great Spartan victory over the Argives in the battle of Thyrea (datable to about 546 B.C.)." He does not, however, comment on the anachronism.

37 Bölte 1929, 130-2. Cf. Choiroboskos 1.297; Hesych s.v. Πάρπαρος; *IG* 5(1).213.63 (5th century B.C.). Jacoby (1955, comm. 646-7 + not. 373-4) argues that Athenaios has confused the two festivals, and that in Sosibios' lost version the subordinate clause ὅτε καὶ etc. described the Parparonia and not the Gymnopaidiai.

38 Wade-Gery 1949. Since the different battles over Thyrea / Kynuria may be seen as a series of ritual wars (cf. Brelich 1961, 22-34), the Parparonia and the Gymnopaidiai had the same occasion, and there would no reason to separate them.

39 Herington 1985, 41.

40 *Leg.* 2, 666d-7a. He has a quotation of Tyrtaios in the first book (*Leg.* 1, 629a-630b = Tyrt. fr. 12 West).

41 There are some examples of η in the quotations of Alkman (but not in the papyri); see Hinge 2004; 2006, 7-16.

42 εἴαρος ὄρνις "bird of the spring" has in all editions been emended to ἱαρὸς ὄρνις "holy bird," but see Giangrande 1971, 102-5; Hinge 1997, 44-5; 2006, 16-7.

43 *Hist.* 6.57.1: ἢν θυσίη τις δημοτελὴς ποιέηται, πρώτους ἐπὶ τὸ δεῖπνον ἵζειν τοὺς βασιλέας, καὶ ἀπὸ τούτων πρώτων ἄρχεσθαι διπλήσια νέμοντας ἑκατέρῳ τὰ πάντα ἢ τοῖσι ἄλλοισι δαιτυμόνεσσι "Whenever there is a public sacrifice, the kings are the first to sit down to the banquet and to be served, and each of them gets the double of what is given to the rest of the dinner guests". Cf. Rosén 1962, 92: "Hdt. stimmt mit Homer im Ausschluß des Sg. aus diesem Substantiv überein, daher ist auch eine Anpassung an die allein im Hexameter zulässige Dat. pl.-Form δαιτυμόνεσσι (χ 12 u.ö.) nicht ausgeschlossen".

44 Schwyzer 1939, 564 n. 1. At *Hist.* 4.8 Ἡρακλέα 'ἐλαύνοντα τὰς Γηρυόναο βόας' ἀπικέσθαι ἐς γῆν ταύτην ἐοῦσαν ἐρήμην "Herakles, driving the kine of Geryones, came to this land, which was desolate", Herodotos makes a similar morphological allusion to Stesichoros (rather than Pindar); see Hinge 2004, 307-310.

45 Herington 1985, 22-4; Nagy 1990a, 353-60.

46 Antig., *Mirab.* 23: φησὶν γὰρ ἀσθενὴς ὢν διὰ τὸ γῆρας καὶ τοῖς χοροῖς οὐ δυνάμενος συμπεριφέρεσθαι οὐδὲ τῇ τῶν παρθένων ὀρχήσει "He says that being weak because of his old age, he cannot carry himself round along with the choruses and the dance of the girls."

47 Vestrheim 2004, 13-5. Calame (1983, 472) rejects the interpretation of Antigonos because Alkman is normally referred to in the third person (cf. 16, 17, 39, 95(b) P); this argumentation presupposes that all fragments ascribed to Alkman were in fact meant for performance by a chorus.

48 τῆς παρθένου "the girl" is probably not a goddess, but a girl praised by the chorus; cf. Calame 1977, vol. 2, 113-4.

49 Von der Muehll 1951, 212-3.

50 In *Suda* he is identified with Sosibios ὁ λυτικός, who was, according to Athen. 11, 493e-f, contemporaneous with Ptolemy Philadelphos (i.e. 288-246 B.C.); this is, however, doubtful. Sosibios the Lakonian must be later than the *Olympionikai* of Timaios (ca. 350-260 B.C.), which he uses, but earlier than Apollodoros of Athens (ca. 180-120 B.C.), who, on the other hand, uses the works of Sosibios. Cf. Jacoby 1955, text 635-6 + comm. 368-9.

51 Cod. -ός; the juxtaposition with θριδακίσκας makes it certain that it should be an accusative plural, and the corruption -ός < -ώς is far more probable than -ός < -ούς.

52 If we estimate that each book contained ca. 1300 lines (i.e. 35-40 columns) and that the average length of the hymns ca. 130 verses, see Hinge 2006, 314-7.

Bibliography

Bölte, F. 1929. "Zu lakonischen Festen." *RhM* 78: 124-43.

Brelich, A. 1961. *Guerre, agoni e culti nella Grecia arcaica.* Bonn: Rudolf Habelt.

Calame, C. 1977. *Les chœurs de jeunes filles en Grèce archaïque*. Filologia e critica 20-21. Rome: Edizioni dell'Ateneo.

Calame, C. 1983. *Alcman. Introduction, texte critique, témoignages, traduction et commentaire*. Lyricorum Graecorum quae exstant 6. Rome: Edizioni dell'Ateneo.

Calame, C. 2000. *Le récit en Grèce ancienne*. Paris: Éditions Belin.

Campbell, D.A. 1988. *Greek Lyric*. Vol. 2. The Loeb Classical Library 143. Cambridge, MA: Harvard University Press.

Davies, M. 1991. *Poetarum melicorum Graecorum fragmenta*. Vol. 1. Oxford: Oxford University Press.

Forrest, W.G. 1968. *A History of Sparta 950-192 B.C.* London: Hutchinson University Library.

Fraser, P. M., and E. Matthews. 1997. *A Lexicon of Greek Personal Names*. Vol. IIIa. Oxford: Clarendon Press.

Giangrande, G. 1971. "Interpretationen griechischer Meliker." *RhM* 114: 97-131.

Harvey, A. E. 1967. "Oxyrhynchus Papyrus 2390 and Early Spartan History." *JHS* 87: 62-73.

Herington, J. 1985. *Poetry into Drama: Early Tragedy and the Greek Poetic Tradition*. Berkeley & Los Angeles: University of California Press.

Hinge, G. 1997. "Kritische Beiträge zum alkmanischen Digamma." *ClMed* 48: 37-51.

Hinge, G. 2003. "Scythian and Spartan Analogies in Herodotos' Representation." In *The Cauldron of Ariantas, Studies Presented to A.N. Ščeglov on the Occasion of His 70th Birthday*, edited by P.G. Bilde, J.M. Højte and V.F. Stolba, 55-74. Black Sea Studies 1. Aarhus: Aarhus University Press.

Hinge, G. 2004. "Dialect Colouring in Quotations of Classical Greek Poetry." In *Dialetti, dialettismi, generi letterari e funzioni sociali: Atti del V Colloquuio Internazionale di Liguistica Greca (Milano, 12-13 settembre 2002)*, edited by G. Rocca, 303-11. ΕΛΛΑΔΑ 1. Alessandria: Edizioni dell'Orso.

Hinge, G. 2006. *Die Sprache Alkmans: Textgeschichte und Sprachgeschichte*. Serta Graeca 24. Wiesbaden: Ludwig Reichert Verlag.

Huxley, G. 1974. "Aristotle's Interest in Biography." *GRBS* 15: 202-13.

Jacoby, F. 1955. *Die Fragmente der griechischen Historiker (FGrH)*. Vol. 3b. Leiden: E. J. Brill.

Kukula, R.C. 1907. "Alkmans Partheneion. Ein Beitrag zum lakonischen Artemiskulte." *Philologus* 66: 202-30.

Nagy, G. 1979. *The Best of the Achaeans. Concepts of the Hero in Archaic Greek Poetry*. Baltimore: Johns Hopkins University Press.

Nagy, G. 1990a. *Pindar's Homer: The Lyric Possession of an Epic Past*. Baltimore: Johns Hopkins University Press.

Nagy, G. 1990b. *Greek Mythology and Poetics*. Ithaca, London: Cornell University Press.

Page, D.L. 1951. *Alcman's Partheneion*. Oxford: Oxford University Press.

Page, D.L. 1962. *Poetae melici Graeci*. Oxford: Oxford University Press.

Pavese, C.O. 1992. *Il grande partenio di Alcmane*. Lexis, Supplemento 1. Amsterdam: Adolf M. Hakkert.

Peponi, A.-E. 2007. "Sparta's Prima Ballerina: *Choreia* in Alcman's Second *Partheneion* (3 *PMGF*)." *CQ* 57: 351-62.

Puelma, M. 1977. "Die Selbstbeschreibung des Chores in Alkmans grossem Parthenion-Fragment." *MusHelv* 43: 1-55.

Rosén, H. B. 1962. *Laut- und Formenlehre der herodotischen Sprachform*. Heidelberg: Carl Winter.

Schneider, J. 1985. "La chronologie d'Alcman." *RÉG* 98: 1-64.

Schwyzer, E. 1939. *Griechische Grammatik*. Vol. 1. Handbuch der Altertumswissenschaft II.1.1. München: C.H. Beck.

Vestrheim, G. 2004. "Alcman fr.26: A Wish for Fame." *GRBS* 44: 15-8.

Von der Muehll, P. 1951. "Kultische und andere Mahlzeiten bei Alkman." *Schweizerisches Archiv für Volkskunde* 47: 208-14.

Wachter, R. 2001. *Non-Attic Greek Vase Inscriptions*. Oxford: Oxford University Press.

Wade-Gery, H.T. 1949. "A note on the origin of the Spartan Gymnopaidiai." *CQ* 43: 79-81.

West, M.L. 1965. "Alcmanica." *CQ* 15: 188-202.

Index

chryselephantine 153-5,
165 n. 8, 169 n. 53, 173
n. 106
chthonic character 111
clamps, double-T 167
n. 19
clamps, dove-tail 167
n. 19
clamps, pi-sharped 131,
166-7 n. 19
clamps, T-clamps 95
clamps, Z-shaped 166
n. 19
claw chisel 95, 131, 166
n. 17
cognition 15
colonialist view 195-6
cult 13-23, 24 ns. 35, 41,
55-7, 59, 60 n. 4, 61
n. 11, 112, 117 n. 35,
146, 155, 162, 172 n. 79,
175 n. 128, 195-6, 198-9,
202-5, 210 n. 22, 215,
220, 224, 227, 233 n. 31
cult images 126, 152
cult of Aphrodite 176
n. 136
cult of Bendis 62 n. 25
cult of Theseus 62 n. 25
cult practice 195, 200, 223
cult statue 103, 125, 165
n. 8
cultural comparisons
198-99
cultural essentialism 202
cultural identity 195, 197,
200, 208
Damaina 219-21
Damareta 216-18, 221
Damotimidas 220
Daochos Monument
(Delphi) 143, 155-6,
174 n. 107

daphnephoric procession
219, 221
Dareios 138
Delian League 56, 61
n. 18
Delos 57, 61 n. 18, 153,
167 n. 19
Delphi 61 n. 16, 136-8,
143, 154-7, 160-1, 163,
166 ns. 16-7, 19, 168
n. 50, 176 n. 130, 177 ns.
144, 150, 178 n. 154, 199
Delphic hymn 196, 208
Demeter 39, 43, 51 n. 12,
67, 70, 114 n. 15, 144,
171 n. 70, 174 n. 107
Demetrios Poliorketes
125-6, 178 n. 154
Demos Acharnai 67, 70
Demos 60 n. 4
Dexion 59-60 n. 3, 84 n. 15
Dillon, Matthew 56
Diodoros 57, 132
Dion Chrysostom 147,
151, 172 n. 85
Dionysion (Thasos) 156-
7, 174 n. 107, 176 n. 133
divine honors 125, 178
n. 154
Doric stoa (Athenian
Asklepieion) 91, 108,
111, 116 n. 7, 117 ns. 28,
34, 37
dowel hole 94-7, 100, 102
drain 92, 97-8, 111, 116
n. 21
Dromos 223
Dymainai 222-3
Dymanes 222-3, 233 n. 31
"dynastic" Monument
(Delphi) 156-7, 176
n. 133

east terrace, Akropolis
91, 113 n. 3, 116 n. 21,
118 n. 37
Eirene and Ploutos,
statue of 144, 147
Eleusinion (Athens) 60
n. 4, 67, 75, 115 n. 15
emic 15
Ephesos 125, 145
Ephoros 226
Epidauria, festival 67-8,
115 n. 15
Epidauros 55-8, 60 ns. 4-5,
8, 61 n. 11, 67, 75, 111,
132, 160-1, 167 n. 29
epiphanies 160
Eponymous Heroes 125,
165 n. 4
Erechteion 78, 83, 85 ns.
43-4, 133, 135
Eresians of Lesbos 146
ethnomusicology 195,
197, 199, 202, 208
etic 15, 21
Euphemos 103
eurocentrism 202
Eurydike 126, 140, 143-5,
151, 153, 165 n. 7, 169
n. 57, 170 n. 63, 171 ns.
66, 69
Eurypontids 220, 223
family 34-5, 37 ns. 18-9, 38
n. 23, 126, 128-9, 136,
138, 151, 154, 158, 162-
3, 168 n. 40, 170 n. 63,
217-8, 220-1, 223
"furrowed work" 105
gender 15
Granikos, battle of 125,
138
"Greek Renaissance" 199
Greekness 208

Contributors

Lisbeth Bredholt Christensen
Department of the Study of Religion
Faculty of Theology
University of Aarhus
Taasingegade 3
8000 Aarhus C, Denmark
E-mail: lbc@teo.au.dk

Richard Hamilton
Department of Greek, Latin and Classical Studies
Bryn Mawr College
101 North Merion Avenue
Bryn Mawr, PA 19010, USA
E-mail: rhamilto@brynmawr.edu

George Hinge
Institute of Language, Literature and Culture
University of Aarhus,
Jens Chr. Skous Vej 5
8000 Aarhus C, Denmark
E-mail: george.hinge@hum.au.dk

Jesper Tae Jensen
Lillegrund 2, 3rd left
2300 Copenhagen S, Denmark
E-mail: klajj@hum.au.dk

Michael Lefantzis
Greek Ministry of Culture
Committee for the Conservation and Restoration of the Odeion of Herodes Attikos and the Stoa of Eumenes at the South Slope of the Akropolis
18 Vironos, 10558 Athens, Greece
E-mail: mlefan@panafonet.gr

Tore Albert Tvarnø Lind
Department of Arts – and Cultural Studies, Musicology
University of Copenhagen
Klerkegade 2
1308 Copenhagen K, Denmark
E-mail: ttlind@hum.ku.dk

Vanda Papaefthymiou
Greek Ministry of Culture
1st Ephoreia of Prehistoric and Classical Antiquities
2-4 Makrygianni
11742 Athens, Greece
E-mail: vada@otenet.gr

Peter Schultz
Department of Art
Concordia College
901 S. 8th St.
Moorhead, MN 56562, USA
E-mail: schultz@cord.edu

Bronwen Lara Wickkiser
Bronwen L. Wickkiser
Department of Classical Studies
Vanderbilt University
VU Station B, 351740
2301 Vanderbilt Place
Nashville, TN 37235-1740, USA
E-mail: bronwen.wickkiser@vanderbilt.edu